advantage interactive cd-rom

Place
Postage
Here

Irwin/McGraw-Hill
Attn: Jodi McPherson, Marketing Manager
699 Boylston Street
10th Floor
Boston MA 02116

Microsoft® Excel 97 for Windows®

Sarah E. Hutchinson

Glen J. Coulthard

THE IRWIN/MCGRAW-HILL ADVANTAGE SERIES FOR COMPUTER EDUCATION

Boston, Massachusetts Burr Ridge, Illinois Dubuque, Iowa
Madison, Wisconsin New York, New York San Francisco, California St. Louis, Missouri

Irwin/McGraw-Hill

A Division of The **McGraw·Hill** *Companies*

MICROSOFT® EXCEL 97 for WINDOWS®

This book is printed on acid-free paper.

6 7 8 9 0 WC/WC 9 0

ISBN 0-07-228255-X

Publisher: *Tom Casson*
Sponsoring editor: *Garrett Glanz*
Developmental editor: *Kristin Hepburn*
GTS production coordinator: *Cathy Stotts*
Marketing manager: *James Rogers*
Senior project supervisor: *Denise Santor-Mitzit*
Production supervisor: *Pat Frederickson*
Art director: *Keith McPherson*
Prepress buyer: *Heather D. Burbridge*
Compositor: *GTS Graphics, Inc.*
Typeface: *11/13 Bodoni Book*
Printer: *Webcrafters, Inc.*

http://www.mhcollege.com

Large figures guide
learning

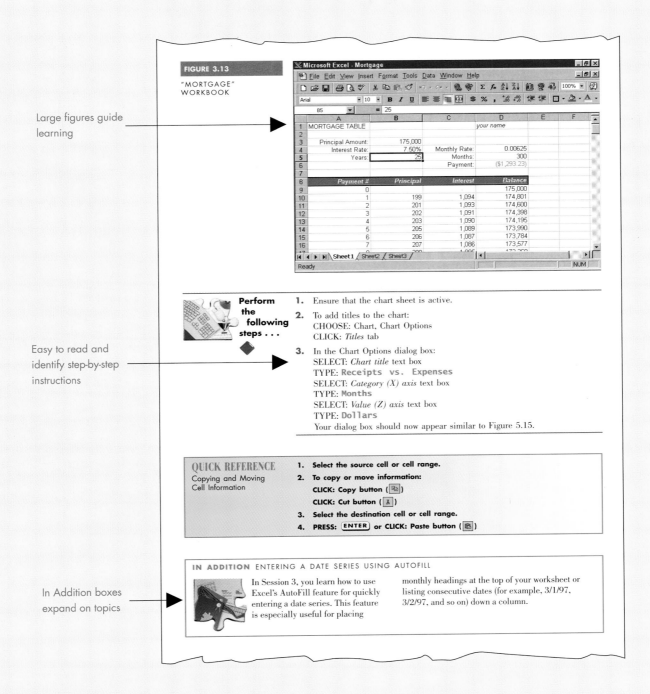

FIGURE 3.13

"MORTGAGE"
WORKBOOK

Easy to read and
identify step-by-step
instructions

Perform the following steps . . .

1. Ensure that the chart sheet is active.

2. To add titles to the chart:
CHOOSE: Chart, Chart Options
CLICK: *Titles* tab

3. In the Chart Options dialog box:
SELECT: *Chart title* text box
TYPE: Receipts vs. Expenses
SELECT: *Category (X) axis* text box
TYPE: Months
SELECT: *Value (Z) axis* text box
TYPE: Dollars
Your dialog box should now appear similar to Figure 5.15.

QUICK REFERENCE
Copying and Moving
Cell Information

1. Select the source cell or cell range.

2. To copy or move information:
CLICK: Copy button (⬚)
CLICK: Cut button (⬚)

3. Select the destination cell or cell range.

4. PRESS: ⬚ENTER⬚ or CLICK: Paste button (⬚)

In Addition boxes
expand on topics

IN ADDITION ENTERING A DATE SERIES USING AUTOFILL

In Session 3, you learn how to use Excel's AutoFill feature for quickly entering a date series. This feature is especially useful for placing monthly headings at the top of your worksheet or listing consecutive dates (for example, 3/1/97, 3/2/97, and so on) down a column.

Students practice with
real life projects

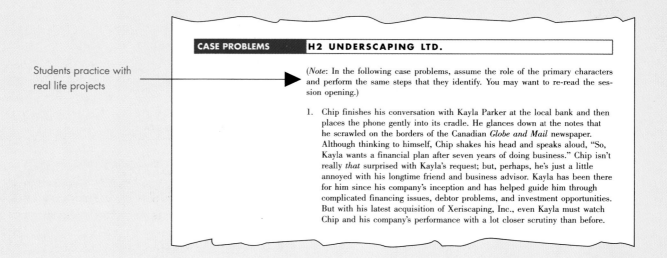

CASE PROBLEMS | **H2 UNDERSCAPING LTD.**

(*Note*: In the following case problems, assume the role of the primary characters and perform the same steps that they identify. You may want to re-read the session opening.)

1. Chip finishes his conversation with Kayla Parker at the local bank and then places the phone gently into its cradle. He glances down at the notes that he scrawled on the borders of the Canadian *Globe and Mail* newspaper. Although thinking to himself, Chip shakes his head and speaks aloud, "So, Kayla wants a financial plan after seven years of doing business." Chip isn't really *that* surprised with Kayla's request; but, perhaps, he's just a little annoyed with his longtime friend and business advisor. Kayla has been there for him since his company's inception and has helped guide him through complicated financing issues, debtor problems, and investment opportunities. But with his latest acquisition of Xeriscaping, Inc., even Kayla must watch Chip and his company's performance with a lot closer scrutiny than before.

TEXT SUPPLEMENTS

ADVANTAGE FILES

Certain hands-on examples and exercises are marked with a disk ◆ icon, indicating the need to retrieve a document file from the **Advantage Files location.** These document files may be provided to you in a number of ways: packaged on a diskette accompanying this text, or on the computer network at your school. You may also download the files from the *Advantage Online* Web site (http://www.irwin.com/cit/adv). *These documents files are extremely important to your success.* Check with your instructor or lab advisor for details on how to acquire the Advantage Files.

In addition to identifying the Advantage Files location, you will also need to specify a **Data Files location.** This location is used to save the documents that you create and may either be a blank diskette or a folder on the network server. Again, your instructor or lab advisor will specify the proper locations. More information on the file locations and the proper techniques for retrieving and saving information is provided inside the back cover of this book.

CD-ROM INTERACTIVE TUTORIALS

In addition to using this book, you may have access to our *Advantage Interactive* software. These interactive multimedia tutorials are fully integrated with the material from each session and make effective use of video clips, screen demonstrations, hands-on exercises, and quizzes. You will enjoy the opportunity to explore these tutorials and learn the software at your own pace. For ordering information, please refer to the coupon inside the front cover.

INSTRUCTOR'S RESOURCE KIT

For instructors and software trainers, each learning guide is accompanied by an **Instructor's Resource Kit (IRK).** This kit provides suggested answers to the short-answer questions, hands-on exercises, and case problems appearing at the end of each session. Furthermore, the IRK includes a comprehensive test bank of additional short-answer, multiple-choice, and fill-in-the-blank questions, plus hands-on exercises. You will also find a diskette copy of the Advantage Files which may be duplicated or placed on your network for student use.

SUPPORT THROUGH THE WWW

The Internet, and more specifically the World Wide Web, is an important component in our approach to software instruction for the Office 97 application series. The *Advantage Online* site at http://www.irwin.com/cit/adv is a tremendous resource for all users, providing information on the latest software and learning guide releases, download options for the Advantage Files, and supplemental files for the Instructor Resource Kits. We also introduce new methods for you to communicate with the authors, publisher, and other users of the series. As a dynamic venture, *Advantage Online* will evolve and improve over time. Please visit us to see the latest developments and contribute your valuable feedback.

NETWORK TESTING

Evaluation and assessment are important components of any instructional series. We are committed to providing quality alternatives to traditional testing instruments. With our Irwin Network Test Interactive software, instructors can select questions, create and administer tests, and then calculate grades—all on-line! Visit the *Advantage Online* site for more information on how we are progressing in this exciting area.

BEFORE YOU BEGIN

As with any software instruction guide, there are standard conventions that we use to indicate menu options, keystroke combinations, and command instructions.

MENU INSTRUCTIONS

In Office 97, all Menu bar options and pull-down menu commands have an under-lined or highlighted letter in each option. When you need to execute a command from the Menu bar—the row of menu choices across the top of the screen—the tutorial's instruction line separates the Menu bar option from the command with a comma. Notice also that the word "CHOOSE" is always used for menu commands. For example, the command for quitting Windows is shown as:

CHOOSE: File, Exit

This instruction tells you to choose the File option on the Menu bar and then to choose the Exit command from the File pull-down menu. The actual steps for choosing a menu command are discussed later in this guide.

KEYSTROKES AND KEYSTROKE COMBINATIONS

When two keys must be pressed together, the tutorial's instruction line shows the keys joined with a plus (+) sign. For example, you can execute a Copy command in Windows by holding down (CTRL) and then pressing the letter c.

The instruction for this type of keystroke combination follows:

PRESS: (CTRL)+c

COMMAND INSTRUCTIONS

This guide indicates with a special typeface and color the data that you are required to type in yourself. For example:

TYPE: Income Statement

When you are required to enter unique information, such as the current date or your name, the instruction appears in italic. The following instruction directs you to type your name in place of the actual words: "your name."

TYPE: *your name*

ACKNOWLEDGMENTS

This series of learning guides is the direct result of the teamwork and heart of many people. We sincerely thank the reviewers, instructors, and students who have shared their comments and suggestions with us over the past few years. We do read them! With this valuable feedback, our guides have evolved into the product you see before you. We also appreciate the efforts of the instructors and students at Okanagan University College who classroom tested our guides to ensure accuracy, relevancy, and completeness.

We also give many thanks to Garrett Glanz, Kristin Hepburn and Tom Casson from Irwin for their skillful management of this text. In fact, special recognition goes to all of the individuals mentioned in the credits at the beginning of this guide. And finally, to the many others who weren't directly involved in this project but who have stood by us the whole way, we appreciate your encouragement and support.

WRITE TO US

We welcome your response to this book, for we are trying to make it as useful a learning tool as possible. Write to us in care of Garrett Glanz, Richard D. Irwin, 1333 Burr Ridge Parkway, Burr Ridge, IL 60521. Thank you.

Sarah E. Hutchinson
sclifford@mindspring.com

Glen J. Coulthard
current@junction.net

Contents

SESSION 1
Fundamentals

SESSION 2
Working with Spreadsheets

SESSION 3
Increasing Your Productivity

SESSION 4
Managing a Workbook

SESSION 5
Creating Charts

APPENDIX
Toolbar Summary 208

INDEX   219

ADDENDUM   A-1
Microsoft Excel 97 for Windows
Additional Microsoft Office User Specialist Certification Topics

Microsoft Excel 97 for Windows

Fundamentals

SESSION

1

HTTP WWW

IRWIN
COMPUTER & INFORMATION TECHNOLOGY

SESSION OUTLINE

INTRODUCTION

Be thankful for the electronic spreadsheet, one of the most commonly used business software tools! Just a few years ago, a spreadsheet existed only in paper form and its 7,500 or so tiny spaces had to be filled in by hand. Many a manager, accountant, and business planner wore down several pencils (and erasers) revising this paper instrument. Today, electronic spreadsheets such as Microsoft Excel enable you to insert and change numbers with ease. This session shows you how to begin using this valuable tool.

THE BONDABLE GROUP

Started in the spring of 1996, The Bondable Group is composed of three friends who formed a partnership after graduating together with degrees in business administration. The group offers investment advice to individuals wanting to expand their portfolios into the bond and stock markets. Jennifer Spalding is the undisputed leader of the group, having graduated with a Finance major. Although they don't possess the same financial skills as their associate, Pancho Valdez and Mackenzie Sherwood are definitely the sales backbone. Both Pancho and Mackenzie are marketing majors with excellent communication and presentation skills.

The group agreed recently to purchase notebook computers for Pancho and Mackenzie, since most of their work entails visiting clients' homes in the evening. To prepare for the arrival of their new computers, Jennifer suggested that the two men develop a simple financial planning tool using Microsoft Excel 97 for Windows. With an electronic spreadsheet, Pancho and Mackenzie could demonstrate the outcomes of different investment strategies to their clients. Unfortunately, neither of the two has ever used Microsoft Excel and they don't know the first thing about creating an electronic spreadsheet.

In this session, you and our two friends are led step-by-step through one of the most popular spreadsheet programs available, Microsoft Excel. You will initially concentrate on spreadsheet fundamentals like entering text, numbers, dates, and formulas. By the end of the session, you will know how to effectively design, create, and save a spreadsheet. You will also know how to retrieve advice from Excel's Help system and how to use the Undo command for reversing data entry and editing mistakes.

INTRODUCING MICROSOFT OFFICE 97

Microsoft Office for Windows combines the most popular and exciting software programs available into a single suite of applications. In the Standard edition, Office 97 includes Microsoft Word, Microsoft Excel, Microsoft PowerPoint, and the all-new Microsoft Outlook, an integrated desktop information tool that manages your e-mail, calendar, contacts, to do lists, journal, and Office documents. In the Professional edition, you also get Microsoft Access, a relational database management system that works directly with the other Office applications. Office 97 also provides shared applications (sometimes called "server applications") that let you create and insert clip art, organizational charts, and mathematical equations into your word processing documents, electronic spreadsheets, and presentations.

All software products are born with specific design goals. For Office 97, Microsoft concentrated on optimizing Office for use in Windows' 32-bit environments, including Windows 95 and Windows NT. In addition to enjoying performance improvements, Office 97 offers integration with the Internet and World Wide Web (WWW) and benefits from many usability enhancements. For example, Office 97 lets you do the following:

- name your documents using up to 250 characters,
- place shortcuts to documents directly on the Windows desktop,
- use the Windows Briefcase program to compare and synchronize files,
- multitask applications with single-click functionality from the taskbar,
- save documents in the web's Hypertext Markup Language (HTML) format, and
- post documents to your internal intranet or to the Web.

All of Office's primary applications use Intellisense technology, helping users to focus on their work and not on their software. Examples of Intellisense are automatic spelling and grammar checking and wizards that lead you through performing basic and complex tasks. Office 97 offers additional Help features, including an animated character called the Office Assistant who provides helpful tips and suggestions as you work.

INTEGRATION FEATURES

Many would say that the essence of Office 97 is its ability to share data among the suite of applications. For example, you can place an Excel chart in a report that you write using Word, a Word document in a presentation created in Power-Point, an Access database in an Excel worksheet, and so on. You can also create objects using shared applications—such as Microsoft Chart, Microsoft Equation Editor, or Microsoft Organization Chart—and insert them in your documents without ever leaving the current Office application.

Further blurring the line between applications, Microsoft Binder allows you to assemble, print, and distribute collections of varied documents. Like working with a real three-ring binder, you can insert documents that you create in Word, Excel, and PowerPoint into a single binder document and withdraw them. Then, you can print the contents of the binder complete with consistent headers and footers and with consecutive page numbering. A binder document also provides an easy way to transfer information from one computer to another, since all the documents are stored in a single file.

INTERNET FEATURES

One of the most exciting innovations in Office 97 is its ability to take advantage of the World Wide Web and the Internet. For those of you new to the online world, the **Internet** is a vast collection of computer networks that spans the entire planet, made up of many smaller networks connected by standard telephone lines, fiber optics, and satellites. More than just an electronic repository for information, the Internet is a *virtual community* with its own culture and tradition. The term **Intranet** refers to a private and usually secure local or wide area network that uses Internet technologies to share information within an organization. To access the Internet, you need a network or modem connection that links your computer to an account on the university's network or to an independent Internet Service Provider (ISP).

Once you are connected to the Internet, you can use web browser software, such as Microsoft Internet Explorer or Netscape Navigator, to access the **World Wide Web (WWW).** The WWW provides a visual interface for the Internet and lets you search for information by simply clicking on highlighted words and images, know as **hyperlinks.** When you click a link, you are telling your computer's web browser to retrieve a page from a web site and display it on your screen. Each web page on the Internet has a unique location or address specified by its *Uniform Resource Locator* or URL. One example of a URL is: http://www.microsoft.com. For more information on the Internet and World Wide Web, visit your local bookstore, campus computing center, or computer users group.

Microsoft Office 97 provides a consistent set of tools for publishing documents, spreadsheets, presentations, and databases to the web and for accessing help information directly from Microsoft's corporate web site. Specifically, each Office application includes a Web toolbar that lets you quickly open, search, and browse through any document on your local computer, corporate or university Intranet, and the Internet. Furthermore, you can create your own hyperlinks and share your documents with the entire world after publishing it to a web server. As you proceed through this manual, look for the Internet integration features found in the In Addition boxes.

WORKING WITH MICROSOFT EXCEL

For years, people used calculators and rolls of paper to perform numerical calculations. With the advancements in computers over the past decade, these manual tools are somewhat obsolete. Accountants, statisticians, and business people now use electronic spreadsheets to analyze their financial and statistical data more accurately and more quickly. However, spreadsheets are much more than glorified calculators; often they are the primary financial tool for a small business.

An electronic spreadsheet is similar to a manual worksheet or an accountant's ledger (Figure 1.1.) With a manual worksheet, you write descriptive labels down the first column or along the top row. Using Microsoft Excel 97, you create a worksheet in much the same way as before, by entering information into cells, or intersections of columns and rows. You can also create formulas, apply formatting options, and save the worksheet to a disk file. An Excel spreadsheet is called a *workbook* and may contain several independent or integrated worksheets. The number of worksheets you can create and store in a workbook is limited only by the memory within your computer.

FIGURE 1.1

PARTIAL VIEW OF AN
ACCOUNTANT'S MANUAL
WORKSHEET

Date	Item	Debit	Credit
19-Jun-96	Sold photocopy machine		
	Dr. Cash in Bank	750.00	
	Cr. Equipment		750.00
25-Jun-96	Sold 20 units of inventory		
	Dr. Accounts Receivable	1000.00	

Some advantages of using Excel over manual worksheets are these:

- *An Excel worksheet is much larger than a manual worksheet.* While a manual worksheet is limited by paper size, each Excel worksheet contains 256 columns and 65,536 rows. Furthermore, you can enter up to 32,000 characters in a single cell!

- *Perform mathematical, statistical, and financial calculations quickly and accurately.* In addition to entering text and numbers into worksheet cells, you can calculate **formulas,** such as 200+350. A formula may consist solely of numbers or it may refer to the contents of other cells.

- *Perform what-if scenarios for planning and budgeting.* Changing a single number in a manual worksheet can mean hours of extra work in recalculating figures. Changing a number in an Excel worksheet, however, instantaneously produces a ripple effect of recalculations for all formulas dependent upon that cell's value. For example, you can quickly test scenarios like "What if my annual sales were only 5,000 units? How would that affect my net income?"

- *Build worksheets quickly using Excel's wizards and templates.* Wizards simplify the process of entering functions, analyzing your data, and working with databases, while templates provide prebuilt workbook solutions.

- *Create charts that visually represent worksheet data.* In addition to the usual line, bar, and pie charts, you can create geographical maps and pinpoint demographics (such as age, income, and education statistics) or analyze regional trends from worksheet information.

PLANNING YOUR WORKSHEET

Would you start building a house or an office building before receiving an architect's plans? Hopefully not! Even experienced builders rely heavily on the planning phase before breaking new ground. Likewise, you wouldn't want to create a spreadsheet without first having a clear objective. This section provides some basic guidelines to help you plan and develop your electronic spreadsheets.

Use the following steps to create a workbook using Excel:

1. Establish your objectives for creating a worksheet.
2. Design the worksheet based on your output or reporting requirements.
3. Construct the worksheet by entering data and creating formulas.
4. Manually test and evaluate the worksheet.
5. Modify, if necessary, and enhance the worksheet.
6. Document the worksheet for other users.

If you are new to electronic spreadsheets, you may not understand the full importance of the above discussion. Don't despair—you'll definitely understand the utility of these steps by the end of this guide. Now, let's begin our journey through Microsoft Excel.

STARTING EXCEL

This session assumes that you are working on a computer with Windows 95 (or Microsoft Windows NT 4.0) and Microsoft Excel 97 loaded on the hard disk drive. Before you load Windows and Excel, let's look at how to use the mouse and keyboard.

USING THE MOUSE AND KEYBOARD

Microsoft Excel 97 for Windows is a complex yet easy-to-learn program. As you proceed through this guide, you will find that there are often three methods for performing the same command or procedure in Excel:

- Menu   Select a command or procedure from the Menu bar.
- Mouse   Point to and click a toolbar button.
- Keyboard   Press a keyboard shortcut (usually CTRL + *letter*).

Although this guide concentrates on the quickest methods, we recommend that you try the others and decide which you prefer. *Don't memorize all of the information in this guide! Be selective and find your favorite methods.*

Although you may use Excel with only a keyboard, much of the program's basic design relies on using a mouse. Regardless of whether your mouse has two or three buttons, you will use the left or primary mouse button for selecting workbook items and menu commands and the right or secondary mouse button for displaying shortcut menus.

The most common mouse actions used in Excel are these:

- Point   Slide the mouse on your desk to position the tip of the mouse pointer over the desired object on the screen.

- Click   Press down and release the left mouse button quickly. Clicking is used to select a cell or an object in the worksheet and to choose menu commands.

- Right-Click   Press down and release the right mouse button. Right-clicking the mouse pointer on a cell or an object displays a context-sensitive shortcut menu.

- Double-Click   Press down and release the mouse button twice in rapid succession. Double-clicking is used to perform in-cell editing and to modify the worksheet tab names in a workbook.

- Drag   Press down and hold the mouse button as you move the mouse pointer across the screen. When the mouse pointer reaches the desired location, release the mouse button. Dragging is used to select a group of cells and to copy or move data.

You may notice that the mouse pointer changes shape as you move it over different parts of the screen. Each mouse pointer shape has its own purpose and may provide you with important information. There are five primary mouse shapes that appear in Excel:

   arrow   Used to choose menu commands and toolbars buttons.

   cross   Used to select cells in a worksheet.

   hourglass   Informs you that Excel is occupied and requests that you wait.

   I-beam   Used to modify and edit text.

   hand   Used to select hyperlinks in the worksheet and in the Help system.

Aside from being the primary input device for creating a worksheet, the keyboard offers shortcut methods for performing commands and procedures. For example, several menu commands have shortcut key combinations listed to the right of the command in the pull-down menu. Therefore, you can perform a command by simply pressing the shortcut keys rather than accessing the Menu bar. Many of these shortcut key combinations are available throughout Windows applications.

LOADING WINDOWS

Because Windows is an operating system, it is loaded automatically into the computer's memory when you turn on the computer. If you haven't already turned your computer on, perform the following steps.

Perform the following steps . . .

1. Turn on the power switches to the computer and monitor. After a few seconds, the Windows desktop will appear (Figure 1.2). (*Note:* The desktop interface on y computer may look different from Figure 1.2.)

2. If a Welcome to Windows dialog box appears, do the following:
   CLICK: Close button (**✕**) in the top corner of the dialog box window

FIGURE 1.2

THE WINDOWS DESKTOP

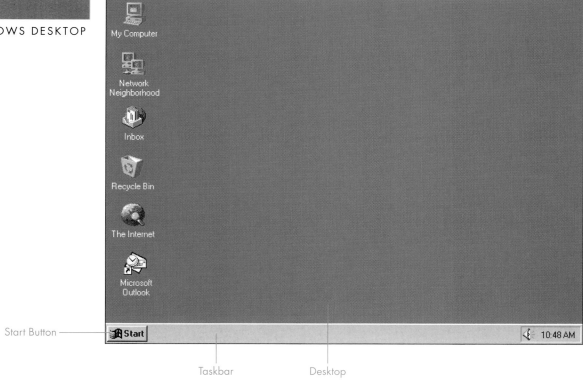

Start Button

Taskbar   Desktop

LOADING MICROSOFT EXCEL 97

Using the Start button (), you can readily access your favorite programs, documents, and system management tools. In this section, you load Microsoft Excel 97 and display a new workbook.

Perform the following steps . . .

1. Position the mouse pointer over top of the Start button ([Start]) and then click the left mouse button once. The Start pop-up menu appears.

2. Point to the Programs command using the mouse. Notice that you do not need to click the left mouse button to display the list of programs in the fly-out or cascading menu.

3. Move the mouse pointer horizontally to the right until it highlights an option in the Programs menu. You can now move the mouse pointer up and down the Programs menu. Notice that you still haven't clicked the left mouse button.

4. Point to the Microsoft Excel menu item and then click the left mouse button once to execute the command. After a few seconds, the Microsoft Excel screen appears.

5. If the Office Assistant window (shown at the right) appears:
   CLICK: Close button ([X]) in its top right-hand corner

The Windows taskbar is usually located on the bottom of your screen below the Status bar. Each application that you are currently working with is represented by a button on the taskbar. Switching between open applications on your desktop is as easy as clicking the appropriate taskbar button, like switching channels on a television set. At this point, you should see a button for Microsoft Excel on the taskbar.

QUICK REFERENCE   1. **CLICK: Start button ([Start])**
Loading Microsoft Excel 97   2. **CHOOSE: Programs, Microsoft Excel**

THE GUIDED TOUR

Software programs designed for Microsoft Windows have many similarities in screen design and layout. Each program operates in its own application window, while the spreadsheets, letters, and presentations you create appear in separate document windows. This section describes the components found in the Excel application and document windows.

APPLICATION WINDOW

When you first load Excel, the screen displays the **application window** and a maximized **document window.** The application window (Figure 1.3) contains the Title bar, Menu bar, Standard toolbar, Formatting toolbar, Formula bar and Name box, and Status bar. You create new worksheets or open existing workbooks in the document area. In Figure 1.3, the document area is covered entirely by a maximized document window.

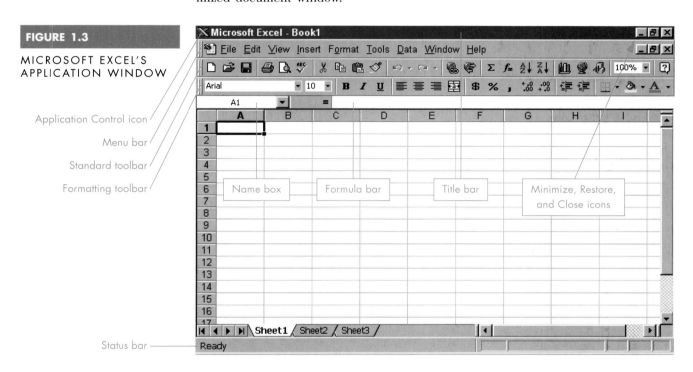

FIGURE 1.3

MICROSOFT EXCEL'S
APPLICATION WINDOW

Application Control icon

Menu bar

Standard toolbar

Formatting toolbar

Status bar

The primary components of the application window are:

Application Control icon ()	Used to identify the application. You can double-click the Control icon to close Microsoft Excel.
Minimize (▭) and Maximize (▢), Restore (▣), and Close (✕) icons	Located in the top right-hand corner, these icons control the display of the application window using the mouse. (*Note*: Since the window is already maximized, the Maximize icon does not appear in Figure 1.3.)
Title bar	The Title bar contains the name of the program and/or workbook file. You can also move a window that is not maximized by dragging its Title bar.
Menu bar	Contains the Excel menu commands.
Standard toolbar	Displays buttons for accessing file management and editing commands using a mouse.
Formatting toolbar	Displays buttons for accessing character and cell formatting commands using the mouse.

| Formula bar | Appears below the toolbars and includes the Name box and Edit Formula button (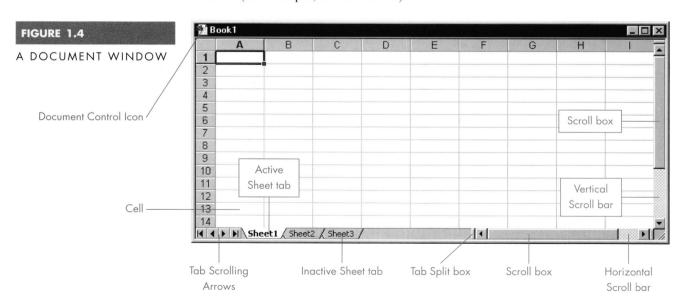). |
| Status bar | Located at the bottom of the application window, the Status bar displays the current status or mode and other helpful information. |

Although the application window is usually maximized, you can reduce it to a window that appears on the desktop. You can then size, move, and manipulate the application window to customize your work environment in Windows. In this guide, we assume that the Excel application window is always maximized.

DOCUMENT WINDOW

You create and store related worksheets and charts in a special file called a **workbook.** You can think of an Excel workbook as a three-ring binder with tabs at the beginning of each new section or topic. In a workbook, you can add and delete sections, copy information from one worksheet section to another, and summarize data in the entire workbook. Each workbook appears in its own document window which can be minimized to an icon, maximized to fill the entire document area, or displayed as a window.

Each new workbook contains three blank worksheets labeled Sheet1, Sheet2, and Sheet3. Similar to a large piece of ledger paper, a worksheet (Figure 1.4) is divided into vertical columns and horizontal rows. The rows are numbered and the columns are labeled from A to Z, then AA to AZ, and so on to column IV. The intersection of a column and a row is called a **cell.** Each cell is given a **cell address,** like a post office box number, consisting of its column letter followed by its row number (for example, B4 or FX400).

FIGURE 1.4

A DOCUMENT WINDOW

A document window consists of the following parts:

Document Control icon ()	Used to size and position the window using the keyboard. You can double-click the Control icon to close the document window.
Scroll bars	Placed at the right and bottom borders of the document window, scroll bars facilitate moving around a worksheet using the mouse.
Sheet tabs	Sheet tabs identify the various pages or sections in a workbook. You click a tab to move to that worksheet or double-click a tab to change its name.
Tab Split box	Drag the tab split box to increase or decrease the space shared by the sheet tabs and the horizontal scroll bar.
Tab Scrolling arrows	Click the tab scrolling arrows to move quickly to the first sheet, previous sheet, next sheet, or last sheet in a workbook.

You should recognize some familiar components in the document window that appear in all windows. For example, the Minimize, Maximize, and Close buttons also appear in the top right-hand corner of the document window. To restore a maximized document to a window, you click the Restore button ([⊟]). To maximize a document window, you click the Maximize button ([☐]). Before proceeding, make sure that the document window is maximized and that you can identify the window icons for both the application and the document window (as shown below):

Application window icons ——— [_ ⊟ X]
Document window icons ——— [_ ⊟ X]

You can display several workbooks concurrently within the application window. For example, you may want to view data from several departments on the screen at the same time. Assuming that the data is divided into separate workbooks, you can open each file in its own document window. Another method for accomplishing this type of summary perspective is to create and store multiple worksheets in a single workbook file. Similar to peeling off pages from a notepad, you enter each department's data on its own worksheet and then consolidate the data in a separate summary worksheet. In Session 4, you learn how to work with multiple workbook files and multiple-sheet workbooks.

MENU BAR

Excel commands are grouped together on the Menu bar, as shown in the example provided below.

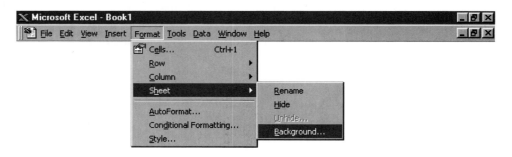

Commands in this guide are written in the following form:

    CHOOSE: Format, Sheet, Background

where Format is the Menu bar option, Sheet is the command on the pull-down menu, and Background is the command on the fly-out menu. To execute a command, click once on the Menu bar option and then click once on the desired menu commands. Commands that are not available for selection appear dimmed. Commands that are followed by an ellipsis (Background..., for example) require further information to be collected in a dialog box.

In the following exercise, you practice accessing the Menu bar.

Perform the following steps . . .

1. To choose the Help command, position the tip of the mouse pointer on the word Help in the Menu bar and click the left mouse button once. A pull-down menu appears below the Help option.

2. To see the pull-down menus associated with other menu options, drag the mouse pointer slowly to the left over the additional options on the Menu bar. (*Note:* You need not hold down the left mouse button as you move the mouse pointer.)

3. To leave the Menu bar without making a command selection, position the pointer in a blank area of the Title bar and click once. On your own, try clicking the Help menu item repeatedly and notice how the pull-down menu appears and disappears.

4. To display the pull-down menu for the File option:
CHOOSE: File
This instruction tells you to click the left mouse button once with the pointer on the File option in the Menu bar. (*Note:* All menu commands that you execute in this guide begin with the word "CHOOSE.")

5. To leave the Menu bar without making a selection:
CLICK: an empty area on the Excel Title bar

SHORTCUT MENUS

Excel provides context-sensitive shortcut menus for quick access to menu commands. Rather than searching for commands in the Menu bar, you position the mouse pointer on an object, such as a cell or toolbar, and click the right mouse button. A pop-up menu appears with the most commonly selected commands for the object.

Let's now practice accessing a shortcut menu.

Perform the following steps . . .

1. To display a shortcut menu, position the mouse pointer over any cell in the worksheet and click the right mouse button. The shortcut menu at the right should appear.

2. To remove the shortcut menu from the screen:
   PRESS: (ESC)
   The shortcut menu disappears.

✂	Cut
📋	Copy
📋	Paste
	Paste Special...
	Insert...
	Delete...
	Clear Contents
📝	Insert Comment
📋	Format Cells...
	Pick From List...

QUICK REFERENCE
Using Shortcut Menus

1. **Position the mouse pointer over an object.**
2. **CLICK: shortcut or right mouse button to display a pop-up menu**
3. **CHOOSE: a command from the menu, or**
   PRESS: (ESC) to remove the menu

TOOLBARS

In the application window, you will see the Standard and Formatting toolbars appear below the Menu bar. Excel provides several toolbars and hundreds of buttons for quick and easy mouse access to its more popular features. Don't worry about memorizing the button names appearing in the following figures, you can simply point to any toolbar button using the mouse and pause until a ToolTip label appears with the button's name.

The Standard toolbar (Figure 1.5) provides access to file management and editing commands, in addition to special features like the Office Assistant and the ChartWizard:

FIGURE 1.5

STANDARD TOOLBAR

The Formatting toolbar (Figure 1.6) lets you access character and cell formatting commands:

FIGURE 1.6

FORMATTING TOOLBAR

To display additional toolbars, you point to a visible toolbar and click the right mouse button to display a shortcut menu. You can show and hide toolbars by choosing their names in the resulting pop-up menu. If a toolbar is currently being displayed, a check mark appears beside its name.

You will now practice displaying and hiding toolbars.

Perform the following steps . . .

1. Position the mouse pointer over any button on the Standard toolbar.

2. To display the Drawing toolbar:
    CLICK: right mouse button to display the shortcut menu
    CHOOSE: Drawing

3. To remove the toolbar:
    RIGHT-CLICK: Drawing toolbar
    This instruction tells you to position the mouse pointer over the Drawing toolbar and click the right mouse button.

4. CHOOSE: Drawing
    The Drawing toolbar disappears from the application window.

IN ADDITION MOVING TOOLBARS

● To undock a toolbar, position the mouse pointer over the Move bar (▥) appearing at the left of the docked toolbar. Click the left mouse button and drag the toolbar into the application window. The toolbar turns into a

floating window, complete with a Title bar and Close box.

● To redock a floating toolbar, position the mouse pointer over its Title bar and drag it toward one of the borders. Release the mouse button when the toolbar snaps into place.

DIALOG BOX

A dialog box is a common mechanism in Windows applications for collecting information before processing a command (Figure 1.7). In a dialog box, you indicate the options you want to use and then click the OK command button when you're finished. Dialog boxes are also used to display messages or to ask for confirmation of commands.

FIGURE 1.7

A DIALOG BOX

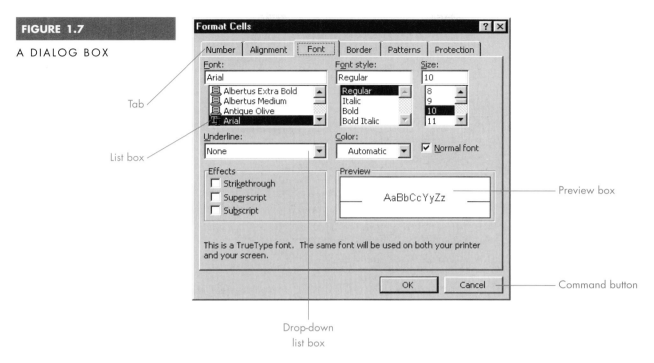

Tab

List box

Preview box

Command button

Drop-down
list box

A dialog box uses several types of controls or components for collecting information. We describe the most common components in Table 1.1.

TABLE 1.1

Dialog Box Components

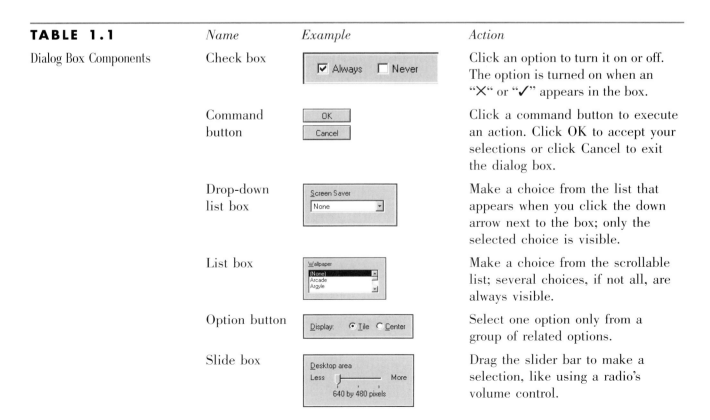

Name	Example	Action
Check box	☑ Always ☐ Never	Click an option to turn it on or off. The option is turned on when an "✕" or "✓" appears in the box.
Command button	OK Cancel	Click a command button to execute an action. Click OK to accept your selections or click Cancel to exit the dialog box.
Drop-down list box	Screen Saver None	Make a choice from the list that appears when you click the down arrow next to the box; only the selected choice is visible.
List box	Wallpaper (None) Arcade Argyle	Make a choice from the scrollable list; several choices, if not all, are always visible.
Option button	Display: ⦿ Tile ○ Center	Select one option only from a group of related options.
Slide box	Desktop area Less ▮— More 640 by 480 pixels	Drag the slider bar to make a selection, like using a radio's volume control.

TABLE 1.1	*Name*	*Example*	*Action*
Continued	Spin box	Wait: 6 ⬍ minutes	Click the up and down arrows to the right of the box until the number you want appears.
	Tab	Contents | Index | Find	Click a named tab to access other pages in the dialog box.
	Text box	File name: untitled	Click inside the text box and then type the desired information.

Most dialog boxes also provide a question mark icon ([**?**]) near the right side of the Title bar. If you have a question about an item in the dialog box, click the question mark and then click the item to display a pop-up help window. To remove the help window, click on it once.

GETTING HELP

Excel provides several **context-sensitive help** features and a comprehensive library of online documentation. Like many developers trying to minimize the retail price of software and maximize profits, Microsoft has stopped shipping volumes of print-based documentation in favor of on-line and web-based Help options. This section describes Excel's help features and how to find more detailed information.

CONTEXT-SENSITIVE HELP

Context-sensitive help refers to a program's ability to present helpful information reflecting your current position in the program. In Excel, you can access context-sensitive help for menu options, toolbar buttons, and dialog box items. The help information is presented concisely in a small pop-up window that you can remove with the click of the mouse. This type of help lets you access information quickly and then continue working without interruption. Table 1.2 describes some methods for accessing context-sensitive help while working in Excel.

TABLE 1.2	To display . . .	Do this . . .
Displaying Context-Sensitive Help Information	A description of a dialog box item	Click the question mark button (?) in a dialog box's Title bar and then click an item in the dialog box. A helpful description of the item appears in a pop-up window. Alternatively, you can often right-click a dialog box item and then chose the What's This? command from the shortcut menu.
	A description of a menu command	Choose Help, What's This? command and then choose a command using the question mark mouse pointer. Rather than executing the command, a helpful description of the command appears in a pop-up window.
	A description of a toolbar button	Point to a toolbar button to display its ToolTip label. You can also choose the Help, What's This? command and then click a toolbar button to display more detailed help information.

In the following exercise, you will access context-sensitive help.

 Perform the following steps . . .

1. To display help for the File, New command, you must first activate the question mark mouse pointer. Do the following:
   CHOOSE: Help, What's This?
   Your mouse pointer should now appear with an attached question mark.
   (*Note:* You can also press **SHIFT** + **F1** to activate this pointer.)

2. Using the question mark mouse pointer (and not the keyboard):
   CHOOSE: File, New
   Rather than executing the command, Excel provides a description of the command in a pop-up window.

3. After reading the description, close the window by clicking on it once.

4. To display a ToolTip for a toolbar button, position the mouse pointer over the AutoSum button (Σ) on the Standard toolbar. After a second or two, a ToolTip will appear showing the button's name.

5. To display additional information for the AutoSum button:
   PRESS: **SHIFT** + **F1**
   This command tells you to hold down the **SHIFT** key and then tap the **F1** key. Then, release the **SHIFT** key.

6. CLICK: AutoSum button (Σ)
The following pop-up window appears:

> **AutoSum**
>
> In Microsoft Excel, adds numbers automatically with the SUM function. Microsoft Excel suggests the range of cells to be added. If the suggested range is incorrect, drag through the range you want, and then press ENTER.
>
> In Word, inserts an = (Formula) field that calculates and displays the sum of the values in table cells above or to the left of the cell containing the insertion point.

7. CLICK: the pop-up window once to remove it

QUICK REFERENCE
Displaying Context-
Sensitive Help

1. **CHOOSE: Help, What's This?**

2. **Using the question mark mouse pointer, select the desired item for which you want to display a help pop-up window.**

OFFICE ASSISTANT

The Office Assistant is your personal and customizable computer guru. When you need to accomplish a particular task, you call up the Assistant by clicking the Office Assistant button (?) on the Standard toolbar. To conduct a search of the entire Help system, you simply type an English phrase in the form of a question. The Assistant analyzes your request and provides a resource list of suggested topics. Furthermore, the Assistant watches your keystrokes and mouse clicks as you work and can offer suggestions and shortcuts to make you more productive and efficient.

Let's put your Assistant to work.

 **Perform
the
following
steps . . .**

1. To display the Office Assistant:
CLICK: Office Assistant button (?)
The Office Assistant and its associated tip window appear as shown in Figure 1.8. Notice that the text in the tip window is selected, ready for you to begin typing your question.

FIGURE 1.8

OFFICE ASSISTANT AND
TIP WINDOW

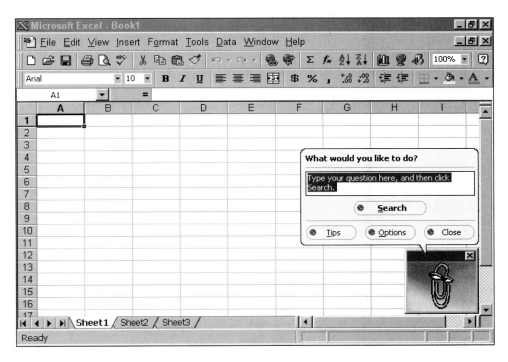

2. Type your request just as you would ask the question out loud. For this example, let's find out what a "function" is in an Excel worksheet.
   TYPE: What is a function?
   CLICK: Search button
   (*Note:* You need not be concerned about typing your questions using perfect grammar or punctuation. However, spelling does count!)

3. A tip window appears with several topics displayed. You must now refine your search by selecting one of these topics. Do the following:
   CLICK: About using functions to calculate values
   A Help Topics window appears with the requested information. You will learn more about working with this window in the next section.

4. CLICK: Close button (🗙) on the Help Topics window
   CLICK: Close button (🗙) on the Office Assistant window

Occasionally an illuminated light bulb will appear in the Office Assistant window. This light bulb informs you that the Assistant wants to share a new tip or suggestion with you. To view the tip, click the light bulb in the Office Assistant window. To close the window, click its Close button.

IN ADDITION CUSTOMIZING THE OFFICE ASSISTANT

- To customize your Assistant's appearance:
  RIGHT-CLICK: Office Assistant window
  CHOOSE: Choose Assistant from the pop-up menu

- To customize your Assistant's behavior:
  RIGHT-CLICK: Office Assistant window
  CHOOSE: Options from the pop-up menu

HELP TOPICS WINDOW

For a complete topical listing of Excel's Help system, choose the Contents and Index command from the Help menu. This command displays the Help Topics window, as shown in Figure 1.9. You can think of the Help Topics window as the front door to Excel's vast help resources.

FIGURE 1.9

HELP TOPICS WINDOW: *CONTENTS* TAB

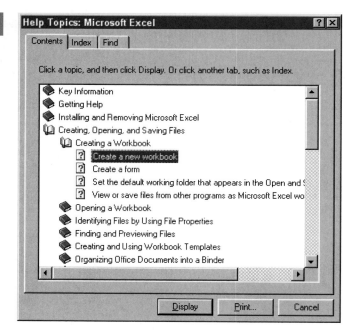

The Help Topics window provides three different tools, each on its own tab, to help you find the information you need quickly and easily. You point to and click a tab using the mouse to make the tab active in the window. Refer to the following tab descriptions to determine which tool you should use when requiring assistance:

- *Contents* tab   Displays a list of help topics organized as a hierarchy of books and pages. This tab is your Table of Contents for the entire Help system. Notice in Figure 1.9 that there are three different types of icons displayed:

  📚 represents a help category; double-click a book icon to view the books and topics it contains represents an open category that is currently displaying its contents; double-click an open book icon to close (or collapse) the book

? represents a help topic; double-click a topic icon to display a help window

● *Index* tab   Displays an alphabetical list of keywords and phrases, similar to a traditional book index. To search for a topic using this tab, type a word (or even a few letters) into the text box which, in turn, makes the list box scroll to the first matching entry in the index. Then, double-click the desired entry to display the help topic. If a keyword has more than one associated topic, a Topics Found window appears and you can select a further topic to narrow your search.

● *Find* tab   Provides the ability to conduct a full-text search of the Help system for finding a particular word or phrase. Although similar to the *Index* tab, this tab differs in its ability to look past indexed keywords and search the help text itself.

When you double-click a help topic, it is displayed in a *secondary* window. You may find that secondary windows include some unfamiliar buttons, like ≫ and ↰, embedded in the help text. The ≫ symbol, which we'll called the Chiclet button, represents a "See Also" link that you can click to move to a related topic. The Show Me symbol (↰) actually initiates the command you're interested in. You may also notice that some words or phrases in the help window have a dotted underline. If you click such a word or phrase, a definition pop-up window appears.

You will now access the Help Topics window.

Perform the following steps . . .

1. To display the Help Topics window:
CHOOSE: Help, Contents and Index

2. CLICK: *Contents* tab
Your screen should now appear similar to Figure 1.9, except that your book categories will appear collapsed. (*Note*: The Help Topics window remembers the tab that was selected when it was last closed. It will automatically return to this tab the next time you access Help.)

3. To display the contents of a book:
DOUBLE-CLICK: "◆ Entering Data and Selecting Cells" book
(*Note*: You can double-click the book icon (◆) or the book's title. If you find it difficult to double-click using the mouse, you can also select or highlight the book by clicking it once and then click the Open command button.) This particular book contains two additional categories.

4. To further clarify the search:
   DOUBLE-CLICK: "📖 Entering Data" book
   Notice that this book contains multiple topics.

5. To display a help topic:
   DOUBLE-CLICK: "❓ Entering data in worksheet cells" topic
   The Help Topics window is removed from view and a secondary window appears with the topic information.

6. To further refine your search:
   CLICK: "➤➤ Enter numbers, text, a date, or a time"
   Notice that the mouse pointer changed to a hand.

7. To print the help topic that appears:
   CLICK: Options command button at the top of the window
   CHOOSE: Print Topic
   (*Note*: You can also print help information directly from the *Contents* tab. If you select a book and then click the Print command button, the entire book, including the additional book categories that may be contained within the book, is sent to the printer.)

8. In the Print dialog box that appears:

   - CLICK: OK command button to print the topic, or

   - CLICK: Cancel command button if you do not have a printer

   Whatever your selection, you are returned to the secondary window. (*Note:* If you selected to print the topic and your computer does not have a printer connected, you may be returned to Excel with an error message. In this case, you can skip the next step.)

9. To close the help window and return to Excel:
   CLICK: Close button (❌)

<table>
<tr>
<td>

QUICK REFERENCE
Searching for Help Using
the Help Topics Window

</td>
<td>

1. **To display the Help Topics window:**

   CHOOSE: Help, Contents and Index

2. **CLICK:** *Contents* **tab to navigate a hierarchical Help system**

   CLICK: *Index* **tab to search for a word or phrase in a keyword index**

   CLICK: *Find* **tab to conduct a full-text search of the Help system**

</td>
</tr>
</table>

If you are connected to the Internet, you can keep current on product and company news by visiting Microsoft's web site. You'll also find helpful productivity tips and online support for all the Office 97 products.

To access this information:

1. Establish an Internet connection.

2. CHOOSE: Help, Microsoft on the Web

3. CHOOSE: *a menu option as shown at the right*

🌐 *F*ree Stuff
🌐 *P*roduct News
🌐 Frequently Asked *Q*uestions
🌐 Online *S*upport
🌐 Microsoft *O*ffice Home Page
🌐 Send Feedbac*k*...
🌐 *B*est of the Web
🌐 Search the *W*eb...
🌐 Web *T*utorial
🌐 Microsoft *H*ome Page

Moving the Cell Pointer

When you first open a new workbook, the **cell pointer** is positioned on cell A1 in Sheet1. For your convenience, Excel displays the current cell address in the Name box at the left-hand side of the Formula bar. In this section, you learn how to move the cell pointer around the worksheet using the mouse and keyboard. Although rudimentary, these skills are vital for efficiently creating and viewing worksheets.

Perform the following steps . . .

1. To move the cell pointer to cell G4 using the keyboard:
    PRESS: ➡ six times
            PRESS: ⬇ three times
    Notice that the cell address appears in the Name box and that the column and row headings are boldface.

2. To move to cell E12 using a mouse:
    CLICK: cell E12
    (*Hint*: Position the cross mouse pointer over cell E12 and click the left mouse button once.)

3. To move to cell E24 using the keyboard:
    PRESS: ⬇ 12 times
    You may notice that the first few rows scroll off the top of the screen.

4. To move to cell E124 using the keyboard, there is an easier method than pressing the ⬇ key 100 times. The **PgUp** and **PgDn** keys are used to move up and down a worksheet by as many rows as fit in the current document window. To move to cell E124, do the following:
    PRESS: **PgDn** until cell E124 is in view
            PRESS: ⬆ or ⬇ arrow keys to move to cell E124

5. To move back to cell E24 using the mouse:

CLICK: ▲ on the vertical scroll bar and hold down the left mouse button
CLICK: cell E24 when it appears after scrolling
(*Note*: You can also drag the scroll box on the vertical scroll bar.)

6. To move to cell AE24:
CLICK: ▶ on the horizontal scroll bar and hold down the left mouse button
CLICK: cell AE24 to move the cell pointer

7. To move back to cell E24:
DRAG: scroll box to the left on the horizontal scroll bar
Notice that a Scroll Tip appears showing the column letter as you drag the mouse. When you see "Column: E" in the Scroll Tip, stop dragging and proceed to Step 8.

8. CLICK: cell E24 to move the cell pointer

9. To move to the first cell (A1) in the worksheet using the keyboard:
PRESS: CTRL + HOME

10. To move the cell pointer in any direction until the cell contents change from empty to filled, filled to empty, or until a border is encountered, press CTRL with an arrow key. To move to column IV:
PRESS: CTRL + ➡

11. To move to row 65,536 (the last cell at the bottom of the worksheet):
PRESS: CTRL + ⬇

12. You can also use the Name box to move directly to any cell in the worksheet. To move to cell AA100, for example:
CLICK: Name box with the I-beam mouse pointer
The cell address in the Name box will appear highlighted.

13. TYPE: aa100
PRESS: ENTER
You are taken immediately to cell AA100.

14. To move back to cell A1:
PRESS: CTRL + HOME

Now you're ready to start entering some information into the worksheet!

OVERVIEW OF DATA ENTRY

You create a worksheet by entering information into the individual cells. A worksheet can be as simple as a five-item household budget or as complex as an order-entry and invoicing application. The remainder of this session explores the basic building blocks for creating a worksheet from scratch, including entering, editing, and deleting cell information.

There are several types of information that may be entered into a worksheet cell: text, numbers, dates and times, formulas, and functions. To begin entering data, you must first move the cell pointer to the desired cell. Then, type the characters that you want to appear in the cell. And finally, you complete the entry by pressing (ENTER) or by clicking the mouse pointer on another cell.

To practice entering data, you will create the worksheet appearing in Figure 1.10 by the completion of this section.

FIGURE 1.10

SAMPLE WORKSHEET

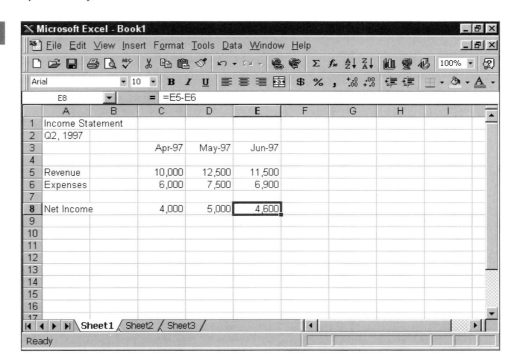

ENTERING TEXT

Text labels enhance the readability of a worksheet with headings, instructions, and descriptive information. Although a typical worksheet column is only eight or nine characters wide, a single cell in a worksheet can hold thousands of characters. With longer entries, the text spills over into the next cell, if it is empty. Later, you will learn how to emphasize important text using different fonts and alignment options.

Let's begin creating the worksheet.

Perform the following steps . . .

1. Move to cell A1. (*Hint*: (CTRL) + (HOME))
   For the remainder of this guide, you can use either the keyboard or mouse to move the cell pointer.

2. As you type the following text, watch the Formula bar. Enter the following heading for the worksheet:
TYPE: Income Statement
Notice that there is an ⊠ and a ▢ to the left of the text in the Formula bar. Rather than pressing (ENTER) to accept the entry or (ESC) to cancel the entry, you can click the ▢ and ⊠ symbols respectively.

3. To accept the entry and deposit it into the current cell:
PRESS: (ENTER)
Notice that the words do not fit in a single cell and must spill over into column B. This is acceptable as long as you do not want to place any information into cell B1. Otherwise, you would have to increase the width of column A. Session 2 discusses changing a column's width.
(*Note*: By default, Excel automatically moves the cell pointer down to the next row when you press (ENTER). If your cell pointer did not move to A2 when you pressed (ENTER), choose the Tools, Options command from the menu and select the *Edit* tab. From the resulting dialog box page, make sure that a "✓" appears in the *Move selection after Enter* check box and that "Down" is selected in the *Direction* drop-down list box. When finished, click the OK command button.)

4. Move the cell pointer into the following cells and type in the corresponding text. When you are finished typing a label, press (ENTER) or an arrow key. If you prefer using the mouse, you can click on the next cell after you have finished typing the label. If you make a mistake while typing, press the (BACKSPACE) key to delete the mistake and then type the correct information.

Enter the following text:

Move to Cell	TYPE:
A2	Q2, 1997
A5	Revenue
A6	Expenses
A8	Net Income

All the text data has now been entered into the worksheet.

ENTERING DATES

You enter dates as values in order to perform date arithmetic, such as calculating how many days have elapsed between two dates. Dates are typically entered into cells using one of the following formats: mm/dd/yy (for example, 12/31/96) or dd-mmm-yy (for example, 31-Dec-96). If you need to display monthly headings across the top of a column, you can enter a date as mmm-yy (for example, Dec-96).

You will now enter dates into the worksheet.

Perform the following steps . . .

1. Move to cell C3.

2. TYPE: Apr-97
   PRESS: ➡

3. Move the cell pointer into the following cells and type in the corresponding dates:

Move to Cell	TYPE
D3	May-97
E3	Jun-97

   With the cell pointer positioned on cell E3, you will notice that the Formula bar contains "6/1/1997" and not "Jun-97." This is one example of how the appearance of a cell can differ from its actual contents. You will encounter other examples later in this session.

All the dates have now been entered into the worksheet.

IN ADDITION ENTERING A DATE SERIES USING AUTOFILL

In Session 3, you learn how to use Excel's AutoFill feature for quickly entering a date series. This feature is especially useful for placing monthly headings at the top of your worksheet or listing consecutive dates (for example, 3/1/97, 3/2/97, and so on) down a column.

ENTERING NUMBERS

Numbers are entered into the worksheet for use in formulas and reports. Whereas text is initially left-aligned with the cell border, numbers and dates are right-aligned. When the cell pointer is positioned on a cell that contains a number, the raw form of the number usually appears in the Formula bar. In other words, the cell may read 8.50% in the worksheet but the value in the Formula bar reads .085. It is important to note that phone numbers, Social Security numbers, and zip codes are not considered numeric values, since they are never used in mathematical calculations.

Let's complete entering the static data into the worksheet.

Perform the following steps . . .

1. Move to cell C5.

2. TYPE: **10,000**
   PRESS: ➡
   (*Note*: When you start constructing formulas, you will enter values without any formatting (for example, 10000). In this step, you have entered a comma in the value to demonstrate an Excel formatting feature and to improve the readability of the worksheet.)

3. Move the cell pointer into the following cells and type in the corresponding numbers:

Move to Cell	TYPE
D5	12,500
E5	11,500

All the numeric data has now been entered into the worksheet. You are ready to enter formulas to calculate the remaining values.

QUICK REFERENCE
Entering Data

1. **Move the cell pointer to the desired cell location.**
2. **Type the information into the Formula bar. If you make a typing or spelling mistake, press the BACKSPACE key to erase the mistake.**
3. **To deposit the information into the cell, press ENTER or an arrow key, or click on a new cell using the mouse.**

ENTERING FORMULAS

A formula is a mathematical calculation that may contain numbers, cell references, and mathematical operators. The basic mathematical operators and rules of precedence apply to an Excel formula. These operators are similar to those found in most electronic spreadsheets (and high school algebra textbooks). For example, in the formula *(3+4)*5*, the *3+4* operation is performed before multiplying the sum by *5* because it appears in parentheses. Table 1.3 lists the common mathematical operators. As for the rules of precedence, Excel calculates what appears in parentheses first, multiplication and division operations (from left to right) second, and, lastly, addition and subtraction (again from left to right).

TABLE 1.3	Symbol	Description
Basic Mathematical Operators	( )	Parentheses
	*	Multiplication
	/	Division
	+	Addition
	−	Subtraction
	%	Percentage
	^	Exponentiation

You enter a formula into the worksheet by positioning the cell pointer where you want the result to appear and then typing an equal sign (=) to precede the expression. You can complete the expression either by typing or by pointing to the cell addresses. Newly introduced in Excel 97, you can use your own worksheet terminology (row and column headings) in constructing formulas rather than using cell references.

In the following exercise, you enter a formula that calculates Expenses as 60% of Revenue. Your first step is to move the cell pointer to where you want the result to appear and then enter the formula into the cell.

Perform the following steps . . .

1. Move to cell C6.

2. TYPE: =c5*60%
   PRESS: ➡
   In this expression, "c5" represents the cell address in the worksheet.

3. Move the cell pointer into the following cells and type in the corresponding formulas.

Move to Cell	TYPE
D6	=d5*60%
E6	=e5*60%

4. Let's create a second formula to subtract Expenses from Revenue, yielding Net Income. When constructing the formula, glance at the Formula bar to see the results of your mouse clicks and keystrokes.
   CLICK: cell C8

5. In this step, you build a formula by pointing:
TYPE: =
CLICK: cell C5
TYPE: –
CLICK: cell C6
CLICK: ▨ in the Formula bar
The answer 4,000 should now appear in the cell.

6. SELECT: cell D8

7. CLICK: Edit Formula button (▨) in the Formula bar
Notice that the equal sign is automatically entered in the Formula bar and
that a display box called the Formula Palette appears.

8. If the Office Assistant appears asking to help create the formula, click the
No option and then proceed with the following steps:
CLICK: cell D5 (12,500)
TYPE: –
CLICK: cell D6 (7,500)
Notice that the Formula Palette displays "Formula result = 5,000" as
shown in Figure 1.11. This feature is useful for checking your work as you
build a long formula.

FIGURE 1.11

EDIT FORMULA
DISPLAY BOX

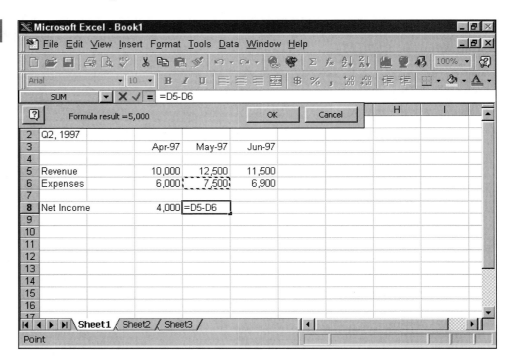

9. To complete the formula:
CLICK: OK command button in the display box

10. To demonstrate that Excel is paying attention, let's create a new *Natural Language Formula*:
CLICK: cell E8
TYPE: **=Revenue-Expenses**
PRESS: **ENTER**
Excel quickly reviews the worksheet, taking note of the column and row headings, and then calculates the formula and displays the result. Your worksheet should now appear similar to Figure 1.10.

QUICK REFERENCE Entering a Formula	1. **Select the cell to contain the formula.** 2. **TYPE: = (an equal sign)** 3. **Enter the desired expression (for example, A4+B4) by typing or by pointing to the cells using the mouse.** 4. **PRESS: ENTER or CLICK: ▨ in the Formula bar**

EDITING A CELL

What if you type a label, a number, or a formula into a cell and then decide it needs to be changed? Novices and experts alike make data entry errors when creating a worksheet. Fortunately, Excel provides several options for editing information that has already been entered.

The primary methods for editing information are these:

- Before you press **ENTER** or click on another cell to deposit an entry, you can correct a typing or spelling mistake using **BACKSPACE**

- You can replace a cell's contents by typing over the original data. When you press **ENTER**, the new data overwrites the original contents.

- If a cell's entry is too long or complicated to retype, you can edit the entry by double-clicking the cell or by selecting the cell and pressing **F2**. A flashing vertical bar appears in the cell, advising you that the entry may be modified. After making the necessary changes, you press **ENTER** to overwrite the original cell or **ESC** to abort the modifications.

● You can also select a cell and then move the mouse pointer into the Formula bar area until it changes into an I-beam. At this point, click the left mouse button once to begin editing the contents of the Formula bar. Clicking ☑ performs the same function as pressing (ENTER) and clicking ☒ performs the same function as pressing (ESC).

Practice editing information in the worksheet.

Perform the following steps . . .

1. CLICK: cell A1

2. TYPE: Profit/Loss Report
   PRESS: (ENTER)

3. To modify the entry in cell A2 to read "Quarter 2" instead of "Q2":
   DOUBLE-CLICK: cell A2
   (*Note*: You can also press (F2) to enter Edit mode.)

4. Using the (◄) and (►) keys or the mouse, position the flashing vertical bar between the "Q" and the "2."

5. TYPE: uarter
   PRESS: Space bar
   PRESS: (ENTER)
   The cell entry should now read "Quarter 2, 1997."

6. DOUBLE-CLICK: cell C8
   Notice that the formula components in the cell are color-coded and that these colors correspond to the cell borders highlighted in the worksheet, as shown below. This feature, called *Range Finder*, is useful when you need to identify whether a calculation is drawing data from the correct cells.

	Apr-97	May-97	Jun-97
	10,000	12,500	11,500
	6,000	7,500	6,900
	=C5-C6	5,000	4,600

7. To cancel the Edit mode:
   CLICK: ☒ in the Formula bar

QUICK REFERENCE
Editing a Cell's Contents

1. DOUBLE-CLICK: the cell that you want to edit (or PRESS: (F2))
2. Use the mouse and arrow keys to edit the entry.
3. PRESS: (ENTER) or CLICK: ☑

ERASING A CELL

Excel allows you to quickly erase a single cell, a group of cells, or the entire worksheet with a few simple keystrokes. To erase a cell's contents, highlight the cell and press the DELETE key. If you would like to delete only the formatting of a cell, you choose Edit, Clear from the Menu bar to display further commands (listed in Table 1.4) on a cascading menu.

	Command	Description
TABLE 1.4		
Edit, Clear Commands	All	Removes the cell contents, formatting (for example, boldface and italic), and comments (reminders that are attached to a cell but do not appear when printed).
	Formats	Removes the cell formatting only, leaving the contents and attached cell comments intact.
	Contents	Removes the cell contents only, leaving the formatting and attached cell comments intact; same as DELETE.
	Comments	Removes the cell comments only, leaving the cell contents and formatting intact.

In the next exercise, you practice erasing information from the worksheet.

Perform the following steps . . .

1. Move to cell A2.

2. PRESS: DELETE to remove the information from the cell

3. Move to cell A8.

4. CHOOSE: Edit, Clear
   CHOOSE: All from the fly-out menu
   Do not perform another command until proceeding to the next section, where you learn how to undo a command.

QUICK REFERENCE
Erasing a Cell

1. **SELECT: the cell that you want to erase**

2. **PRESS:** DELETE

USING THE UNDO COMMAND

The **Undo command** allows you to cancel up to the last 16 actions you performed in the worksheet. There are three methods for executing the Undo command. You can choose Edit, Undo from the menu, press the keyboard shortcut of **CTRL**+z, or click the Undo button (🔄▾) on the Standard toolbar.

Let's practice two of these methods in the next exercise.

Perform the following steps . . .

1. To undo the last command that you executed in the previous section:
CLICK: Undo button (🔄▾)
Ensure that you click the main arrow portion of the toolbar button and not the drop-down triangle to the right. The words "Net Income" reappear in the worksheet.

2. SELECT: cell A1

3. PRESS: **DELETE**

4. CLICK: drop-down triangle on the Undo button (🔄▾)
Your screen should now appear similar to Figure 1.12.

FIGURE 1.12

PERFORMING A
MULTIPLE UNDO

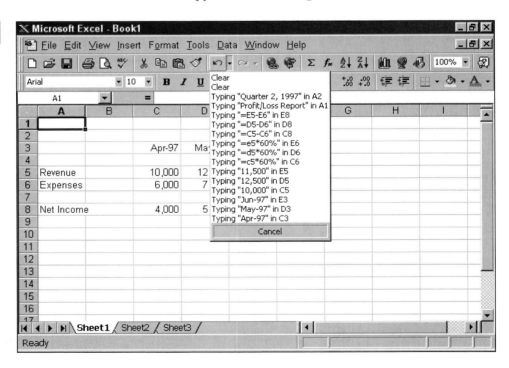

5. Move the mouse pointer downward in the Undo drop-down list until the first four items are highlighted.

QUICK REFERENCE	•	**CHOOSE: Edit, Undo, or**
Undo a Command	•	**PRESS:** CTRL +z, **or**
	•	**CLICK: Undo button (** 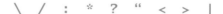 **) on the Standard toolbar**

6. To perform the multiple undo:
   CLICK: mouse pointer on the fourth item in the drop-down list

SAVING AND CLOSING A WORKBOOK

When you are creating a workbook, it exists only in the computer's RAM (random access memory), which is highly volatile. To permanently store your work, you must save the workbook to the local hard disk, a network drive, or to a floppy diskette. Saving your work to a disk is similar to placing it into a filing cabinet. For important workbooks (ones that you cannot risk losing), you should save your work at least every 15 minutes, or whenever you're interrupted, to protect against an unexpected power outage or other catastrophe.

To save a workbook to a disk, click the Save button (🖫) on the Standard toolbar or select the File, Save command from the menu. In the dialog box that appears, type a new filename using less than 255 characters, including spaces, and then press **ENTER** or click the Save command button. Do not use the following characters in filenames:

$$\backslash \quad / \quad : \quad * \quad ? \quad `` \quad < \quad > \quad |$$

In the next few steps, you will save the current workbook to one of the following locations:

- *Advantage Files location* - This location may be on a diskette, a folder on your local hard drive, or a folder on a network server. The Advantage Files are the workbook files that have been created for you and that you will retrieve in the remaining exercises in this guide.

- *Data Files location* - This location may also be on a diskette, a hard drive folder, or a network folder. You will save the workbooks that you create or modify in the Data Files location.

   IMPORTANT: *Before continuing, ensure that you know the location of your Advantage Files and where to store your Data Files. If necessary, ask your instructor or lab assistant for additional information.*

Let's save the current workbook to your Data Files location.

Perform the following steps . . .

1. Make sure that you have identified the location for storing your data files. If you require a diskette, place it into the diskette drive now.

2. CLICK: Save button (□)
   Excel displays a dialog box similar to the one shown in Figure 1.13; the filenames and directories may differ from your dialog box.

FIGURE 1.13

SAVE AS DIALOG BOX

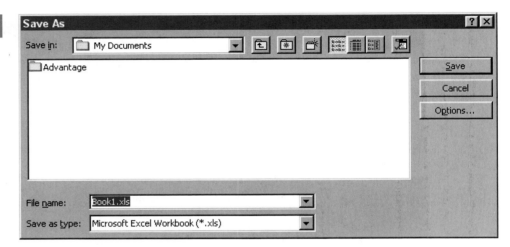

3. To specify a filename for the workbook:
   TYPE: My First Workbook

4. To specify where the workbook will be saved, do the following:
   CLICK: down arrow beside the *Save in* drop-down list box
   SELECT: *your Data Files location*
   PRESS: (ENTER) or CLICK: Save command button

   In this guide, we save workbooks to the "My Documents" folder on the hard disk and retrieve workbooks from the "Excel97" subfolder, which is located at the following path: \My Documents\Advantage\Excel97

5. When you are finished working with a workbook, you close the file to free up valuable RAM. To close the "My First Workbook" file:
   CHOOSE: File, Close

There are times when you'll want to save an existing workbook under a different filename. For example, you may want to keep different versions of the same workbook on your disk. Or, you may want to use one workbook as a template for future workbooks that are similar in style and format. Rather than retyping an entirely new workbook, you can retrieve an old workbook file, edit the information, and then save it under a different name using the File, Save As command. If you want to replace the old file instead, choose File, Save or click the Save button (🖫).

QUICK REFERENCE	● **CLICK: Save button (🖫), or**
Saving a File	● **CHOOSE: File, Save, or**
	● **CHOOSE: File, Save As**

QUICK REFERENCE	● **CHOOSE: File, Close, or**
Closing a File	● **CLICK: Close button (☒) on the document window**

IN ADDITION USING LONG FILENAMES IN DOS (AND WINDOWS 3.1)

 Because DOS can't understand file-names that are longer than eight characters, it changes a Windows filename when it tries to use a file with a long filename. For example, the Windows filename "Multitasking Workbook" would be changed to "MULTIT~1.XLS" in DOS or when saved to a network drive that did not support long filenames.

IN ADDITION SAVING A WORKBOOK AS AN HTML DOCUMENT

 To publish your Excel workbook on the Web, you must first save it as an HTML document using the File, Save as HTML command. *HTML* is an abbreviation for *Hypertext Markup* *Language*, a convention used for marking textual documents with special formatting codes so that they display nicely in web browser software. For more information, ask the Office Assistant to search for information on "Publishing to HTML."

OPENING A WORKBOOK

Now that your workbook is stored in this electronic filing cabinet called a disk, how do you retrieve it for editing? To open a new workbook, you click the New button (🗋) on the Standard toolbar. To modify or print an existing workbook, click the Open button (📂) or choose the File, Open command from the menu. Once the Open dialog box appears, you select the file's location by clicking in the *Look in* drop-down list box. You then double-click the workbook's name appearing in the file list.

Perform the following steps . . .

1. Make sure that you have identified the location for retrieving the Advantage Files. If you require a diskette, place it into the diskette drive now.

2. To open a new workbook:
   CLICK: New button ([◻])
   (*Note*: You can also choose File, New from the menu and then double-click the blank Workbook template icon (⬛) to load a new workbook.)

3. To practice using the Open dialog box:
   CLICK: Open button (📂) on the Standard toolbar

4. To view the Advantage Files:
   CLICK: down arrow beside the *Look in* drop-down list box
   SELECT: *your Advantage Files location*
   Your screen should now appear similar to Figure 1.14.

FIGURE 1.14

OPEN DIALOG BOX

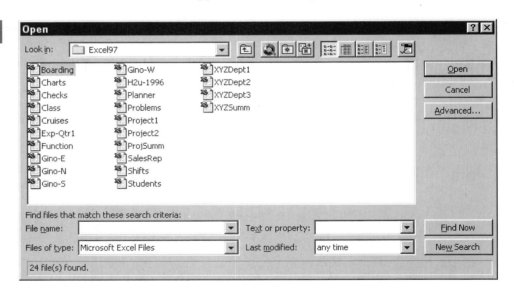

5. To change the display in the Open dialog box, try the following:
   CLICK: Detail button (▦) to see each workbook's file size and date
   CLICK: Properties button (▦) to see summary information
   CLICK: Preview button (▦) to see a workbook preview
   CLICK: List button (▦) to see a multiple-column format

6. Let's open a workbook:
   DOUBLE-CLICK: Students
   The "Students" workbook is loaded into memory and Sheet1 is displayed maximized in the application window.

QUICK REFERENCE
Opening a New Workbook

- **CLICK: New button ( ), or**
- **CHOOSE: File, New**
  DOUBLE-CLICK: Workbook template icon ( )

QUICK REFERENCE
Opening an Existing
Workbook

1. **CLICK: Open button ( ), or**
   CHOOSE: File, Open from the Menu bar
2. **CLICK: down arrow beside the *Look in* drop-down list box**
3. **SELECT: a file location**
4. **DOUBLE-CLICK: the desired workbook**

IN ADDITION OPENING AN OFFICE DOCUMENT FROM THE DESKTOP

You can open an existing document using one of the following methods:

- CHOOSE: **Start**, Documents and then select the desired document from the 15 most recently-used files listed (if available)

- CHOOSE: **Start**, Find, Files or Folders and then perform a search for the desired document name

- CHOOSE: **Start**, Open Office Document and then select the desired document in the Open dialog box

IN ADDITION EXCEL ON THE WEB

- *Excel as a Web browser:* You can open documents that are based on the Web's native Hypertext Markup Language (HTML). In the Open dialog box, select "HTML Documents" from the *Files of type* drop-down list box. Then, select a storage location and double-click the desired filename. Excel displays the document complete with hypertext links.

- *Excel reaches the Web:* With the appropriate connection, you can open and save Excel workbooks on the Internet. In the Open or Save dialog boxes, select an FTP Internet site location from the *Look in* or *Save in* drop-down list boxes, respectively. Once connected to a remote FTP server, you work with files the same as if they were on your local hard disk. This feature lets you share and update Excel workbooks with users from around the world.

LEAVING EXCEL

When you are finished using Excel, save your work and exit the program by clicking the Close button ( ) or by choosing the File, Exit command. If you have made modifications to a workbook and have not yet saved the changes, Excel asks whether the workbook should be saved or abandoned before exiting.

Perform the following steps . . .

1. To exit Excel:
CHOOSE: File, Exit
Assuming that no changes were made to the "Students" workbook, the application is closed and you are returned to the Windows desktop.

2. To exit Windows:
CLICK: Start button ()
CHOOSE: Shut Down
SELECT: *Shutdown the computer?* option button
CLICK: Yes command button

QUICK REFERENCE	• **CHOOSE: File, Exit or**
Exiting Excel	• **CLICK: Close button () of the Excel application window**

SUMMARY

This session introduced you to using Microsoft Excel 97, an electronic spreadsheet program. We began the session exploring the advantages of electronic spreadsheets over manual worksheets, comparing the size of work areas and the speeds at which calculations and corrections are performed. The importance of planning the construction of a spreadsheet was also emphasized.

After you loaded Windows and Excel, this session presented an overview of Excel's major components, including the application and document windows. As well, you were introduced to data entry techniques for entering text, numbers, and formulas into the worksheet cells. Because even experts require some assistance now and then, this session also demonstrated some of Excel's Help features.

For easy reference, many of the commands and procedures appearing in this session are provided in Table 1.5, the Command Summary.

TABLE 1.5

Command Summary

Command	Description
Edit, Clear	Erases the contents and formatting of a cell.
Edit, Undo ()	Reverses up to the last 16 actions performed.
File, Close	Closes a workbook file.
File, Exit (or)	Leaves Excel.
File, New ()	Opens a new workbook file.
File, Open ()	Opens an existing workbook file.
File, Save ()	Saves a workbook file to the disk.

TABLE 1.5	*Command*	*Description*
Continued	File, Save As	Saves a workbook file, specifying the filename.
	Help, Contents and Index	Displays the Help Topics window.
	Help, What's This?	Accesses context-sensitive help mouse pointer.
	Programs, Microsoft Excel	Launches Excel from the [Start] menu.

KEY TERMS

application window

In Microsoft Windows, each running application program appears in its own application window. These windows can be sized and moved anywhere on the Windows desktop.

cell

In an electronic spreadsheet program, this marks the intersection of a column and a row.

cell address

The location of a cell on a worksheet given by the intersection of a column and a row. Columns are labeled using letters. Rows are numbered. A cell address combines the column letter with the row number (for example, B9 or DF134).

cell pointer

The cursor on a worksheet that points to a cell. The cell pointer is moved using the arrow keys or the mouse.

context-sensitive help

A Help feature that provides a concise description for a particular menu option, toolbar button, or dialog box item.

document window

In Excel, each open workbook file appears in its own document window. These windows can be sized and moved anywhere within the Excel application window.

formulas

Mathematical expressions that define the relationships among various cells in a worksheet.

hyperlinks

In Microsoft Office 97, text or graphics that when clicked take you to another resource location, either within the same document or to a separate document stored on your computer, a network server, an Intranet resource, or onto the Internet.

Internet

A worldwide network of computer networks that are interconnected by standard telephone lines, fiber optics, and satellites.

Intranet

A local or wide area network that uses Internet protocols and technologies to share information within an institution or corporation.

Undo command

In Excel, a command that makes it possible to reverse up to the last 16 commands executed.

workbook

The Excel file where you create your work. A workbook appears in a document window and may contain worksheets and chart sheets.

World Wide Web (WWW)

A visual interface to the Internet based on *hyperlinks*. Using web browser software, you click on hyperlinks to navigate the resources on the Internet.

EXERCISES

SHORT ANSWER

1. Name two Office 97 Internet integration features.

2. List some of the advantages of using Excel over manual worksheets.

3. List the suggested planning steps for constructing a spreadsheet.

4. Explain the *context-sensitive help* features found in Excel.

5. Name the Help feature that provides a natural language interface for asking questions. What two areas of this feature can be customized?

6. How do you reverse the last three commands executed?

7. What is the fastest method for moving to cell DF8192?

8. What is the difference between a toolbar and a menu bar?

9. What is the significance of an ellipsis (...) after a menu option?

10. In Excel, how do you enter a formula into a cell? Provide an example.

HANDS-ON

(*Note*: Ensure that you know the storage location of your Advantage Files and your Data Files before proceeding.)

1. In this exercise, you will produce a worksheet for managing your personal credit cards. The tasks include entering text and numbers and then editing worksheet cells. Perform the following steps.

    a. Load Windows and Excel to begin working with a new workbook.

    b. Move the cell pointer to the following cells: (a) A21, (b) K50, (c) IV50, (d) IV16384, (e) AA1000, (f) A1

c. With your cell pointer in cell A1:
    TYPE: **Personal Financial Planner**
    PRESS: (ENTER)

d. Enter the following text labels:

Move to Cell	TYPE:
C3	**Budget**
D3	**Actual**
A6	**VISA**
A7	**Chevron**
A8	**AMEX**
A9	**M/C**

e. Enter the following numbers:

Move to Cell	TYPE:
C6	**1200**
C7	**500**
C8	**200**
C9	**75**
D6	**1200**
D7	**450**
D8	**215**
D9	**135**

f. Change the label in cell A6 from "VISA" to "Discover" by typing over the existing entry.

g. Change the label in cell A8 from "AMEX" to "AMEX Gold" using the mouse to edit the text in the cell.

h. Change the label in cell A9 from "M/C" to "Mastercard."

i. Change the budgeted value for Chevron in cell C7 to 400.

j. Reverse the change in the last step using the Undo button (⤺).

k. Change the Actual value for AMEX Gold in cell D8 to 210.

l. Reverse the change in the last step by pressing (CTRL) + z.

2. This exercise uses the same worksheet to practice entering formulas.

    a. Move to cell A11.

    b. TYPE: **Total Balances**

    c. Move to cell C11. Enter a formula that adds the Budget values in column C.

    d. Move to cell D11. Enter a formula that adds the Actual values in column D.

    e. Move to cell E3.

    f. TYPE: **Variance**

    g. In cell E6, enter a formula to subtract the actual Discover card balance from the budgeted value. (*Hint*: Budget − Actual.)

    h. In cell E7, enter a formula to subtract the actual Chevron balance from the budgeted value.

    i. Enter formulas to calculate the variance for the remaining cards.

    j. Using the Edit Formula button (**=**), enter a formula to calculate the variance for the Total Balances.

    k. Save the workbook as "My Financial Plan" onto your Data Files diskette or into your Data Files folder. Your worksheet should now appear similar to Figure 1.15.

    l. Close the workbook before proceeding.

FIGURE 1.15

"MY FINANCIAL PLAN" WORKBOOK

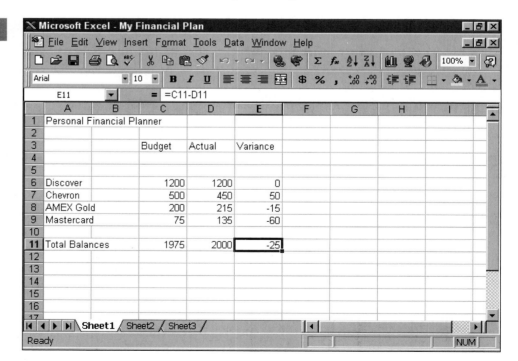

3. **On Your Own:** Your Personal Phone Book
   Create a new workbook called "Personal Phone Book" that stores personal information for some of your closest friends. Include their given names in column A, surnames in column B, phone numbers in column C, and their age in column D. Add at least five entries and then create a formula that calculates the average age of your friends. Save the workbook to your Data Files location.

4. **On Your Own:** Explore a Microsoft Excel Help Topic
   Pick a Microsoft Excel Help topic that interests you and write about it in a few paragraphs. Make sure to explain why you chose the topic and how to perform the procedures described. For example, you may be interested in learning how to publish a worksheet on the World Wide Web or how to customize the Office Assistant. You may want to look through the In Addition boxes in this session for more ideas.

CASE PROBLEMS | **THE BONDABLE GROUP**

(*Note*: In the following case problems, assume the role of the primary characters and perform the same steps that they identify. You may want to reread the session opening.)

1. Realizing that Pancho and Mackenzie need some help getting started on their spreadsheet, Jennifer calls a meeting for that afternoon. At 3:00 PM precisely, the three friends congregate in the boardroom around a small oval table. "Okay, let's review what our objectives are," Jennifer says, opening the meeting with her usual sentence. "First, we want to develop a spreadsheet that we can show to clients on the screen to help them better understand financial planning concepts. Second, we want to develop a single template that we can re-use for all of our clients. Is everyone with me so far?" The two gentlemen nod in agreement as Jennifer writes down the points on a flip chart. "Great, now let's brainstorm about what information we want to include." After more than an hour, the three partners emerge from the boardroom with a list of features that they want to appear in the spreadsheet.

   The following list is a summary of the points written on the flip chart during the partners' afternoon meeting. Your job is to implement these points in an Excel spreadsheet.

   - Enter the title of the worksheet "Your Guide to Financial Planning Success," in the top left-hand corner (cell A1).

   - Enter the company's name, "The Bondable Group," immediately below the title of the worksheet.

   - Leaving two blank lines after the company's name, enter the text label "Five Principles of Successful Investing:" in column A.

- Below this title, enter each of the five principles on a separate row:
  (1) Establish your goals.
  (2) Start early.
  (3) Make saving part of your regular routine.
  (4) Invest for the long term.
  (5) Diversify your portfolio.

- Leaving two more blank lines, enter the text label "Scoring Your Investment Objectives:"

- Below this title, enter the following information in columns A and B:

POINTS	QUESTION
	What is your age?
	What is your income?
	When will you need the money?
	How much risk can you take?
	TOTAL SCORE

- Save the workbook as "Bondable Plan" to your Data Files location.

2. On Friday morning, Pancho and Mackenzie receive their new notebook computers and immediately launch Microsoft Excel. They are very pleased with their new toys and don't even try to suppress their grins as they click away at the keyboards. "Hey Pancho, I've got a client meeting with Garrett Buggey before lunch. I'll try out the "Bondable Plan" workbook and let you know how it works." Pancho thanks Mackenzie and scurries from the office to make his own appointments.

   Mackenzie arrives early at Garrett's office and is led to a small meeting room. While waiting for his client, Mackenzie opens the notebook computer and loads the "Bondable Plan" workbook. "Hiya Mac!" Garrett calls as he enters the room. "Hey, that's a nice system you've got there. When did you get it?" Mackenzie explains that the computer had arrived that morning and that he wants to show Garrett a new spreadsheet. Based on his personal information and a point-scoring system developed by Jennifer, Mackenzie enters the following information into the spreadsheet:

POINTS	QUESTION
5500	What is your age?
4320	What is your income?
1745	When will you need the money?
7500	How much risk can you take?
	TOTAL SCORE

After he enters the numbers into the spreadsheet, Mackenzie realizes that they forgot to create a formula for the TOTAL SCORE line. This is the most important figure in the entire spreadsheet! Fortunately, Mackenzie remembers how to total a column of numbers using an addition formula. With the total score displaying in the worksheet, Garrett changes his mind on how much risk he is prepared to take in his investments. Mackenzie changes the point score from 7500 to 6275, and they both watch as the TOTAL SCORE line changes instantaneously.

Perform the same steps Mackenzie did after loading the "Bondable Plan" workbook. Save the new workbook as "Garrett Buggey" and then close the workbook before proceeding.

3. Mackenzie returns to the office after a successful meeting with Garrett. After telling Pancho about the forgotten formula, they decide to review and revise the entire "Bondable Plan" workbook. Refer to the following list and implement the changes in your worksheet:

- Open the original "Bondable Plan" workbook.

- Edit the title "Your Guide to Financial Planning Success" to read "The Personal Guide to Financial Planning Success."

- Add a sixth principle to the "Successful Investing" list called "(6) Make adjustments over time." Make sure that you edit this area's title, as well.

- Edit the question about risk in the "Scoring Your Investment Objectives:" area to read "How much risk do you want to take?"

- Add a new area titled "Determining Your Asset Mix:" to the spreadsheet, two lines below the "Scoring Your Investment Objectives:" area.

- Enter the following information, in three columns, below this area's title.

ANSWER	RESULT	QUESTION
		What is your monthly salary?
		a. % of monthly salary for Investment
		b. % of investment for Savings
		c. % of investment for Income Funds
		d. % of investment for Growth Funds

- Pancho and Mackenzie will enter a client's information into the ANSWER column. You must create formulas for the RESULT column that will provide the proper calculation results. Looking at the example provided below, ensure that items b., c., and d. in the ANSWER column add up to 100%. Also, ensure that the same items in the RESULT column add up to the *monthly salary for investment* value (in this example, 500).

ANSWER	RESULT	QUESTION
$5,000		What is your monthly salary?
10%	**500**	a. % of monthly salary for Investment
30%	**150**	b. % of investment for Savings
30%	**150**	c. % of investment for Income Funds
40%	**200**	d. % of investment for Growth Funds

- Practice using the new table by inputting several combinations of figures into the ANSWER column. Manually check that the calculations in the RESULTS column are correct.

Save the revised "Bondable Plan" workbook, updating the existing version. Close the workbook and then exit Excel.

Microsoft Excel 97 for Windows

Working with Spreadsheets

SESSION

2

IRWIN
COMPUTER & INFORMATION TECHNOLOGY

INTRODUCTION

Spreadsheets may look complicated, but even a new user can begin to construct one in a short period of time. With Microsoft's IntelliSense® technology, Excel provides several "Auto" features that can correct your spelling mistakes, format worksheet cells, and calculate formulas automatically. This session shows you how to set up a new workbook and enter data efficiently, and how to use AutoCalculate, AutoComplete, AutoCorrect, and AutoFormat. Once your spreadsheet is created, you can easily modify it and use it over and over.

MADRID CLOTHING COMPANY

Suriya Amin opened the first mall location for the Madrid Clothing Company in 1988. Since then the company has expanded into six locations across the Pacific Northwest, from the Alderwood Mall near Seattle to the Pacific Center in Vancouver, British Columbia. The Madrid Clothing Company supplies European casual wear for a middle- to upper-class clientele.

Suriya's younger brother Khalid, who is also one of her store managers, wants to expand the operation into California. Realizing that Suriya would never accept a serious proposal from her younger brother, Khalid decides to create and submit an anonymous "what-if" spreadsheet that compares the worst-case and best-case scenarios for such an expansion. To ensure that she takes the proposal seriously, Khalid must strive to give the report a very professional appearance. To this end, he must learn how to format a worksheet in Microsoft Excel and how to print the report with headers and footers.

In this session, you and Khalid will improve your efficiency working with Excel. You will create, proof, customize, enhance, save, and then print a workbook. By the end of this session, you will know how to apply these skills to any workbook you create.

CREATING A NEW WORKBOOK

When you first load Excel, an empty workbook called Book1 appears in the document window. To create a workbook, you simply enter information into the worksheets labeled from Sheet1 to Sheet3 and then save the workbook under a new filename. (*Note:* In Session 4, you learn how to add and delete sheets in a workbook.) If you've already entered information into Book1 and want to create a new workbook, choose the File, New command or click the New button ([D]) on the Standard toolbar. Because each workbook that you open consumes memory, you should save your work and close all unnecessary documents before creating a new workbook.

In the next two sections, you will create the worksheet shown in Figure 2.1. You will use this worksheet throughout the session to practice several spreadsheet procedures.

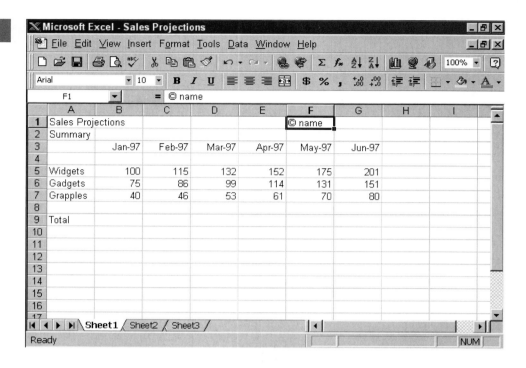

Perform the following steps . . .

1. Make sure that you've loaded Excel and that a new workbook appears in the document window. Enter the following text labels for headings on the worksheet:

Move to Cell	TYPE:
A1	Sales Projections
A5	Widgets
A6	Gadgets
A7	Grapples
A9	Total

2. Enter the following dates as column headings:

Move to Cell	TYPE:
B3	Jan-97
C3	Feb-97
D3	Mar-97
E3	Apr-97
F3	May-97
G3	Jun-97

Before entering the numeric values for the spreadsheet, proceed to the next section to learn about cell ranges.

IN ADDITION USING TEMPLATES

Rather than creating a worksheet from scratch, you can open and then modify a *template*. A template is simply a worksheet that serves as the starting point for the creation of a new worksheet. You can create and save your own templates or access some of Excel's professionally designed built-in templates, including an Invoice, Expense Statement, and Purchase Order worksheet. To view the installed templates, choose the File, New command and select the *Spreadsheet Solutions* tab. For more information, ask the Office Assistant about "Using a Template."

INTRODUCING CELL RANGES

In most Windows programs, you select objects and then choose commands to act on the objects, such as a copy or format operation. To enhance an Excel worksheet, for example, you select a cell or group of cells—called a **cell range**—and then choose a formatting command. After executing the command, Excel leaves the selected range highlighted for you to choose additional commands. You can use either the keyboard or the mouse to select a cell range in a worksheet.

A cell range is a single cell or a rectangular block of worksheet cells. Each cell range has a beginning and an ending cell address. The top left-hand cell is the beginning cell and the bottom right-hand cell is the ending cell in a range. To specify a range in a worksheet formula, you enter the two cell addresses separated by a colon (for example, B4:C6). Figure 2.2 illustrates some cell ranges.

FIGURE 2.2

CELL RANGES

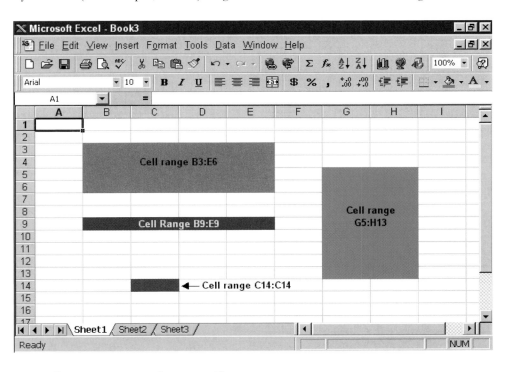

You will now practice selecting cell ranges.

Perform the following steps . . .

1. Move to cell B3.

2. To select the range of cells from B3 to G3 using the keyboard:
   PRESS: (**SHIFT**) and hold it down
   PRESS: (➡) five times
   If the highlight does not extend from cell B3 to G3, make sure that you are holding down the (**SHIFT**) key as you press (➡).

3. When the range is highlighted, release the (**SHIFT**) key.

4. To remove the range selection, you can press any arrow key:
   PRESS: (⬅)
   (*Note:* You can also click on any cell to remove the highlighting from the cell range.)

5. To select the range of cells from B5 to G7 using a mouse:
   CLICK: cell B5 and hold down the left mouse button
   DRAG: the mouse pointer down and to the right until you reach G7

6. When the range is highlighted, release the mouse button. A selected range is highlighted in reverse (white text on a black background) from the rest of the worksheet. The exception is the active cell with the cell pointer, in this case cell B5 in the range B5:G7.

7. Using cell ranges makes your job of entering data easier and more accurate. As you type information into a highlighted cell range, the cell pointer is automatically moved to the next cell in the range when you press (**ENTER**). For example, do the following while the cell range remains selected:
   TYPE: **100**
   PRESS: (**ENTER**)
   Notice that the cell pointer moves down to cell B6. When the cell pointer reaches the last cell at the bottom of the selected column, it will move to the top of the next column in the range.

8. With the cell range still highlighted, complete the data entry as follows:

	B	C	D	E	F	G
5	100	115	132	152	175	201
6	75	86	99	114	131	151
7	40	46	53	61	70	80

9. With the cell range still highlighted, practice moving from cell to cell:
PRESS: (ENTER) to move down one cell at a time; when you reach the bottom cell, the cell pointer moves to the top of the next column
PRESS: (SHIFT)+(ENTER) to move up one cell at a time; when you reach the top cell, the cell pointer moves to the previous column
PRESS: (TAB) to move right one cell; when you reach the rightmost cell in a row, the cell pointer moves to the next row
PRESS: (SHIFT)+(TAB) to move left one cell; when you reach the leftmost cell, the cell pointer moves to the previous row

10. To remove the highlighting and return to cell A1:
PRESS: (CTRL)+(HOME)

QUICK REFERENCE	
Selecting a Range of Cells Using the Mouse	1. **Click once on the cell in the top left-hand corner of the range.**
	2. **Hold down the left mouse button and drag the mouse pointer to the bottom right-hand corner of the range.**
	3. **Release the mouse button.**

QUICK REFERENCE	
Selecting a Range of Cells Using the Keyboard	1. **Position the cell pointer in the top left-hand corner of the cell range.**
	2. **PRESS: (SHIFT) key and hold it down**
	3. **Extend the highlight over the desired group of cells using the arrow keys (◄, ►, ▲, and ▼).**
	4. **Release the (SHIFT) key.**

SPELL-CHECKING A WORKSHEET

This section introduces the Spelling Checker for correcting typographical errors and misspellings. You can perform a spelling check on a particular cell range, a single sheet, several sheets, or the entire workbook. When a spelling check is requested, Excel begins scanning the cells with textual information. In addition to comparing each word to entries in Excel's main dictionary, you can create a custom dictionary that contains proper names, abbreviations, and technical terms.

Besides running a spelling check, Excel's **AutoCorrect** utility can automatically correct your typographical and capitalization errors as you type. You will find this feature extremely handy if you habitually misspell or mistype particular words. For example, people often type "thier" instead of "their"—making a simple but common typing mistake. Excel's AutoCorrect utility provides corrections for this word and hundreds of other commonly misspelled words. It also lets you easily insert complex symbols like © and ™ into your worksheet cells.

To start a spelling check, click the Spelling button () on the Standard toolbar. When the Spelling Checker cannot identify a word and believes it to be misspelled, a dialog box appears allowing you to correct or ignore the entry, or to add the word to the custom dictionary or AutoCorrect list. The Spelling Checker also flags errors relating to repeated words (for example, "the ball was was red") and mixed case (for example, "the baLL was rEd"). An added benefit for users of Office 97 is that the terms you add to the custom dictionary and to AutoCorrect are shared by all applications.

Let's practice spell-checking a worksheet.

Perform the following steps . . .

1. Move to cell A2.

2. Enter a misspelled word:
TYPE: **Summury**
PRESS: **ENTER**

3. PRESS: **CTRL** + **HOME** to move to the top of the worksheet

4. To begin the spelling check:
CLICK: Spelling button ()
(*Note:* You can also choose the Tools, Spelling command on the Menu bar to start a spelling check.) When Excel finds the first misspelled word, it displays the dialog box shown in Figure 2.3 and waits for further instructions:

FIGURE 2.3

SPELLING DIALOG BOX

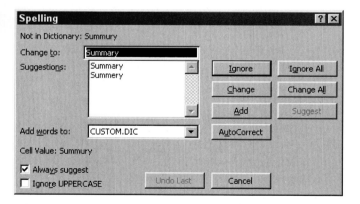

5. You have several options when the Spell Checker cannot find a word:
- Select the correctly spelled word in the *Suggestions* list box and then click the Change command button.
- Type the correct spelling of the word in the *Change to* text box and then click the Change command button.
- If the word is spelled correctly and not frequently used, click the Ignore or Ignore All buttons to proceed to the next word.
- If the word is spelled correctly and frequently used, click the Add button to add it to the custom dictionary.

- If the word is one that you frequently mistype and the correct spelling appears in the *Change to* text, click the AutoCorrect command button to have Excel correct this mistake automatically in the future.

To correct the spelling of Summary and proceed:
CLICK: Change command button

6. Continue the spelling check for the remainder of the worksheet. A message box will appear notifying you when the spelling check is finished. To proceed:
PRESS: **ENTER** or CLICK: OK

7. To demonstrate using AutoCorrect:
CLICK: cell F1
TYPE: (c)
PRESS: Space bar
AutoCorrect replaces "(c)" with the proper copyright symbol "©" automatically when you press the Space bar.

8. To complete the cell entry:
TYPE: *your name*
PRESS: **ENTER**
(*Hint:* Do not take the above instruction literally. Enter your own name and not the text "your name.")

9. To review some of the other entries available in AutoCorrect:
CHOOSE: Tools, AutoCorrect
In the dialog box (Figure 2.4) that appears, notice the two columns in the list box: *Replace* and *With*. What you type into a worksheet cell is presented in the Replace column and what AutoCorrect replaces your typing with is presented in the *With* column. On your own, scroll through the list box and review the commonly misspelled words that AutoCorrect will automatically correct for you.

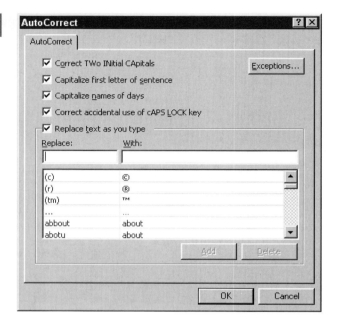

10. To proceed, ensure that all the check boxes are selected (as shown in Figure 2.4) and then do the following:
CLICK: OK command button

11. PRESS: (CTRL) + (HOME) to move to the top of the worksheet

12. Make sure that you have identified the location for saving your Data Files. If you require a diskette, place it into the diskette drive now. Save your worksheet as "Sales Projections" and then close the workbook.

QUICK REFERENCE
Spell-Checking a Worksheet

1. **CLICK: Spelling button (🔤), or**

 CHOOSE: Tools, Spelling

2. **When a misspelled word is located, Excel suggests alternative spellings.**
 Select a suggestion and then click a command button to change the entry,
 add it to the dictionary, add it to AutoCorrect, or ignore the word for the
 remainder of the spelling check.

Data ENTRY USING AUTOCOMPLETE

Have you ever experienced a conversation with a person who insisted on finishing your sentences for you? Perhaps it was a friend, a business associate, or even your spouse. Although tremendously annoying in a social situation, this type of imposition proves to be an exceptional software feature—and it's called AutoComplete!

AutoComplete second-guesses what you are about to type into a worksheet cell by reviewing your past entries in that cell's column. Similar to the AutoCorrect feature, AutoComplete watches your keystrokes and then jumps in when it thinks it can help. While AutoCorrect at least lets you finish typing a word before correcting a mistake, AutoComplete lets only a few letters go by before completing a matching entry.

The following exercise illustrates using the AutoComplete feature.

 **Perform the following steps . . .**

1. Open the workbook called "Problems" stored in the Advantage Files location. (*Remember:* This location may be on a diskette or in a folder on your hard disk or on a network drive.) The "Problems" workbook contains a single worksheet that is used to record problems in a computer lab. Notice that there are repeating entries beneath the columns labeled Shift, Supervisor, and Machine.

2. Let's add two new items to the worksheet. First, enter a date:
CLICK: cell A15
TYPE: 4/1/97
PRESS: ➡

3. To add "Blue" in the Shift column:
TYPE: b
AutoComplete scans the existing entries in the column and then fills in the remaining letters in the word "blue." (*Note:* If "blue" does not appear, press **ENTER** and then choose the Tools, Options command. Click the *Edit* tab in the dialog box and then ensure that the *Enable AutoComplete for cell values* check box is selected. Click the OK command button to complete the dialog box.)

4. To move to cell C15 and accept the AutoComplete entry:
PRESS: ➡
Notice that the "b" is now capitalized in "Blue" so as to conform to the existing entries in the column.

5. Watch closely as you type each letter to add a new Supervisor to column C:
TYPE: Brandon
Notice that AutoComplete fills in "Bradley" as you type the "Bra" portion of the name. When you type the "n," AutoComplete realizes that you are entering a new Supervisor's name and removes the letters it had previously inserted for "Bradley."

6. To move to cell D15:
PRESS: ➡

7. An additional feature of AutoComplete is its ability to generate an up-to-date list of the unique entries from a column. To illustrate:
RIGHT-CLICK: cell D15

8. On the shortcut menu that appears:
CHOOSE: Pick From List
AutoComplete generates a list of items contained in the column and then displays its results in a pop-up list box.

9. SELECT: "Tower CPU" from the Pick List
Your screen should now appear similar to Figure 2.5.

10. To finish the line item:
RIGHT-CLICK: cell E15
SELECT: "15 - RAM parity error on boot" from the Pick List

11. Practice using the typing method and the Pick List to enter the following item to the Problem Report:

Move to Cell	Entry
A16	5/15/97
B16	Green
C16	Kineshanko
D16	Laser printer
E16	13 - Low toner

12. Save the workbook as "Problem Report" to your Data Files location. Then, close the workbook.

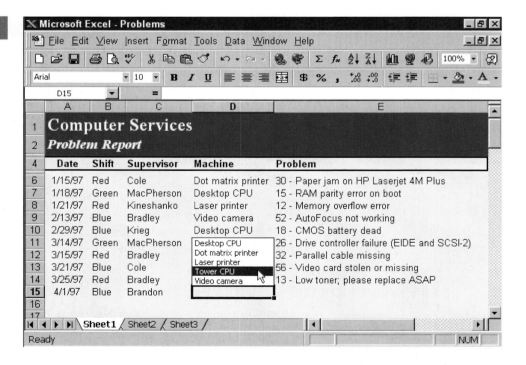

CALCULATING TOTALS

Adding together a few numbers on your worksheet is easy using a simple addition formula. Imagine the time it would take, however, to sum a column of 100 numbers with a formula such as =A1+A2+A3...+A99. Fortunately, Excel has anticipated many of these repetitive operations and provides a library of electronic shortcuts called **functions,** organized into the following categories:

- Database
- Date & Time
- Financial
- Information
- Logical
- Lookup & Reference
- Math & Trig
- Statistical
- Text

The mathematical and statistical functions are the most commonly used, enabling you to sum or average a range of numbers, count cell entries, and extract maximum and minimum results from a cell range. This section introduces the SUM function which is used as a replacement for long addition formulas. To enter the SUM function into a cell, you can type the expression or click the AutoSum button (Σ) on the Standard toolbar. Thanks to Excel's new **AutoCalculate** utility, you can view the sum of a selected cell range in the Status bar without even entering the SUM function!

THE SUM FUNCTION

The first step in using the SUM function is to move to the cell where you want the result to appear. Functions, like formulas, begin with an equal sign to inform Excel to expect a function name as opposed to a text label. The syntax for the SUM command is "=SUM(cell range)" where the cell range is the block of cells to be summed. You can enter the cell range by typing the cell addresses or by highlighting the block of cells using the mouse.

The objective of the following exercise is to demonstrate these two methods for entering the SUM function. Normally, you would not use a different method to sum each column. However, this example provides an opportunity to practice some important skills.

Perform the following steps . . .

1. Ensure that there are no open workbooks in the document area.
2. Open the "Sales Projections" workbook that you created earlier in this session.
3. Move to cell B9.

4. To calculate the total sales for the month of January, enter the SUM function by typing the cell addresses:
TYPE: =sum(b5:b7)
PRESS: ➡
The value 215 appears in the cell. (*Note:* You can enter the function name and cell range using uppercase or lowercase letters.)

5. To calculate the total sales for February, enter the SUM function into cell C9 by pointing to the cell range using the keyboard:
TYPE: =sum(
PRESS: ⬆ four times to move to cell C5
PRESS: **SHIFT** and hold down
PRESS: ⬇ twice to extend the range to cell C7
TYPE:) and release the **SHIFT** key
PRESS: ➡
The number 247 appears in cell C9.

6. To calculate the total sales for March, enter the SUM function into cell D9 by pointing to the cell range using the mouse:
TYPE: =sum(
CLICK: cell D5 and hold down the left mouse button
DRAG: mouse pointer to cell D7 and then release the mouse button
TYPE:)
PRESS: ➡
The number 284 appears in cell D9.

7. SELECT: cell range from E9 to G9

8. To calculate the total sales for April through June, enter the SUM function once and copy the formula to the remaining cells in the range using a keyboard shortcut:
TYPE: =sum(e5:e7)
PRESS: **CTRL** + **ENTER**
When you press **CTRL** + **ENTER**, Excel copies the entry in the active cell to the remaining cells in the highlighted range; in this case, F9 and G9.

9. To demonstrate using AutoCalculate:
CLICK: cell B9 and hold down the left mouse button

10. DRAG: mouse pointer to C9 and keep the mouse button depressed
The Status bar now displays "Sum=462", the sum of the selected cell range B9:C9. AutoCalculate provides an immediate summation of the selected cells without entering a formula or using a function.

11. DRAG: mouse pointer to G9 slowly, watching the Status bar as you move the cell pointer from D9 through to G9
The Status bar should now display "Sum=1881", the sum of the selected cell range B9:G9.

12. On your own, select other cell ranges using the mouse and watch the "Sum=" portion of the Status bar change to reflect the results.

IN ADDITION FORMULA AUTOCORRECT

Excel automatically corrects some common mistakes that novice users make when entering formulas and functions. For example, if you enter `==sum(b9:g9)` into a cell, Excel displays a dialog box with the proposed correction of `=sum(b9:g9)`. You simply click the Yes command button to have Excel edit the formula.

THE AUTOSUM BUTTON

Rather than entering an addition formula or the SUM function manually, you can use the AutoSum button (Σ) to automatically sum a cell range. To AutoSum a cell range, you position the cell pointer where you want the result to appear and click the AutoSum button (Σ) once. Excel enters the SUM function with its best guess of the desired cell range. If the range is correct, press **ENTER** to complete the entry. You can also bypass the need to press **ENTER** by double-clicking the AutoSum button (Σ) with the cell pointer in the desired cell.

Let's complete the "Sales Projections" workbook by calculating the total sales for each product.

Perform the following steps . . .

1. Move to cell H3.

2. TYPE: Total

3. Move to cell H9.

4. To calculate the total sales for all products:
    CLICK: AutoSum button (Σ)
    Verify that the cell range appearing in the cell and in the Formula bar is correct before proceeding to the next step.

5. To proceed:
    CLICK: ☑ in the Formula bar
    (*Note:* You can also press **ENTER** or click the AutoSum button (Σ) a second time to accept the cell range.)

6. To calculate the total sales for each individual product, select the cell range from H5 to H7. Ensure that the entire range is highlighted.

7. CLICK: AutoSum button (Σ)
    Because more than one cell is highlighted, the SUM function is automatically entered for all three cells. Your worksheet should now appear similar to Figure 2.6.

FIGURE 2.6

ENTERING THE SUM
FUNCTION AND USING
AUTOSUM

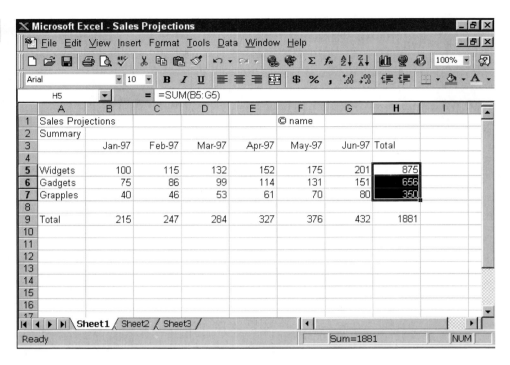

8. Using the mouse, click each of the cells H5, H6, and H7 and read the cell references in the Formula bar. Ensure that each SUM function sums the correct cell range.

9. Save the "Sales Projections" workbook to your Data Files location.

QUICK REFERENCE	1. **Move the cell pointer to where you want the result to appear.**
AutoSum Button	2. **CLICK: AutoSum button (Σ)**

CHANGING COLUMN WIDTHS

You can increase the **column width** of your worksheet columns to allow for long text labels, numbers, and date formats. To change a column's width from the default or standard width, move the cell pointer to any cell in the desired column and then choose the Format, Column, Width command from the Menu bar. In the *Column Width* text box, you type the desired width (up to 255) and then click on OK.

To change the width of more than one column at a time, you highlight cells within the columns (on any row) before you issue the command. You can also choose the Format, Column, AutoFit Selection command to have Excel calculate the best width for the column based on its entries. As with most procedures, there are keyboard and mouse methods for changing a column's width. Using the mouse, you can modify a column's width by dragging the column borders within the frame area.

You will now change the width of several columns in a worksheet.

Perform the following steps . . .

1. Move to cell A1.

2. To change the width of column A to 15 characters:
   CHOOSE: Format, Column, Width

3. In the *Column Width* text box, enter the number of characters:
   TYPE: 10
   PRESS: (ENTER) or CLICK: OK
   The column's width is changed and you are returned to the worksheet.

4. To change the width of column B to 12 characters using the mouse, first move the mouse pointer into the column frame area where the column letters (A, B, and so on) appear.

5. Position the mouse pointer over the borderline between column B and column C. The mouse pointer changes shape from a cross to a black vertical line split by a horizontal double-headed arrow.

6. CLICK: the borderline and hold down the mouse button
   DRAG: the mouse pointer to the right to increase the width to 12
   (*Hint:* The width is displayed in a ToolTip. This method takes a very steady hand and good mouse control to get an exact width.)

7. Release the mouse button.

8. To concurrently change multiple columns to the same width, you must first select the columns by dragging the mouse pointer over the column letters in the frame area. For this step, select columns B through H using the mouse by clicking on the letter B and then dragging the mouse pointer to column H. The columns will appear highlighted.

9. To have Excel select the best width for each of the columns:
   CHOOSE: Format, Column, AutoFit Selection

10. Although the columns are adjusted to best fit their cell entries, most appear too narrow. With the columns still selected, drag any border (for example, the border between columns D and E) in the highlighted frame area to increase the width of all columns to 8 characters. When you release the mouse button, notice that all of the highlighted columns are sized to 8 characters wide.

QUICK REFERENCE
Changing a Column's Width

1. Select a cell in the column that you want to format.
2. CHOOSE: Format, Column, Width
3. Type the desired column width in the text box.
4. PRESS: (ENTER) or CLICK: OK

CHANGING ROW HEIGHTS

You can change the row height of any worksheet row to customize borders and line spacing. To change a row's height, move the cell pointer to any cell in the desired row and then choose Format, Row, Height from the Menu bar. In the *Row Height* text box, you type the desired height in points (where 72 points is equal to one inch) and then click on OK. Similar to changing a column's width, you can use a mouse to drag the row borders within the frame area to increase or decrease a row's height.

You will now change the height of several rows in a worksheet.

Perform the following steps . . .

1. Move to cell A1.

2. To change the height of row 1 to 25 points (approximately ⅜ inch), issue the formatting command:
   CHOOSE: Format, Row, Height

3. In the *Row Height* text box, enter a number for the height in points:
   TYPE: 25
   PRESS: ENTER or CLICK: OK
   The row's height is changed, and you are returned to the worksheet.

4. To change the height of row 3 to 21 points using a mouse, first move the mouse pointer into the frame area where the row numbers appear.

5. Position the mouse pointer over the borderline between row 3 and row 4. The mouse pointer changes shape from a cross to a black horizontal line split by a vertical double-headed arrow.

6. CLICK: the borderline and hold down the mouse button
   DRAG: the mouse pointer down to increase the row height to 21
   (*Hint:* The height is displayed in a ToolTip.)

7. Release the mouse button.

8. To change multiple rows to the same height, you must first select the rows by dragging the mouse in the frame area. For this step, select the range from row 5 to row 9 by clicking on the number 5 and then dragging the mouse pointer to row 9.

9. To change the row height to 16 points:
   CHOOSE: Format, Row, Height
   TYPE: 16
   PRESS: ENTER or CLICK: OK

10. Move to cell A1. Your worksheet should now appear similar to Figure 2.7.

FIGURE 2.7

CHANGING THE COLUMN
WIDTHS AND ROW
HEIGHTS

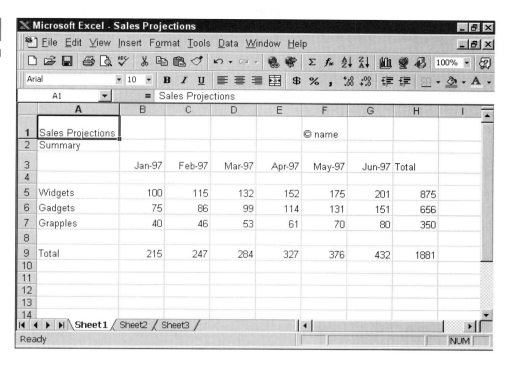

Unlike column widths, row heights are automatically adjusted to their best fit according to the font size of entries in the row. However, you can still modify the spacing in your worksheets by adjusting row heights manually. If you want to reset the row height back to the standard or default setting, choose the Format, Row, AutoFit command from the menu.

QUICK REFERENCE
Changing a Row's Height

1. **Select a cell in the row to format.**
2. **CHOOSE: Format, Row, Height**
3. **Type the desired row height in the text box.**
4. **PRESS: ENTER or CLICK: OK**

FORMATTING YOUR WORKSHEET

With Excel's spreadsheet publishing capabilities, you can enhance your worksheets with a variety of fonts, borders, and shading. You can also format numbers to display currency and percentage symbols and to specify the number of decimal places. The combination of these features enables you to produce professional-looking reports and presentations using Excel.

SELECTING CELL RANGES

To format your worksheet, select the cells that you want to enhance and then issue a formatting command. To this point in the guide, you've learned how to select a single cell and a block of cells called a range. There are several additional methods for selecting cells in a worksheet that will improve your productivity. For example, you can select multiple cell ranges in different areas of a worksheet and then apply a single command to format them all. Some common selection methods are provided below.

- To apply formatting changes to an entire worksheet, select the worksheet by pressing **CTRL**+a or by clicking once on the Select All button (▭), located in the top left-hand corner of the frame area.

- To select multiple cell ranges, select the first cell range as usual and then hold down the **CTRL** key as you select the additional cell ranges using the mouse.

- To select a cell range that spans a large area of the worksheet (for example, A1:M300), select the first cell (top left-hand corner of the range) and then scroll to the last cell (bottom right-hand corner of the range) using the scroll bars. When the last cell is visible, press and hold down the **SHIFT** key and click the cell once. All the cells in between the first and last are highlighted.

Because a cell range remains highlighted after issuing a command, you can choose additional formatting commands without having to reselect cells. To remove the highlighting from a cell range, press an arrow key or click on any cell in the worksheet using the mouse.

USING FONTS

One of the most effective means of enhancing a worksheet is to vary the **fonts**—that is, the **typefaces** and point sizes—that are used in titles, column headings, row labels, and other worksheet cells. Although fonts are effective at drawing the reader's attention to specific topics, don't feel that you must use every font in each worksheet. Remember, a worksheet must be easy to read and understand—too many fonts are distracting.

To enhance your worksheet, select the cell or range of cells to format and then issue the Format, Cells command from the menu. (*Hint:* You can also select the Format Cells command from a shortcut menu.) For fonts and styles, select the *Font* tab (Figure 2.8) by clicking on it using the mouse. After making the desired selections from the dialog box, click the OK command button.

FIGURE 2.8

FORMAT CELLS DIALOG
BOX: *FONT* TAB

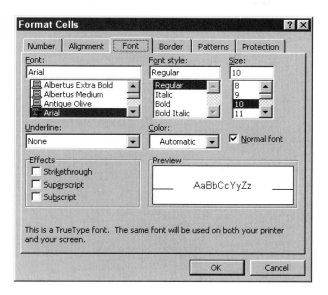

Rather than accessing the Format Cells dialog box from the menu, you can click buttons on the Formatting toolbar: Font (Arial ▾), Font Size (10 ▾), Bold (**B**), Italic (*I*), and Underline (U). These buttons provide single-step access to the most popular features found in the Format Cells dialog box.

You will now change fonts and styles in the worksheet.

Perform the following steps . . .

1. SELECT: cell range from B3 to H3

2. To emphasize the column headings, make the dates bold:
CLICK: Bold button (**B**)

3. SELECT: cell range from A5 to A9

4. To italicize the product names:
CLICK: Italic button (*I*)

5. RIGHT-CLICK: cell A1
A shortcut menu appears.

6. To enhance the title:
CHOOSE: Format Cells
CLICK: *Font* tab

7. SELECT: Times New Roman from the *Font* list box
SELECT: Bold Italic from the *Font style* list box
SELECT: 18 from the *Size* list box
PRESS: (**ENTER**) or CLICK: OK

8. SELECT: cell A2

9. To enhance the sub-title using the Formatting toolbar:
SELECT: Times New Roman from the Font drop-down list box
(Arial ▾)
SELECT: 14 from the Font Size drop-down list box (10 ▾)
(*Hint:* To display the options in a drop-down list, click the down arrow
beside the drop-down list on the toolbar.)

10. Save the "Sales Projections" workbook to your Data Files location.

QUICK REFERENCE
Using Fonts

1. **SELECT: the cell or cell range that you want to format**
2. **CHOOSE: Format, Cells**
3. **CLICK:** *Font* **tab**
4. **SELECT: a font, font style, size, color, and effects**
5. **PRESS:** ⟨ENTER⟩ **or CLICK: OK.**

IN ADDITION USING CONDITIONAL CELL FORMATTING

New in Excel 97, you can flag results in your worksheet based on specific conditions. For example, you could highlight those salespeople who sell under 100 units by changing the font color of their name. To access this feature, choose the Format, Conditional Formatting command from the menu. For more information, ask the Office Assistant to search for help on "Conditional Formats."

FORMATTING VALUES

Numeric formats improve the appearance and readability of numbers in a worksheet by inserting dollar signs, commas, percentage symbols, and decimal places. Although the number appears differently on the worksheet when formatting is applied, the value in the Formula bar does not change—only the appearance of the number changes. In addition to dollar figures and percentages, Excel stores date and time entries as values and allows you to customize their display in the worksheet.

To enhance your worksheet with value formatting, select the desired cell range and then issue the Format, Cells command. When the dialog box appears, click the

Number tab to display a variety of numeric formatting options. Figure 2.9 provides an example of the Format Cells dialog box with the *Number* tab and the Currency category selected.

FIGURE 2.9

FORMAT CELLS DIALOG
BOX: *NUMBER* TAB

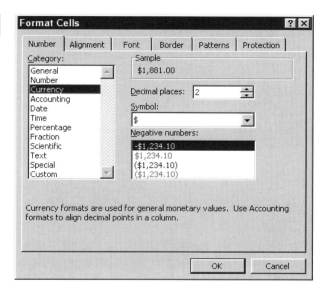

To format the values in your worksheet, select a *Category* from the list box and then make selections from that category's formatting options. You can also format values by clicking the following buttons on the Formatting toolbar: Currency Style ($), Percent Style (%), Comma Style (,), Increase Decimal (.00), and Decrease Decimal (.00). These buttons provide single-step access to the most popular features found in the dialog box. (*Note:* Although its name implies differently, the Currency Style ($) toolbar button formats values to the Accounting style, which lines up the dollar symbols and decimal points in a column.)

In this exercise, you change the visual appearance of several cells.

Perform the following steps . . .

1. SELECT: cell range from B9 to H9

2. To display the dialog box of numeric formatting options:
   RIGHT-CLICK: any cell in the highlighted cell range
   CHOOSE: Format Cells
   CLICK: *Number* tab

3. To view the currency formatting options:
   SELECT: Currency in the *Category* list box

4. To format the values with dollar signs, commas, and decimal places:
   SELECT: 2 in the *Decimal places* spin box
   SELECT: $ in the *Symbol* drop-down list box
   SELECT: ($1,234.00) in the *Negative numbers* list box (red option)
   PRESS: ENTER or CLICK: OK
   Notice that the value in H9 is unable to display in the cell. Instead, a series of "#" appears. This is Excel's way of informing you that the cell is not wide enough to display the value using the selected format. Your options are to either increase the column's width or select a different numeric format.

5. To increase the width of column H only to 10 characters:
   CLICK: cell H9
   CHOOSE: Format, Column, Width
   TYPE: **10**
   PRESS: ENTER or CLICK: OK

6. SELECT: cell range from B5 to H7

7. To select a number format with commas:
   CLICK: Comma Style button (,)

8. If there are no decimals displaying for the Comma style:
   CLICK: Increase Decimal button ( ) twice
   Otherwise, proceed to the next section.

QUICK REFERENCE
Formatting Numbers and Dates

1. **SELECT: the cell or cell range that you want to format**
2. **CHOOSE: Format, Cells**
3. **CLICK: *Number* tab**
4. **SELECT: a format from the *Category* list box**
5. **SELECT: formatting options for the selected category**
6. **PRESS: ENTER or CLICK: OK**

ALIGNING A CELL'S CONTENTS

Excel automatically aligns text against the left edge of a cell and values against the right edge. However, you can easily change the **cell alignment** for any type of information in the worksheet. You can even rotate text in a cell to any angle or orientation. Together with merging cells, you can create some interesting labels for your worksheet. Using the menu, choose the Format, Cells command and then make selections from the *Alignment* tab in the dialog box (Figure 2.10). Using the Formatting toolbar, click the Align Left ( ), Center ( ), Align Right ( ), and Merge and Center ( ) buttons to align cell information.

FIGURE 2.10

FORMAT CELLS DIALOG
BOX: *ALIGNMENT* TAB

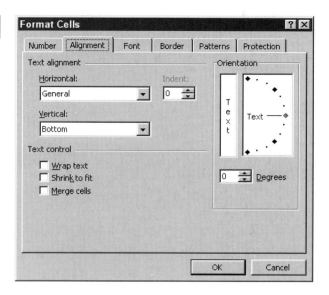

Let's change the alignment of some worksheet information.

Perform the following steps . . .

1. SELECT: cell range from B3 to H3

2. To center the date headings in their respective columns:
   CHOOSE: Format, Cells
   CLICK: *Alignment* tab
   SELECT: Center from the *Horizontal* drop-down list box
   SELECT: Center from the *Vertical* drop-down list box
   PRESS: [ENTER] or CLICK: OK

3. SELECT: cell range from A5 to A9

4. To right-align the product or row headings:
   CLICK: Align Right button (▤)

5. To center the sub-title in A2 across the width of the worksheet:
   SELECT: cell range from A2 to H2

6. CLICK: Merge and Center button (▦)
   Notice that the cells are merged into one cell and that the contents are centered. Your screen should now appear similar to Figure 2.11.

7. Save the "Sales Projections" workbook to your Data Files location.

FIGURE 2.11

THE "SALES PROJECTIONS" WORKSHEET AFTER FORMATTING

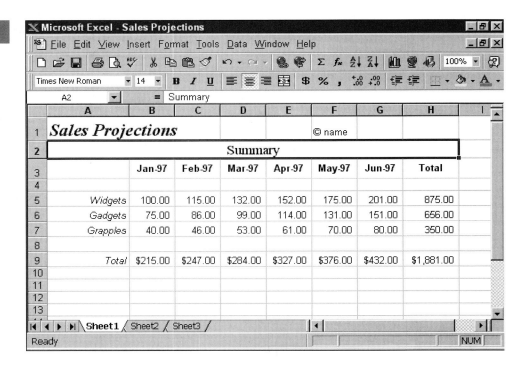

	A	B	C	D	E	F	G	H	I
1	*Sales Projections*					© name			
2	Summary								
3		Jan-97	Feb-97	Mar-97	Apr-97	May-97	Jun-97	Total	
4									
5	*Widgets*	100.00	115.00	132.00	152.00	175.00	201.00	875.00	
6	*Gadgets*	75.00	86.00	99.00	114.00	131.00	151.00	656.00	
7	*Grapples*	40.00	46.00	53.00	61.00	70.00	80.00	350.00	
8									
9	*Total*	$215.00	$247.00	$284.00	$327.00	$376.00	$432.00	$1,881.00	
10									
11									
12									
13									

QUICK REFERENCE

Changing a Cell's Alignment

1. **SELECT: the cell or cell range that you want to format**
2. **CLICK: an alignment button on the Formatting toolbar, such as Align Left ( ), Center ( ), Align Right ( ), or Merge and Center ( ) buttons**

IN ADDITION INDENTING TEXT IN A WORKSHEET CELL

New in Excel 97, you can indent text appearing in a worksheet cell up to 15 steps. To do so, select the desired cell and then click the Increase In-

dent button ( ) on the Formatting toolbar. To remove an indentation, you click the Decrease Indent button ( ).

ADDING BORDERS AND SHADING CELLS

The gridlines that appear in the document window are nonprinting lines, provided only to help you line up information in the worksheet. To enhance the readability of your printed worksheets, you can add borders, underlines, and shading to cells. Borders are used to separate data into logical sections and to emphasize titles. As well, these features allow you to create professional-looking invoice forms, memos, and tables.

To add borders and shaded patterns to your worksheet, select the desired cell or cell range and issue the Format, Cells command. In the dialog box that appears, select the *Border* tab or the *Patterns* tab. You can also click the Borders drop-down list ( ) on the Formatting toolbar to quickly apply borders to a selection or use the Fill Color button ( ) and the Font Color button ( ) to change the background and font colors.

You will now practice creating borders and shading cells.

Perform the following steps . . .

1. SELECT: cell range from B3 to H3
2. To add a border to the worksheet:
   CLICK: down arrow beside the Borders drop-down list ( )
   Make sure that you click the down arrow and not the button itself. You should see a list of sample border formats appear.
3. SELECT: a thick outline border (in the bottom right-hand corner)
   The formatting is immediately applied to the selection.
4. To apply a color to the cells' background:
   CLICK: down arrow beside the Fill Color drop-down list ( )
   SELECT: a light yellow color
5. To change the text color:
   CLICK: down arrow beside the Font Color drop-down list ( )
   SELECT: a dark blue color
6. SELECT: cell range from B9 to H9
7. To add two different borders to this range:
   CHOOSE: Format, Cells
   CLICK: *Border* tab
   SELECT: a single line in the *Style* group
   SELECT: a top location ( ) in the *Border* group
   SELECT: a double line in the *Style* group
   SELECT: a bottom location ( ) in the *Border* group
   PRESS: ENTER or CLICK: OK
   Notice that you select a new line style before choosing the border group to which you want it applied.
8. In order to get a full appreciation of fonts and borders, Excel lets you temporarily remove the **gridlines** from the worksheet. This provides a more accurate view of how the worksheet will look when printed. To temporarily remove the gridlines from your worksheet:
   CLICK: cell A12
   CHOOSE: Tools, Options
   CLICK: *View* tab
   SELECT: *Gridlines* check box to remove the "✓"
   PRESS: ENTER or CLICK: OK
   (*Note:* This option provides a cleaner view of your worksheet on the screen, but it does not affect how the worksheet will print. The print options for gridlines and headings are specified in the Page Setup dialog box, described later in this session.)

Your worksheet should now appear similar to Figure 2.12.

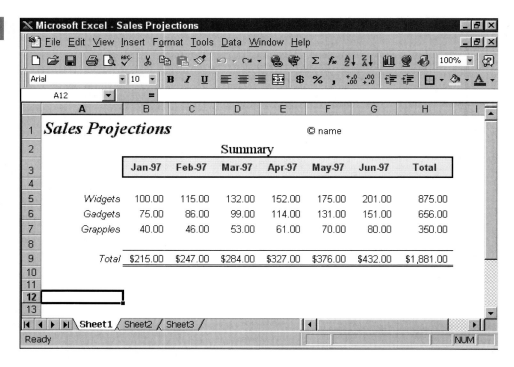

9. To return the display to normal:
   CHOOSE: Tools, Options
   CLICK: *View* tab (if it is not already selected)
   SELECT: *Gridlines* check box so that a "✓" appears
   PRESS: (ENTER) or CLICK: OK

10. Save the "Sales Projections" workbook to your Data Files location.

QUICK REFERENCE
Adding Borders, Colors,
and Patterns

1. **SELECT: the cell or cell range that you want to format**
2. **CHOOSE: Format, Cells**
3. **CLICK: *Border* tab to specify border lines**
4. **CLICK: *Patterns* tab to specify a shading level or color**
5. **PRESS: (ENTER) or CLICK: OK**

IN ADDITION ADDING A BACKGROUND BITMAP TO A WORKSHEET

Similar to specifying wallpaper for your Windows desktop, you can now add a texture or bitmap graphic image to an Excel 97 worksheet. To do so, choose Format, Sheet, Background from the Menu bar and then select a bitmap file. Excel will tile the selected graphic image across the entire worksheet.

COPYING FORMATTING OPTIONS

Excel's Format Painter button (⬚) lets you copy the formatting styles from one area in your worksheet to another. To copy a cell's formatting, select the cell and click the Format Painter button (⬚). To apply the formatting, you click on a single cell or drag the paintbrush mouse pointer to format an entire cell range. When you release the mouse button, the formatting styles are copied from the original selection to your new selection. Not only does this feature speed formatting operations, it ensures consistency among the cell formatting in your worksheet.

You will now practice using the Format Painter.

Perform the following steps . . .

1. To practice copying styles, let's format a cell with new options:
   SELECT: cell B5
   CLICK: Decrease Decimal button (⬚) twice
   The entry in cell B5 will now appear as 100.

2. To copy this formatting change to the rest of the values:
   CLICK: Format Painter button (⬚)

3. Move the mouse pointer into the document window. Notice that the mouse pointer is now a cross with a paintbrush.

4. SELECT: the cell range from B5 to H9

5. Release the mouse button. Notice that all the values in the range are now formatted with the same features as cell B5.

6. To undo the last operation:
   CLICK: Undo button (⬚) three times
   PRESS: ESC to remove the dashed marquee from around cell B5
   The cells now appear with their original formatting (two decimals).

7. PRESS: CTRL + HOME to move to cell A1

QUICK REFERENCE
Copying a Cell's Formatting

1. **SELECT: the cell whose formatting you want to copy**
2. **CLICK: Format Painter button (⬚) on the Standard toolbar**
3. **SELECT: the cell range that you want to format**
4. **Release the mouse button to complete the operation.**

IN ADDITION COPYING FORMATTING TO SEVERAL RANGES

You can copy a cell's formatting to several cell ranges at the same time by double-clicking the Format Painter button (⬚). After you apply the first coat to a cell range in the worksheet, the mouse pointer remains a cross with a paintbrush so that you can paint other cell ranges. When you are finished, click the Format Painter button (⬚) to return to the cross mouse pointer.

REMOVING FORMATTING OPTIONS

If you want to remove the formatting features applied to an area on your worksheet, select the cell or range of cells and then choose the Edit, Clear command from the menu. On the cascading menu that appears, select the Formats command. This command removes the formatting options only, not the contents of the cell or range of cells.

In this exercise, you practice removing formatting options.

Perform the following steps . . .

1. SELECT: cell A1

2. To remove the formatting for this cell:
CHOOSE: Edit, Clear, Formats
Notice that the cell's formatting is stripped while its contents are left intact.

3. To undo the last command:
CLICK: Undo button (⬚)

QUICK REFERENCE
Removing a Cell's Formatting

1. **SELECT: a cell or cell range**
2. **CHOOSE: Edit, Clear, Formats**

USING THE AUTOFORMAT COMMAND

The **AutoFormat** command lets you apply a predefined table format, complete with numeric formats, alignments, borders, shading, and colors, to a group of cells on your worksheet. This feature assumes that your data is organized in the worksheet as a table, with labels running down the left column and across the top row. To automatically format your worksheet, select a cell range and then choose the Format, AutoFormat command.

Let's apply a few different formats to our worksheet.

Perform the following steps . . .

1. SELECT: cell range from A3 to H9

2. To display the AutoFormat dialog box:
CHOOSE: Format, AutoFormat

3. In the *Table format* list box:
SELECT: Colorful 2
PRESS: (**ENTER**) or CLICK: OK

4. To remove the highlighting from the range:
SELECT: cell A12
Your screen should now appear similar to Figure 2.13.

FIGURE 2.13

APPLYING THE
AUTOFORMAT COMMAND

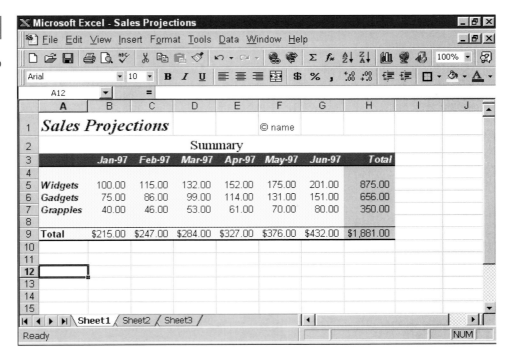

	A	B	C	D	E	F	G	H	I	J
1	*Sales Projections*					© name				
2				Summary						
3		*Jan-97*	*Feb-97*	*Mar-97*	*Apr-97*	*May-97*	*Jun-97*	*Total*		
4										
5	*Widgets*	100.00	115.00	132.00	152.00	175.00	201.00	875.00		
6	*Gadgets*	75.00	86.00	99.00	114.00	131.00	151.00	656.00		
7	*Grapples*	40.00	46.00	53.00	61.00	70.00	80.00	350.00		
8										
9	Total	$215.00	$247.00	$284.00	$327.00	$376.00	$432.00	$1,881.00		
10										
11										
12										
13										
14										
15										

5. Practice choosing some of the other table format options from the AutoFormat dialog box. Before proceeding, reselect the Colorful 2.

6. Save the "Sales Projections" workbook to your Data Files location.

QUICK REFERENCE
Using AutoFormat

1. **SELECT: the cell or cell range that you want to format**
2. **CHOOSE: Format, AutoFormat**
3. **SELECT: an option from the *Table format* list box**
4. **PRESS: (ENTER) or CLICK: OK**

PRINTING THE WORKBOOK

This section introduces the commands for printing a workbook, including options for setting up the page and previewing the output.

DEFINING THE PAGE LAYOUT

You define the page layout settings for printing a workbook using the File, Page Setup command. In the dialog box that appears, you specify **margins, headers, footers,** and whether gridlines or row and column headings should appear on the final printed document. To make the process more manageable, Excel organizes the page layout settings under four tabs in the Page Setup dialog box (Figure 2.14):

- *Page* tab   The *Page* tab lets you specify the paper size, print scale, and the workbook's print orientation (for example, portrait or landscape).

- *Margins* tab   You specify the top, bottom, left, and right page margins in inches using this tab. Excel also lets you center the worksheet both horizontally and vertically.

- *Header/Footer* tab   You use a header and a footer to print static information at the top and bottom of each page, respectively.

- *Sheet* tab   Besides specifying the actual print area on this tab, you can tell Excel whether to print gridlines, titles, or row and column headings.

FIGURE 2.14

PAGE SETUP DIALOG BOX:
PAGE TAB DISPLAYED

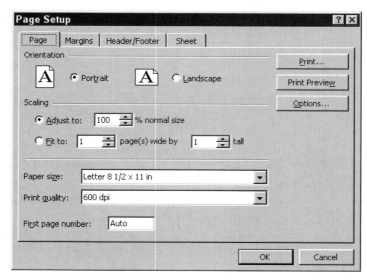

In this section, you define the page layout specifications for the "Sales Projections" workbook.

Perform the following steps . . .

1. Before changing options in the Page Setup dialog box, let's specify the print area for the worksheet:
   SELECT: cell range from A1 to H9
   CHOOSE: File, Print Area, Set Print Area
   PRESS: CTRL + HOME
   The print area on the worksheet is now surrounded by dashed lines.

2. To specify the page layout settings:
CHOOSE: File, Page Setup
CLICK: *Page* tab

3. Make the following selections:
SELECT: Portrait in the *Orientation* group
SELECT: Adjust to 100% normal size in the *Scaling* group
SELECT: "Letter 8½ × 11 in" in the *Paper Size* drop-down list box

4. To specify the margins:
CLICK: *Margins* tab

5. Make the following selections:
SELECT: 1.5 inches for the *Top* margin
SELECT: 1.5 inches for the *Bottom* margin
SELECT: 1 inch for the *Left* margin
SELECT: 1 inch for the *Right* margin
(*Hint:* To increase and decrease the margin values, you click the up and down triangles that appear to the right of each spin box.)

6. To center the worksheet between the left and right margins:
SELECT: *Horizontally* check box in the *Center on page* group

7. To specify a header and a footer:
CLICK: *Header/Footer* tab

8. To create a custom header:
SELECT: "(none)" at the top of the *Header* drop-down list box
CLICK: Custom Header command button
Figure 2.15 shows the Header dialog box and labels the buttons used for inserting information into the different sections.

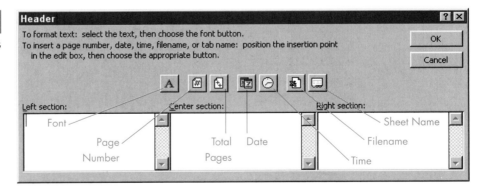

9. To create a header that prints the current date against the right margin:
CLICK: the mouse pointer in the *Right section* once
TYPE: `Printed on:`
PRESS: Space bar once
CLICK: Date button (as labeled in Figure 2.15)
CLICK: OK command button
You will see the custom header appear in the Page Setup dialog box.

10. To select a predefined footer:
SELECT: "Sales Projections, Page 1" from the *Footer* drop-down list box

11. To confirm that the print area is correct and that no gridlines will appear on the printed worksheet:
CLICK: *Sheet* tab

12. Confirm that the cell range from A1 to H9 appears in the *Print area* text box. Also, ensure that there are no check boxes selected in the *Print* group. (*Note:* By default, Excel does not print gridlines on your worksheet.)

13. To complete the Page Setup dialog box and return to the worksheet:
PRESS: (**ENTER**) or CLICK: OK

14. Save the "Sales Projections" workbook to your Data Files location.

QUICK REFERENCE
Preparing to Print

1. **SELECT: the cell range that you want to print**
2. **CHOOSE: File, Print Area, Set Print Area**
3. **CHOOSE: File, Page Setup**
4. **In the Page Setup dialog box, specify options for page layout settings, margins, headers and footers, and whether to print gridlines or column and row headings.**
5. **PRESS: (ENTER) or CLICK: OK**

PREVIEWING THE OUTPUT

You can preview a workbook in a full-page display by choosing the File, Print Preview command or clicking the Print Preview button (⊡). Once the preview is displayed, use the Next and Previous command buttons near the top of the screen to move through the document page by page. Use the magnifying glass mouse pointer to zoom in and out on the page. If you need to modify some page layout options, click the Setup button to display the Page Setup dialog box or the Margins button to drag margin lines in the Preview window. You can also click the Page Break Preview button to adjust the page breaks in your worksheet and to resize the print area. A watermark appears in the background with "Page 1," "Page 2," and so on. This feature lets you visually arrange the print boundaries using the mouse.

Let's preview the worksheet.

Perform the following steps . . .

1. To preview how the "Sales Projections" workbook will print:
CLICK: Print Preview button (⊡)

2. To zoom in on the page:
CLICK: Zoom command button

3. To zoom out, move the mouse pointer over the preview page and then click the left mouse button once.

4. When you are finished previewing the worksheet:
PRESS: (**ESC**) or CLICK: Close

---

1. **CLICK: Print Preview button ( )**
2. **CLICK: Zoom command button to zoom in and out on a page**
3. **CLICK: Page Setup command button to modify the page layout**
4. **CLICK: Margins command button to modify the margin settings**
5. **PRESS: (ESC) or CLICK: Close**

PRINTING THE SELECTED RANGE

When you are satisfied with your worksheet in the Preview mode, choose the File, Print command to display the Print dialog box (Figure 2.16) or click the Print button ( ) to send it directly to the printer. In the Print dialog box, you can specify what to print (a selected cell range or the entire workbook, for example) and how many copies.

FIGURE 2.16

PRINT DIALOG BOX

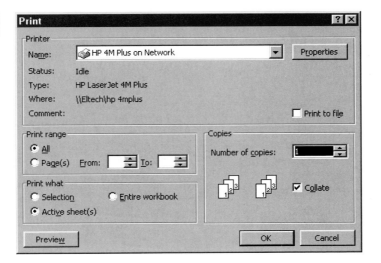

Let's print your worksheet.

Perform the following steps . . .

1. To send the worksheet to the printer and bypass the Print dialog box:
CLICK: Print button ( )
The document is printed using the default settings. This produces the same result as choosing the File, Print command and then clicking the OK command button, without changing any settings in the dialog box.

2. Save the "Sales Projections" workbook to your Data Files location.

3. Close the workbook and then exit Excel.

QUICK REFERENCE   1. **CLICK: Print button (🖨)**
Printing a Worksheet   2. **SELECT: additional print options, as desired**
                          3. **PRESS: ⟦ENTER⟧ or CLICK: OK**

SUMMARY

This session introduced you to the everyday procedures required to effectively work with Microsoft Excel. You created a workbook from scratch and then practiced entering formulas and using the SUM function. You also learned to use some of Excel's "Auto" features, including AutoCalculate, AutoComplete, AutoCorrect, and AutoFormat. The majority of the session, however, dealt with Excel's formatting capabilities. Column widths, row heights, fonts, numeric formats, cell alignments, borders, colors, and shading were all modified in customizing the sample workbook. Toward the end of the session, you concentrated on setting up and previewing a workbook for printing.

Many of the commands introduced in the session are provided in Table 2.1, the Command Summary.

TABLE 2.1

Command Summary

Command	Description
Edit, Clear, Formats	Removes formatting from the selected cell range.
File, Page Setup	Sets the print area, margins, headers, and footers.
File, Print (🖨)	Prints the workbook.
File, Print Preview (🔍)	Previews the workbook before printing.
Format, AutoFormat	Formats the selected range using predefined styles.
Format, Cells	*Font* tab: Applies fonts, styles, and point sizes to cells. *Number* tab: Changes the appearance of values. *Alignment* tab: Changes the alignment of a cell. *Border* tab: Applies borders to cells. *Patterns* tab: Applies shading to cells.
Format, Column, AutoFit Selection	Changes the column width to the best fit.
Format, Column, Width	Changes the column width.
Format, Row, Height	Changes the row height.
Tools, Options	Removes gridlines from the screen display.
Tools, Spelling (🔤)	Spell-checks a cell range, worksheet, or a workbook.

KEY TERMS

AutoCalculate

In Excel, a software feature that sums the selected range of cells and displays the result in the Status bar.

AutoComplete

In Excel, a software feature that assists you in entering data into a worksheet by filling in letters from existing entries in the column as you type.

AutoCorrect

In Excel, a software feature that corrects common typing and spelling mistakes automatically as you type. It also enables you to enter complex symbols quickly and easily.

AutoFormat

In Excel, a software feature that applies professionally designed formatting styles to your worksheet tables.

cell alignment

The positioning of data entered into a worksheet cell in relation to the cell borders.

cell range

One or more cells in a worksheet that together form a rectangle.

column width

The width of a worksheet column measured in characters. Because the actual width of a group of characters changes depending on the font size, it is often used only as a relative measure.

font

All the characters of one size in a particular *typeface;* includes numbers, punctuation marks, and upper- and lowercase letters.

footer

Descriptive information (such as page number and date) that appears at the bottom of each page of a document.

functions

Shortcuts that can be used in formulas to perform calculations.

gridlines

The lines on a worksheet that assist the user in lining up the cell pointer with a particular column letter or row number.

header

Descriptive information (such as page number and date) that appears at the top of each page of a document.

margins

Space between the edge of the paper and the top, bottom, left, and right edges of printed text.

row height

The height of a worksheet row measured in points. Points are the measurement unit for type—there are 72 points to the inch.

SUM function

Function used to add values stored in a range of spreadsheet cells.

typeface

The shape and appearance of characters. There are two categories of typefaces: serif and sans serif. Serif type (for example, Times Roman) is more decorative and, some say, easier to read than sans serif type (for example, **Arial**).

EXERCISES

SHORT ANSWERS

1. Why use the SUM function rather than a simple addition formula?

2. What is meant by a "best fit" or "AutoFit" column width?

3. How do you apply formatting changes to an entire worksheet?

4. How do you select multiple cell ranges in a worksheet?

5. What does "#########" in a cell indicate?

6. What unit of measure is used to specify the height of a row?

7. What unit of measure is used to specify the width of a column?

8. How does AutoCorrect differ from AutoComplete?

9. Name the tabs in the Page Setup dialog box.

10. Does turning the gridlines off for the screen display affect the way the document prints? Explain.

HANDS-ON

(*Note:* Ensure that you know the storage location of your Advantage Files and your Data Files before proceeding.)

1. This exercise retrieves an existing workbook, edits the information, and saves the workbook under a new filename. You also send a copy of the updated file to the printer.

     a. Open the "Exp-Qtr1" workbook that is stored in the Advantage Files location.

     b. Modify the worksheet to reflect the second quarter's expenses by editing the following cells listed.

Move to Cell	TYPE
D1	*your name*
B2	Apr-97
C2	May-97
D2	Jun-97
B6	43.44
C4	39.65
C7	119
D6	83.91
D8	98.60

   c. Save this workbook to your Data Files location under the name "Exp-Qtr2". (*Hint*: Use the File, Save As command.)

   d. Specify a header that prints only the current date in the top left-hand corner of the page.

   e. Specify a footer that prints only the page number in the bottom right-hand corner of the page.

   f. Review the worksheet in Print Preview mode.

   g. Select the cell range from A1 to E10 and then set the print area.

   h. Print the workbook.

   i. Save the workbook, replacing the old version of the file.

2. This exercise uses the formatting commands covered in this session to enhance the "Exp-Qtr2" workbook.

   a. If the workbook is not already loaded into memory, open the "Exp-Qtr2" workbook.

   b. Make the following changes to column widths:

Column	Width
A	15
B	10
C	10
D	10
E	12

c. Make the following changes to row heights:

Row	Height
1	25
2	20
3	6
9	6
10	18

d. Make the headings from cell B2 to E2 bold and italic.

e. Center the headings horizontally and vertically in their columns.

f. Make the Expense items (the row labels) from A4 to A10 bold.

g. Right-align the Expense items.

h. Increase the size of the font for the title (in cell A1) to 18 points.

i. Select the cells from B2 to E2.

j. Place an outline border around these cells and then shade the interior a light green color.

k. Select the cells from B4 to E8.

l. Place a border grid around each of these cells and then shade the interior a light yellow color.

m. Change the screen display by removing the column and row headers and the gridlines. Then, clear the print area using the File, Print Area, Clear Print Area command.

n. Delete the word "Type" in cell A2.

o. Save the workbook as "Expenses - Formatted" to your Data Files location. Your screen should now appear similar to Figure 2.17.

p. Set the print area again and then print the workbook.

q. Close the workbook.

FIGURE 2.17

"EXPENSES - FORMATTED"
WORKBOOK

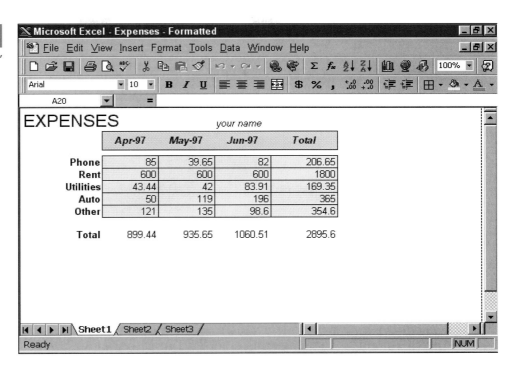

3. This exercise provides a step-by-step approach for using the formatting commands covered in this session to create a memo or fax form.

a. Open a new workbook.

b. Move to cell A1.

c. TYPE: **Memorandum**

d. Center the title between columns A and E.

e. Choose an interesting font with boldface and a size of at least 24 points for the title.

f. Make columns A through E at least 12 characters wide.

g. Enter the following information:

Move to cell	TYPE
A3	DATE:
A4	TO:
A5	FROM:
A6	SUBJECT:

h. Increase the row height to 30 points for rows 3 through 6.

i. Right-align, italicize, and make bold each of the row headings in column A.

j. Select an interesting font and a size of at least 12 points.

k. Color the cell range from A1 to E1 and then change the font color.

l.   Color the cell range from A8 to E8 with the same fill color.

m.   Move to cell A1.

n.   Save this workbook as "Memorandum" to your Data Files location. Your worksheet should appear similar to Figure 2.18.

o.   Print and then close the workbook.

FIGURE 2.18

"MEMORANDUM"
WORKBOOK

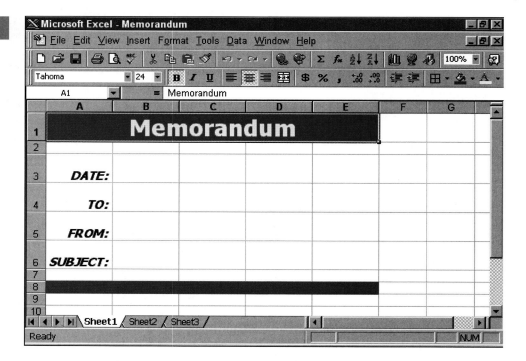

4.   **On Your Own:** Creating a Custom Invoice Form
     For this exercise, you are to create a custom invoice form for your home-based business. The form should include your company name and address at the top of the form, an area for the customer's name and address, and then the following column headings:

     Quantity Item # Description   Unit Price Total Price

     Outline the columns with borders to visually separate the itemized information. As desired, apply additional formatting to make the invoice professional and attractive. Save the workbook as "My Invoice Form" to your Data Files location and then print a copy of the worksheet. Finally, close the workbook before proceeding.

5.   **On Your Own:** Formatting Your Personal Phone Book
     Retrieve the "Personal Phone Book" workbook that you created at the end of Session 1. Format the worksheet using the commands learned in this session and then print a copy of your phone book for review. When you are satisfied with the output, save the workbook back to your Data Files location. Close the workbook and then exit Excel.

CASE PROBLEMS | **MADRID CLOTHING COMPANY**

(*Note:* In the following case problems, assume the role of the primary characters and perform the same steps that they identify. You may want to re-read the session opening.)

1. It's 10 o'clock on a Sunday morning and Khalid's one day off will be spent in front of his computer. He must create, format, and print the spreadsheet for his expansion proposal today. He will venture to the company's main office tomorrow and place the proposal strategically on Suriya's desk before anyone else arrives. With the caffeine from a fourth cup of coffee tingling through his veins, Khalid opens his folder of handwritten notes. His first task is to create the basic spreadsheet layout.

    From the following table that Khalid has drawn by hand, create a spreadsheet called "Lucky 7" and then save it to your Data Files location.

California Expansion	Q1/98	Q2/98	Q3/98	Q4/98
Best-Case Scenario:				
Sales Revenue	22,500	38,000	52,800	85,700
Cost of Goods Sold				
Gross Margin				
Variable Expenses				
Fixed Expenses	6,000	6,000	6,000	6,000
Net Profit				
Worst-Case Scenario:				
Sales Revenue	15,800	18,900	26,500	36,000
Cost of Goods Sold				
Gross Margin				
Variable Expenses				
Fixed Expenses	7,500	7,500	7,500	7,500
Net Profit				

2. Looking over the spreadsheet, Khalid realizes how much work is still ahead of him. But instead of diving into the spreadsheet haphazardly, he contemplates the steps that he needs to perform. First of all, he must complete the missing information. For example, the Cost of Goods Sold and Variable Expenses for the Best-Case Scenario are 55 percent and 10 percent of the Sales Revenue, respectively. For the Worst-Case Scenario, the Cost of Goods Sold and Variable Expenses are 60 percent and 15 percent of the Sales Revenue. He must also enter a formula for each quarter to calculate the Gross Margin (Sales Revenue minus Cost of Goods Sold) and the Net Profit (Gross Margin minus Variable and Fixed Expenses). Lastly, Khalid decides to add a column called YTD that totals the figures from the four quarters.

Complete the "Lucky 7" spreadsheet following the steps that Khalid has outlined and then save the file to the Advantage Diskette.

3. Knowing that the presentation style is sometimes as important as the information itself, Khalid decides to format the "Lucky 7" worksheet to give it a professional appearance. Having worked through the examples in this session, Khalid applies fonts, styles, and numeric formats to the worksheet, aligns the cell contents of the column headings, applies some border lines and colors, and changes column widths and row heights. When satisfied with its appearance, Khalid checks the spelling in the spreadsheet and then prints it with the current date and page number appearing in the footer of the page.

    Following Khalid's lead, format, spell-check, and print the workbook, and then save the file to the Advantage Diskette. Make sure that you test the accuracy of the spreadsheet's formulas using the AutoCalculate feature. You should also insert some new values for the Sales Revenue and watch the Net Profit result adjust. Check at least one of the columns manually using a calculator before saving and then closing the workbook. When finished, exit Excel and shut-down Windows.

Increasing Your Productivity

SESSION

HTTP WWW

3

IRWIN

COMPUTER & INFORMATION TECHNOLOGY

SESSION OUTLINE

INTRODUCTION

Electronic spreadsheets are timesavers compared to the old pencil-and-paper spreadsheets. Now let us demonstrate some timesavers for the time-saver. Instead of building a worksheet cell by cell, Excel provides you with some data entry and command shortcuts that work with cell ranges. You will also learn how to enter built-in functions for performing complex calculations.

CASE STUDY	**RIVERSIDE FORD, INC.**

Riverside Ford is one of New Jersey's largest car dealerships. Located near the Meadowlands Arena, Riverside has always maintained a high profile in the community and has easily met Ford's contractual obligations for selling new cars and trucks. One of Zachary Rempel's duties as a business manager with Riverside is to generate the month-end summary report that must be submitted to Ford's regional office.

Just last week, the owner, Jackson L. Davies, purchased a new computer for Zachary and made him personally responsible for generating all of the dealership's reports. With an increased workload, Zachary knew that he would have to streamline operations and find a more efficient method for summarizing the data he received. Fortunately, the computer came with Microsoft Excel installed and, after only a few days, Zachary is now creating, formatting, and printing worksheets. However, Zachary has also become a little frustrated with Excel. He doesn't like entering long and complex formulas to perform standard calculations, like finding the average value for a column of numbers, picking the highest salesperson's commission in the month, or showing the monthly payment for a financed vehicle. And though he knows that there must be a better way, he doesn't have time to figure out these other methods on his own.

In this session, you and Zachary learn to improve your productivity in creating and editing worksheets. In addition to learning how to copy and move information and how to insert and delete columns and rows, you are introduced to Excel's built-in functions for performing standard calculations. This session provides you with some of the most powerful productivity tools that Excel has to offer.

ABSOLUTE AND RELATIVE CELL ADDRESSES

This section adds a new twist to referencing cells in formulas. In previous sessions, you typed the cell address or clicked on the cell that you wanted to include in a formula. You should be aware, however, that there are two types of cell addresses that can be entered into formulas: *relative* and *absolute*. The differences between the two types become important when you start copying and moving information in your worksheet.

When a formula is copied from one worksheet location to another, Excel automatically adjusts the cell references in the copied formula to reflect their new location. This adjustment spares you from having to type many similar formulas into the worksheet and thus saves a tremendous amount of time. A cell reference that adjusts when it is copied is referred to as a **relative cell address.** On the other hand, there are times when you don't want a cell reference to automatically adjust when it is copied. A cell reference that refers to an exact location on the worksheet and does not adjust is called an **absolute cell address.**

By default, formulas that you enter in Excel use relative cell references. To use an absolute cell reference, you must precede the column letter and the row number of the cell address with a dollar sign. For example, to make cell B5 an absolute cell reference in a formula, you would type dollar signs before the B and before the 5, such as B5. If you wanted to have the cell reference automatically adjust the row number when it was copied but not the column letter, then you would use *mixed cell addressing* and type a dollar sign before the column letter only, such as $B5. You will practice using these types of cell references in the next section on copying and moving worksheet information.

COPYING AND MOVING INFORMATION

To efficiently construct a worksheet, you need tools that reduce the number of repetitive entries you are required to make. For example, once you have created a formula that adds figures in one column, why not copy that formula to sum the adjacent column as well? Two of the most common editing activities in a worksheet are copying and moving data.

There are several different methods for copying and moving information in a worksheet. Similar to most Windows applications, Excel provides the **Clipboard** for sharing information within a workbook, among workbooks, and among applications. For quick "from-here-to-there" copy and move operations, Excel provides the **drag and drop** method where you use the mouse to drag cell information in a worksheet. This section provides examples using both methods for copying and moving information.

USING THE CLIPBOARD

If the drag and drop method is quicker and easier, why use the Clipboard to copy and move information? The Clipboard provides greater flexibility, allowing you to copy information to multiple locations in a worksheet. To use this method, you first select the cell range that you want to copy or move and then cut or copy the selection to the Clipboard. After moving the cell pointer to the desired destination, you paste the data from the Clipboard into the worksheet. You can then repeat the paste operation multiple times, if required.

The Clipboard commands, toolbar buttons, and keyboard shortcuts for copying and moving information appear in Table 3.1.

TABLE 3.1

Copying and Moving
Information Using the
Clipboard

Task Description	Menu Command	Toolbar Button	Keyboard Shortcut
Moves the selected cell range from the worksheet to the Clipboard	Edit, Cut	✂	**CTRL** +X
Copies the selected cell range to the Clipboard	Edit, Copy	📋	**CTRL** +C
Inserts the contents of the Clipboard at the cell pointer	Edit, Paste	📋	**CTRL** +V

FIGURE 3.1

THE "SALESREP"
WORKBOOK

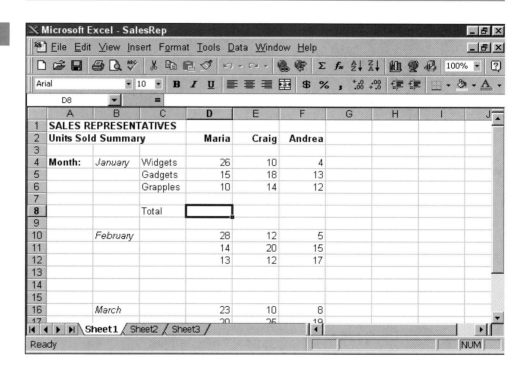

To practice using the Clipboard, you will open and then modify the "SalesRep" workbook (Figure 3.1). This workbook provides an incomplete summary for three sales representatives.

Perform the following steps . . .

1. Make sure that you know the storage location of your Advantage Files and your Data Files before proceeding. Open the "SalesRep" workbook, located in your Advantage Files location.

2. Let's cancel Excel's option for moving the cell pointer down one row each time you press **ENTER**. Do the following:
CHOOSE: Tools, Options
CLICK: *Edit* tab
SELECT: *Move selection after Enter* check box so that no "✓" appears
PRESS: **ENTER** or CLICK: OK

3. The first step in completing this worksheet is to sum the January data for each salesperson. Do the following:
CLICK: cell D8

4. TYPE: =d4+d5+d6
PRESS: ENTER
The cell should now include the sum of the figures in column D (51).

5. To copy this formula onto the Clipboard:
CLICK: Copy button (🖺)
A dashed marquee now surrounds the cell range.

6. To place a copy of the formula into cell E8:
CLICK: cell E8
PRESS: ENTER
Notice that the result of the formula is the sum of the figures in column E (42). Because the formula uses relative cell addresses, it automatically adjusts the cell references to the new column. Look in the Formula bar to see the new formula (=E4+E5+E6).

7. To see the effect of using absolute cell references, let's edit the formula in cell E8:
DOUBLE-CLICK: cell E8
You will see the formula appear in the cell ready for editing and the color-coded borders around the appropriate cells.

8. PRESS: HOME
PRESS: ➡ once
The cursor now appears to the right of the equal sign.

9. To make a cell address absolute, you type a dollar sign in front of the column letter and row number. However, there is a shortcut method, as demonstrated below:
PRESS: F4 (Absolute key)
PRESS: ➡
PRESS: F4 (Absolute key)
PRESS: ➡
PRESS: F4 (Absolute key)
PRESS: ENTER

10. To copy this new formula onto the Clipboard using the shortcut menu:
RIGHT-CLICK: cell E8
CHOOSE: Copy

11. To place a copy of the Clipboard's contents into cell F8:
CLICK: cell F8
PRESS: ENTER
Notice that the result of the formula is still the sum of the figures in column E. The formula did not automatically adjust because it uses absolute cell references.

12. Now let's clean up the Total line. You are going to enter a new formula in
cell D8 and then copy it to columns E and F. To begin:
CLICK: cell D8
PRESS: DELETE

13. DOUBLE-CLICK: AutoSum button (Σ)

14. To copy and then paste the formula:
CLICK: Copy button (🗐)
SELECT: cell range from E8 to F8
PRESS: ENTER

QUICK REFERENCE
Copying and Moving
Cell Information

1. **Select the source cell or cell range.**

2. **To copy or move information:**

   CLICK: Copy button (🗐)

   CLICK: Cut button (✂)

3. **Select the destination cell or cell range.**

4. **PRESS: ENTER or CLICK: Paste button (🗐)**

USING DRAG AND DROP

One of Excel's most popular features is drag and drop. This method uses the mouse
to copy and move information from one location to another without using the Clipboard. Although you cannot perform multiple pastes, it is by far the easiest method
for copying and moving information short distances. You can even use drag and
drop to copy information between sheets in a workbook by holding down the
ALT key and dragging the selection over a sheet tab.

You will now practice using drag and drop.

**Perform
the
following
steps . . .**

1. To demonstrate how you can move cells using drag and drop:
SELECT: cell range from D2 to F2

2. Position the mouse pointer over a border of the selected cell range until a
white arrow appears.

3. CLICK: left mouse button and hold it down
DRAG: mouse pointer downward one row until a shaded outline appears
around cells D3 to F3

4. Release the left mouse button. The contents are moved to the newly highlighted cell range.

5. To undo the last move operation:
CLICK: Undo button (↶ ▾)

6. To copy cells using drag and drop:
SELECT: cell range from C4 to C8

7. Position the mouse pointer over a border of the selected cell range until a white arrow appears.

8. PRESS: CTRL and hold it down
CLICK: left mouse button and hold it down
DRAG: mouse pointer downward until a shaded outline appears around cells C10 to C14
(*Note*: When you hold down the CTRL key, a plus sign appears at the tip of the mouse pointer to inform you that dragging and dropping the selection will result in a copy operation.)

9. Release the left mouse button. Using the same process, copy the cell range from C10 to C14 to the cell range C16 to C20. Your screen should appear similar to Figure 3.2.

FIGURE 3.2

THE "SALESREP"
WORKBOOK AFTER
COPYING AND MOVING
CELL INFORMATION

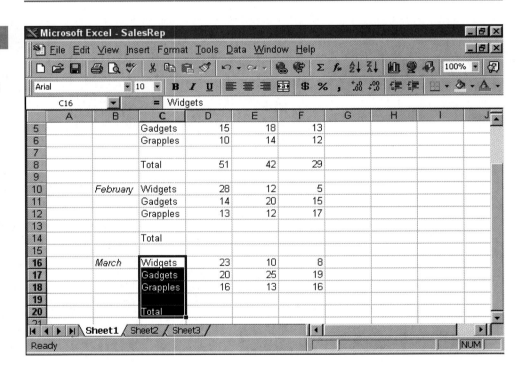

QUICK REFERENCE
Move and Copy Cells
Using Drag and Drop

1. Select the cell or cell range to copy or move.

2. Position the mouse pointer (a white arrow) over any border of the selected cells. (To copy the cells, hold down the CTRL key.)

3. Drag the selected cells to their destination. (To move between sheets in a workbook, hold down the ALT key.)

4. Release the mouse button and, if necessary, CTRL and/or ALT.

USING FILL RIGHT AND FILL DOWN

Excel provides two commands specially designed for copying formulas: Edit, Fill, Right and Edit, Fill, Down. These commands are used when you have entered a single formula or function that needs to be extended across a row (Fill Right) or down a column (Fill Down). Rather than choosing the menu commands, you can select the cell range and press the keyboard shortcuts (CTRL)+r for Fill Right or (CTRL)+d for Fill Down. If you prefer using the mouse, you can select a cell to copy and then drag the cell's **fill handle,** which is the black square that appears in the lower right-hand corner of a cell or cell range. This copies the formula across or down the selected range. You will practice using the fill handle in the next section.

Let's demonstrate the Fill Right command.

Perform the following steps . . .

1. To begin, let's create the first formula:
   CLICK: cell D14
   DOUBLE-CLICK: AutoSum button (Σ)

2. To copy the formula in cell D14 to the remaining cells:
   SELECT: cell range from D14 to F14
   CHOOSE: Edit, Fill, Right
   (*Note*: Ensure that the cell with the formula appears in the top left-hand corner of the selected range.)

3. You will now copy the formulas to the cell range D20 to F20. Before proceeding, ensure that cells D14 to F14 remain highlighted:
   CLICK: Copy button ()
   CLICK: cell D20
   PRESS: (ENTER)

4. Save the workbook as "Sales Rep Report" to your Data Files location.

QUICK REFERENCE
Using Fill Right and
Fill Down

1. **Select the cell that contains the information to copy.**
2. **Extend the cell range downward or to the right, depending on where you want to place the copies. (*Hint:* The cell to copy always appears in the top left-hand corner of the cell range.)**
3. **CHOOSE: Edit, Fill, Right or Edit, Fill, Down, depending on where you want to place the copies.**

CREATING A SERIES WITH AUTOFILL

With Excel's AutoFill feature, you can quickly enter a series into a worksheet. A **series** is simply a sequence of data that follows a pattern, typically mathematical (1, 2, 3,...) or date (Jan, Feb, Mar,...). From the menu, you enter a series using the Edit, Fill, Series command. If you prefer using the mouse, you can drag a cell's fill handle.

You will now practice using AutoFill.

 **Perform the following steps . . .**

1. In this exercise, we move to a blank area of the worksheet to demonstrate some uses for the fill handle. To begin, do the following:
   CLICK: Name box in the Formula bar
   TYPE: a50
   PRESS: **ENTER** or CLICK: OK

2. Move the cell pointer up to cell A40.

3. TYPE: Jan
   PRESS: **ENTER**
   You have to type in at least one cell entry as the starting point for a series. Make sure that your cell pointer remains on cell A40.

4. Position the mouse over the small black square in the bottom right-hand corner of the cell pointer. The mouse pointer will change to a black cross hair.

5. CLICK: left mouse button and hold it down
   DRAG: the cell range outline to cell F40
   Notice the yellow ScrollTip that appears when you drag the range.

6. Release the mouse button to complete the AutoFill operation. Since Jan was the starting entry for the series, Excel increments the series by one month for each column.

7. Move to cell A42.

8. TYPE: Quarter 1
   PRESS: **ENTER**

9. DRAG: fill handle for A42 to cover the range to F42

10. Release the mouse button. Notice that Excel understands that the word "Quarter" refers to one in four. After Quarter 4, Excel begins again with Quarter 1.

11. Move to cell A44.

12. To create a custom data series:
    TYPE: Jan-97
    PRESS: ➡
    TYPE: Apr-97
    PRESS: **ENTER**
    You must enter values into the first two cells so that Excel can extrapolate the value needed to increment the series further.

13. SELECT: cell range from A44 to B44
    Make sure that both cells are selected before proceeding. Notice that there is only one fill handle for the range even though two cells are selected.

14. DRAG: fill handle to cover the cell range from A44 to F44

15. Release the mouse button.

16. Move to cell A46. Your worksheet should now appear similar to Figure 3.3.

17. Save the "Sales Rep Report" workbook to your Data Files location.

FIGURE 3.3

USING AUTOFILL TO
COMPLETE A SERIES

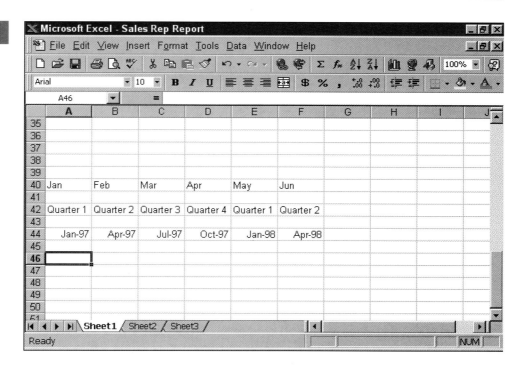

QUICK REFERENCE		
Using AutoFill	**1.**	**Select the cell that contains the data to continue in a series.**
	2.	**Position the mouse on the cell's fill handle, a small black square in the bottom right-hand corner of the cell, until it changes to a black cross hair mouse pointer.**
	3.	**Drag the fill handle to extend the series.**
	4.	**Release the mouse button to complete the operation.**

INSERTING AND DELETING ROWS AND COLUMNS

One way that you can quickly modify the layout of a worksheet is to add or delete rows and columns. As we mentioned in Session 1, people often create worksheets or design a report without fully understanding the problem that they are trying to solve. Therefore, worksheets must evolve as needs change and as the initial objectives become better defined. The ability to reorganize a worksheet by inserting and deleting rows and columns is an important part of this evolution.

To add a row or column to the worksheet, you choose the Insert, Rows or Insert, Columns command. To delete a row or column, you select a row or column and then choose the Edit, Delete command. The easiest method for selecting a row or column is to click its row number or column letter in the frame area. And the easiest method for choosing the Insert or Delete command is by right-clicking the row number or column letter in the frame area to display the shortcut menu.

You will now practice modifying the "Sales Rep Report" workbook.

Perform the following steps . . .

1. To view the top of the worksheet page:
   PRESS: CTRL + HOME

2. To add a blank column, move the cell pointer into the column frame area and do the following:
   RIGHT-CLICK: column E
   Notice that the entire column is highlighted and a shortcut menu appears.

3. CHOOSE: Insert
   The new column is inserted and the original information is moved one column to the right.

4. To insert another column:
   RIGHT-CLICK: G in the column frame
   CHOOSE: Insert
   The column is immediately inserted into the worksheet.

5. To delete a column:
   RIGHT-CLICK: B in the column frame
   CHOOSE: Delete

6. To undo the last command issued:
   CLICK: Undo button ( )

7. To delete a row between the product figures and the total monthly sales lines, do the following:
   RIGHT-CLICK: 7 in the row frame
   CHOOSE: Delete
   RIGHT-CLICK: 12 in the row frame
   CHOOSE: Delete
   RIGHT-CLICK: 17 in the row frame
   CHOOSE: Delete
   Your worksheet should now appear similar to Figure 3.4.

8. Close the "Sales Rep Report" workbook without saving the changes.

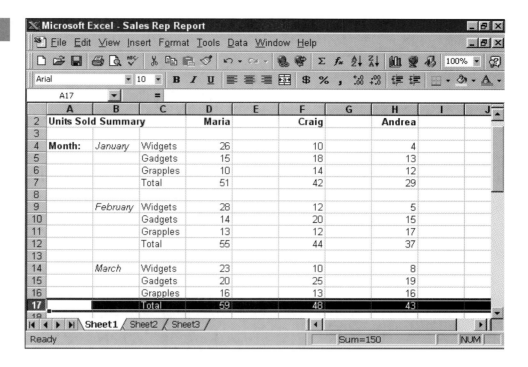

1. **RIGHT-CLICK: column letter or row number in the frame area**

2. **CHOOSE: Insert to insert a row or column**

   CHOOSE: Delete to delete a row or column

FUNCTIONS

This section introduces you to some very useful functions that can save you a tremendous amount of time in creating worksheets. And don't let the word *function* conjure up visions of your last algebra or calculus class; Excel's 300 or so functions are substitutes for entering lengthy formulas. Using functions, you can create formulas that calculate mortgage payments or analyze variances without having to first take a Finance or Statistics course.

For easy access, Excel groups its functions into the following categories: Database, Date & Time, Financial, Information, Logical, Lookup & Reference, Math & Trig, Statistical, and Text. You can enter a function by clicking the Paste Function button (ƒ*) on the Standard toolbar or by accessing the Formula Palette with the Edit Formula button (=). You can also enter a function like any other formula. First, type an equal sign followed by the function name. Then, depending on the type of function, you enter numbers, cell references, or range names within parentheses after the function name. In the next section, you learn how to name a cell range.

CREATING RANGE NAMES

A **range name** is a label that you give to a group of cells on the worksheet. This label or name can be used in formulas and functions to refer to a cell or cell range. As demonstrated in Session 1, Excel lets you create *Natural Language Formulas* by reviewing your worksheet headings and implementing range names on the fly. For example, with named ranges, you can enter a self-explanatory function like "=SUM(widgets)" rather than "=SUM(B3:B7)." Not only do named ranges make it easier to construct a worksheet, they make a worksheet easier to understand.

To create a range name, select the cell range and then click once on the Name box in the Formula bar. When the existing information appears highlighted in the Name box, type a new name and press (ENTER). To display a drop-down list of all the named ranges in a workbook, you can click the down arrow beside the Name box. This list is useful for entering range names into formulas and for moving quickly to a particular range.

QUICK REFERENCE Naming a Cell Range	
1.	Select a cell or cell range to name.
2.	CLICK: Name box in the Formula bar
3.	Type a name for the selected range.
4.	PRESS: (ENTER) or CLICK: OK

USING MATH AND STATISTICAL FUNCTIONS

Mathematical and statistical functions are among the most commonly used categories of functions in spreadsheets. They are also the easiest functions to learn how to use. As described in Table 3.2, the SUM, AVERAGE, MAX, and MIN functions provide a great deal of flexibility and power for the typical application.

TABLE 3.2

Math and Statistical Functions

Function	*Description*
=SUM(range)	Adds together a range of cells.
=AVERAGE(range)	Determines the average value in a range of cells.
=MAX(range)	Determines the maximum value in a range of cells.
=MIN(range)	Determines the minimum value in a range of cells.

Let's practice using statistical functions.

 **Perform the following steps . . .**

1. Open the "Function" workbook, located in your Advantage Files location. This workbook uses tabs to separate the exercises for Statistical, Financial, and Miscellaneous functions.

2. CLICK: Statistical sheet tab (if it is not already selected)
(*Hint*: Using the mouse, click the worksheet tab named Statistical, located at the bottom of the document window.)

3. Let's start by assigning a name to the range of cells containing the student grades. To begin:
SELECT: cell range from B3 to B12

4. CLICK: Name box in the Formula bar
(*Note*: When selected properly, the "B3" appears highlighted.)

5. TYPE: grades
PRESS: [ENTER]
You can now reference this cell range as GRADES, using uppercase or lowercase letters.

6. CLICK: cell F4

7. To sum the column of results, use the SUM function:
TYPE: =sum(grades)
PRESS: [ENTER]
The answer 756 appears in cell F4.

8. To enter a function using the Formula Palette:
CLICK: cell F6
CLICK: Edit Formula button ([=])
The Formula Palette appears under the Formula bar.

9. To display a list of the most commonly used functions:
CLICK: down arrow adjacent to the Name box

10. To select the AVERAGE function:
CLICK: AVERAGE
The Formula Palette now displays helpful information for the AVERAGE function.

11. With the information in the Number1 text box highlighted:
TYPE: grades
Notice that the actual cell contents appear at the right of the text box and that the result is calculated near the bottom of the Formula Palette. Your worksheet should now appear similar to Figure 3.5.

FIGURE 3.5

ENTERING THE AVERAGE
FUNCTION USING
THE FORMULA PALETTE

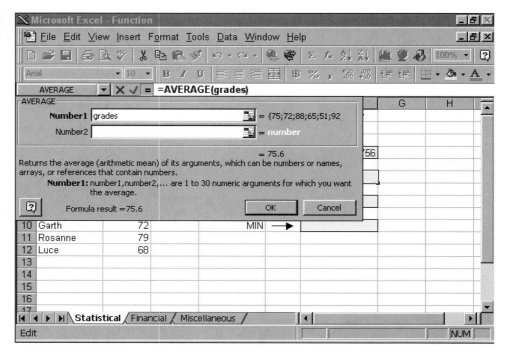

12. To complete the entry:
CLICK: OK command button

13. To enter a function using the Paste Function tool:
CLICK: cell F8
CLICK: Paste Function button (f_*) on the Standard toolbar

14. In the Paste Function dialog box (Figure 3.6):
SELECT: Statistical in the *Function category* list box
SELECT: MAX in the *Function name* list box
CLICK: OK command button
Notice that the Formula Palette appears, similar to using the Edit Formula
button (=).

FIGURE 3.6

PASTE FUNCTION
DIALOG BOX

Paste Function	? X
Function category:	Function name:
Most Recently Used	LOGINV
All	LOGNORMDIST
Financial	MAX
Date & Time	MAXA
Math & Trig	MEDIAN
Statistical	MIN
Lookup & Reference	MINA
Database	MODE
Text	NEGBINOMDIST
Logical	NORMDIST
Information	NORMINV

MAX(number1,number2,...)

Returns the largest value in a set of values. Ignores logical values and text.

OK   Cancel

15. With the information in the Number1 text box highlighted:
TYPE: grades
CLICK: OK command button
The answer 94 appears in cell F8.

16. Using the Paste Function button (f_x), complete the entry in cell F10 for the MIN function. The answer 51 should appear in the cell before proceeding.

17. Let's use AutoCalculate to find some statistical results. As you may remember from Session 2, you selected a cell range and AutoCalculate displayed the sum of the range in the Status bar. You can also display a count of the values in a selected range, or the average, minimum, and maximum values. To demonstrate:
SELECT: cell range from B3 to B12
Notice that "Sum=756" appears in the Status bar.

18. To display a count of the values in the selected range:
RIGHT-CLICK: on the "Sum=756" AutoCalculate display area
CHOOSE: Count from the pop-up menu
The answer "Count=10" appears in the Status bar. Also, notice the other options that are available on the Shortcut menu.

19. Let's reset the AutoCalculate display area:
RIGHT-CLICK: on the AutoCalculate display area
CHOOSE: Sum

20. On your own, change some of the numbers in the grades column (column B) to see the effects on the statistical functions in column F. When ready to move on to the next section, save the workbook as "Completed Functions" to your Data Files location.

USING FINANCIAL FUNCTIONS

Excel's financial functions enable you to confidently use complex financial formulas in your worksheets. And the best part is that you don't even need to understand the difference between a stock and a bond! Some of the more popular financial functions, listed in Table 3.3, are devoted to making investment decisions and solving **annuity** problems. An annuity is a series of equal cash payments over a given period of time, such as an investment contribution or a loan payment.

TABLE 3.3	*Function*	*Description*
Financial Functions		
	=PV(rate,periods,payment)	Calculates the **present value** (the principal) of a series of equal cash payments made at even periods in the future and at a constant interest rate.
	=FV(rate,periods,payment)	Calculates the **future value** of a series of equal cash payments made at even periods in the future and at a constant interest rate.
	=NPV(rate,cell range)	Calculates the **net present value** of a series of investments and returns (cash flows) appearing in a cell range, given a constant discount or interest rate.
	=IRR(cell range,guess)	Calculates the **internal rate of return** for a series of periodic investments and returns (cash flows) appearing in a cell range.
	=PMT(rate,periods,pv)	Calculates the payment amount for a loan or mortgage, given a constant interest rate and number of periods.

Let's practice using financial functions. The worksheet that you will use includes a loan payment calculation, an annuity, and an investment scenario.

 **Perform the following steps . . .**

1. CLICK: Financial sheet tab of the "Completed Functions" workbook

2. CLICK: cell F3

3. As an example of a payment calculation, you will now calculate the monthly payments for a $20,000 car loan. The payments are made over three years (36 periods) at an annual interest rate of 8.5 percent. In other words, the *Present Value* or PV for the calculation is $20,000; the periods are 36 (3 years × 12 months); and the rate is 8.5 percent divided by 12 months (in order to change the annual rate to a monthly rate.) Let's use the Formula Palette to help us enter this equation:
   TYPE: =pmt
   CLICK: Edit Formula button (■)

4. You should see the flashing insertion point in the *Rate* text box. If you don't know the cell address, you can click the Dialog Collapse button (▦) at the right and then click the desired cell in the worksheet. Let's practice selecting a cell using this method. Do the following:
   CLICK: Dialog Collapse button (▦) to withdraw the dialog box
   CLICK: cell B4
   CLICK: Dialog Expand button (▦) to re-display the Formula Palette
   Notice that the cell address B4 appears in the text box with its value appearing to the right.

5. Now you must ensure that the rate is calculated on a monthly basis:
TYPE: /12

6. To complete this function, you must provide values for all the text box labels that appear in boldface. Therefore, the next item to enter is the number of periods. Do the following:
SELECT: *Nper* text box
CLICK: Dialog Collapse button (⬛)
CLICK: cell B5
CLICK: Dialog Expand button (⬛)

7. To enter the present value:
SELECT: *Pv* text box
CLICK: Dialog Collapse button (⬛)
CLICK: cell B3
CLICK: Dialog Expand button (⬛)
Notice that the worksheet values that correspond to the cell references appear in the dialog box along with the function's result. Your screen should appear similar to Figure 3.7.

FIGURE 3.7

FORMULA PALETTE:
PMT FUNCTION

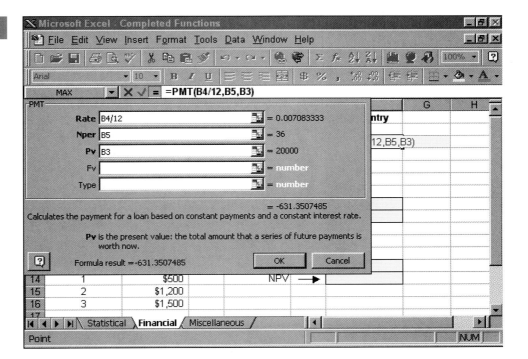

8. To complete the entry:
CLICK: OK command button
The answer ($631.35) appears in cell F3. The payment appears in parentheses to indicate it is a negative number, since it is a cash outflow from yourself to the bank.

9. In this scenario, an altruistic stranger offers you a choice between receiving a flat $6,000 at the end of five years or an annuity of $1,000 per year for the next five years. With an interest rate of 8 percent per year, you must determine which would be the better offer? This problem requires that you enter a future value calculation using the following syntax: FV(rate,periods,payment). Do the following:
CLICK: cell F8
TYPE: =fv(b9,b10,b8)
PRESS: (ENTER)
The better offer is $6,000 at the end of five years, since the future value of the annuity is only worth $5,866.60. With the majority of these calculations, you are concerned with the absolute or positive value for the number. Therefore, you can ignore the negative sign or parentheses.

10. Now, picture this: The same stranger offers you a choice between receiving $4,000 today or an annuity of $1,000 per year for the next five years. With an interest rate of 8 percent per year, you must determine which would be the better offer. This problem requires that you enter a present value calculation using the following syntax: PV(rate,periods,payment). Do the following:
CLICK: cell F9
TYPE: =pv(b9,b10,b8)
PRESS: (ENTER)
The better offer is $4,000 today, compared to receiving $3,992.71 in today's dollars over the next five years.

11. Some friends have just asked you to invest in a wonderful opportunity! The deal is simple. You give them $2,000 now and they will pay you $500 at the end of the first year, $1,200 in the second year, and $1,500 in the third year. In total, you are receiving $3,200 for your $2,000 investment. But is this a good investment? The *net present value* and *internal rate of return* are two profitability measures for such investments. Let's use the Formula Palette to help us in entering these functions:
CLICK: cell F13
TYPE: =irr
CLICK: Edit Formula button (=)

12. To specify the range of cash flow figures:
CLICK: Dialog Collapse button ( ) for the *Values* text box
SELECT: cell range from B13 to B16
CLICK: Dialog Expand button ( )

13. To calculate the internal rate of return, you should also enter an estimate of your expected rate of return. Do the following:
SELECT: *Guess* text box
TYPE: 20%
CLICK: OK command button
Not a bad deal at all! This calculation shows that you would make a return of over 23 percent on your investment.

14. Another test for the profitability of an investment is the net present value. We will use 10 percent as the expected interest rate:
CLICK: cell F14
TYPE: **=npv**
CLICK: Edit Formula button (**=**)

15. To specify the parameters for this function:
TYPE: **10%** in the *Rate* text box
SELECT: *Value1* text box
CLICK: Dialog Collapse button ( ) for the *Value1* text box
SELECT: cell range from B13 to B16
CLICK: Dialog Expand button ( )
CLICK: OK command button
This calculation confirms that it is a wise investment opportunity. An investment is profitable if the net present value result is a positive number. Your worksheet should now appear similar to Figure 3.8.

FIGURE 3.8

"COMPLETED FUNCTIONS" WORKBOOK: *FINANCIAL* TAB

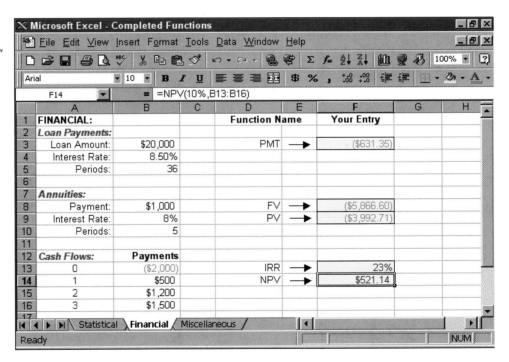

16. Change some numbers in the loan payments, savings account, and cash flow sections to see their effects on the functions that you entered. For example, what would the monthly payment be for a $15,000 car loan over four years? What if your friends needed $2,500 for their startup capital in Step 11? Would it still be a wise investment?

USING MISCELLANEOUS FUNCTIONS

This section describes some miscellaneous functions that you may find quite useful. Although often considered an intermediate-to-advanced topic, the IF function is one of the most useful available. With this function, you can evaluate a cell's value and then perform a calculation based on its contents. The miscellaneous functions covered in this section are described in Table 3.4.

TABLE 3.4	Function	Description
Miscellaneous Functions	=NOW( )	Provides the current date and time.
	=TODAY( )	Provides the current date only.
	=ABS(cell)	Provides the **absolute value** of a cell. For example, =ABS(−4.5) returns 4.5.
	=ROUND(cell,digits)	Provides the **rounded value** of a cell to the number of digits specified. For example, =ROUND(3.9275,2) returns 3.93.
	=INT(cell)	Provides the **integer value** of a cell. For example, =INT(3.75) returns 3.
	=IF(condition,true,false)	Performs a calculation based on the condition being met.

In this exercise, you practice using some additional functions.

Perform the following steps . . .

1. CLICK: Miscellaneous sheet tab of the "Completed Functions" workbook

2. CLICK: cell E3

3. TYPE: =now()
   PRESS: (ENTER)
   (*Note:* This cell is formatted to display the date in a d-mmm-yy format. You can apply a different format to the cell, including one that displays the current time, without changing the function.)

4. In this scenario, you want cell E4 to display a commission rate that is based on a salesperson's unit sales. If sales are less than 10,000 units, the commission is 5 percent; otherwise, the commission is 6 percent. To enter this function, let's use the Formula Palette. Do the following:
   CLICK: cell E4
   TYPE: =if
   CLICK: Edit Formula button ()

5. To specify the test condition:
   CLICK: Dialog Collapse button (🔲) for the *Logical_test* text box
   CLICK: cell B4 ($15,000)
   TYPE: <10000
   CLICK: Dialog Expand button (🔲)

6. To complete the other parameters for this function:
SELECT: *Value_if_true* text box
TYPE: **5%**
SELECT: *Value_if_false* text box
TYPE: **6%**
CLICK: OK command button
You should see the result 6 percent appear in cell E4.

7. Copy the expression in cell E4 to cells E5 and E6 using the fill handle.

8. Let's enter the ROUND function:
CLICK: cell E11
TYPE: **=round(**
CLICK: cell A11
TYPE: **,2)**
PRESS: **ENTER**

9. You will now learn to *nest* a function, meaning to place a function within a function. In this step, you enter a formula that returns the absolute, rounded value for the number in cell A13. Do the following:
TYPE: **=abs**
CLICK: Edit Formula button (**=**)

10. In the Formula Palette:
CLICK: down arrow adjacent to the Name box
SELECT: More Functions from the drop-down list
The Paste Function dialog box should now appear.

11. To enter the ROUND function:
SELECT: Math & Trig from the *Function category* list box
SELECT: ROUND from the *Function name* list box
CLICK: OK command button
Your worksheet should appear similar to Figure 3.9.

FIGURE 3.9

FORMULA PALETTE:
ROUND FUNCTION
NESTED IN THE ABS
FUNCTION

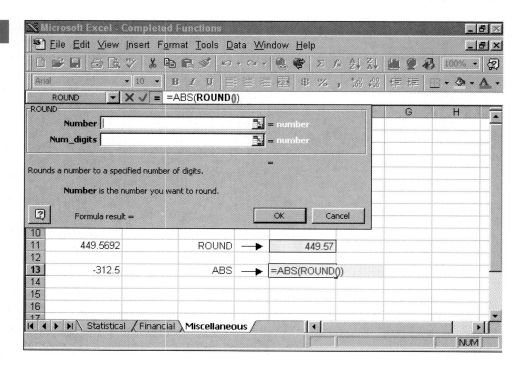

12. To complete the ROUND function:
CLICK: Dialog Collapse button (▣) for the *Number* text box
CLICK: cell A13 (−312.5)
CLICK: Dialog Expand button (▣)
SELECT: *Num_digits* text box
TYPE: **0**
CLICK: OK command button
The value 313 appears in cell E13.

13. Change some numbers in the worksheet to see the effects on the functions that you entered. You can also edit a function that you've entered by double-clicking the cell or by selecting the cell and clicking the Edit Formula button (▣).

14. Save the workbook as "Completed Functions" to your Data Files location.

USING GOAL SEEK

The Goal Seek command is a powerful "what-if" tool that lets you find questions for answers—similar to playing Jeopardy on television. For example, you can state exactly what you need as a bottom line profit and Goal Seek automatically calculates the sales required to meet this goal. How does Goal Seek work? Since profit is dependent on sales (*Sales* less *Expenses* equals *Profit*), Goal Seek quickly substitutes values into the sales variable until the desired profit is achieved.

To use Goal Seek, you choose the Tools, Goal Seek command from the menu. In the dialog box that appears, you enter the cell that contains the formula for calculating the target value (for example, *Profit*) and then enter the target value itself. You also need to tell Goal Seek what variable it is allowed to change in order to achieve this target value (for example, *Sales*). Once completed, you press **ENTER** or click on OK.

Let's practice using Goal Seek.

Perform the following steps . . .

1. CLICK: Financial sheet tab in the "Completed Functions" workbook

2. If you changed any of the original values on this page, ensure now that the Loan Amount is $20,000 (in cell B3), the Interest Rate is 8.50 percent (in cell B4), and the Periods is 36 (in cell B5) before proceeding.

3. Let's use Goal Seek to calculate the maximum loan amount that we can afford with monthly payments of $500. To start Goal Seek:
CLICK: cell F3
CHOOSE: Tools, Goal Seek

4. In the *Set cell* text box, make sure that the cell address is F3.

5. To enter the monthly payment that we can afford:
SELECT: *To value* text box
TYPE: −500
Notice that we enter −500, since it is a cash outflow to the bank.

6. To specify that the loan amount is the variable to change:
SELECT: *By changing cell* text box
CLICK: cell B3
If the dialog box is covering cell B3, use the Dialog Collapse (▦) and Expand (▣) buttons. Your screen should now appear similar to Figure 3.10.

FIGURE 3.10

ENTERING VALUES INTO
THE GOAL SEEK
DIALOG BOX

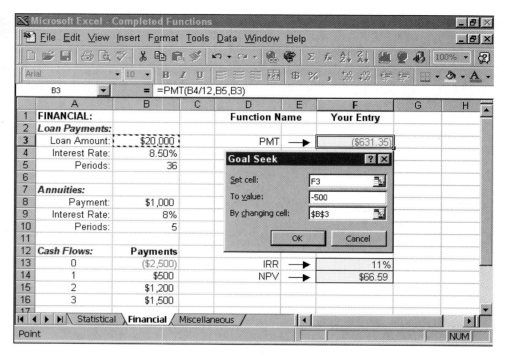

7. To solve the equation:
   CLICK: OK to accept the Goal Seek dialog box
   CLICK: OK to bypass the Goal Seek Status dialog box
   When you return to the worksheet, the Loan Amount has been changed to
   $15,839 in cell B3 and the payment in cell F3 is now $500.

8. Save the workbook as "Completed Functions" to your Data Files location.

9. Close the workbook and exit Excel.

QUICK REFERENCE
Using Goal Seek

1. **CHOOSE: Tools, Goal Seek**
2. **Specify the formula or expression which contains the target value.**
3. **Enter the desired target value.**
4. **Specify the variable to change.**
5. **PRESS: ENTER or CLICK: OK**

IN ADDITION SOLVING MORE COMPLEX "WHAT-IF" SCENARIOS

For more complex problems, Excel
provides the **Solver** tool which
allows you to specify more than
one variable to change in order to

meet multiple goals and constraints. For more
information, ask the Office Assistant for help on
"Using Solver for What-Ifs."

SUMMARY

This section explored several new commands for increasing your productivity. After a discussion on absolute and relative cell addresses, you were introduced to the commands and shortcut keys for copying and moving information around your worksheet. Some final formatting commands were also introduced for inserting and deleting columns and rows in your worksheet.

The latter half of the session introduced several of Excel's built-in functions. The Statistical and Financial categories were emphasized with the SUM, AVERAGE, MAX, MIN, PV, FV, IRR, NPV, and PMT functions. Several miscellaneous functions were also introduced, including the IF function for calculating an expression based on a set of conditions.

Many of the commands used in the session are provided in Table 3.5, the Command Summary. See Tables 3.2 to 3.4 for the Function summaries.

TABLE 3.5	*Command*	*Description*
Command Summary	Edit, Copy or (🖹)	Places a copy of a cell or cell range onto the Clipboard.
	Edit, Cut or (✂)	Moves a cell or cell range from the worksheet to the Clipboard.
	Edit, Delete	Deletes a column or row from the worksheet.
	Edit Formula (▣)	Opens the Formula Palette for creating and editing a formula.
	Edit, Fill, Down	Copies a cell to adjacent cells down the worksheet.
	Edit, Fill, Right	Copies a cell to adjacent cells across the worksheet.
	Edit, Paste or (📋)	Pastes the contents of the Clipboard into the active cell or selected cell range.
	Insert, Column/Row	Inserts a column or row in the worksheet.
	Paste Function (*fx*)	Displays the Paste Function dialog box for selecting a function for use in an equation.
	Tools, Goal Seek	Launches the Goal Seek tool for performing "what-if" analysis.

KEY TERMS

absolute cell address

Cell reference in a worksheet that does not adjust when copied to other cells.

absolute value

The value of a real number, disregarding its sign. For example, the absolute value of the number −5 is 5.

annuity

A series of equal cash payments over a given period of time.

Clipboard

In Windows, the Clipboard is a program that allows you to copy and move information within an application or among applications. The Clipboard temporarily stores the information in memory before you paste the data in a new location.

drag and drop

An Excel feature that allows you to copy and move information by dragging cell information from one location to another using the mouse.

fill handle

The small black square that is located in the bottom right-hand corner of a cell or cell range. You use the fill handle to create a series or to copy cell information.

future value

The value in future dollars of a series of equal cash payments.

integer value

The value of a number to the left of the decimal point. For example, the integer of 125.978 is the number 125.

internal rate of return

The rate of return at which the net present value is 0.

net present value

A calculation used to determine whether an investment provides a positive or negative return, based on a series of cash outflows and inflows.

present value

The value in present-day dollars of a series of equal cash payments made sometime in the future.

range name

A name that is given to a range of cells in the worksheet. This name can then be used in formulas and functions to refer to the cell range.

relative cell address

Cell reference in a worksheet that automatically adjusts when copied to other cells.

rounded value

The value of a number rounded to a specific number of decimal places. For example, the number 2.378 rounded to a single decimal returns the number 2.4.

series

A sequence of numbers or dates that follows a mathematical or date pattern.

Solver

An Excel tool that facilitates "what-if" analysis. Although similar to Goal Seek, Solver enables you to specify more than one variable to modify and more than one goal to attain.

EXERCISES

SHORT ANSWER

1. What is the difference between an absolute cell address and a relative cell address? How is this difference expressed in an Excel formula?

2. What is the primary difference between using the Edit, Copy command and the drag and drop method to copy information?

3. Explain the fastest way to put semi-annual headings at the top of your worksheet (i.e., Jan-97, Jul-97, Jan-98,...).

4. Why would you want to name a range of cells?

5. List the function categories in Excel.

6. Describe four statistical functions.

7. Describe five financial functions.

8. What is the purpose of the NOW function?

9. What is the purpose of the IF function?

10. How do you access the Paste Function dialog box from within the Formula Palette?

HANDS-ON

(*Note:* Ensure that you know the storage location of your Advantage Files and your Data Files before proceeding.)

1. The objective of this exercise is to create a new workbook, reorganize its layout, construct formulas, and then practice copying and moving information. Perform the following steps.

   a. Ensure that Excel is loaded and that a blank worksheet appears on the screen.

   b. Set column A's width to 20 characters.

   c. Set columns B through E to 10 characters wide.

d. Type the text and numbers as displayed in Figure 3.11 into the appropriate cells. Make sure that you type your name into cell C1.

e. Perform a spelling check and then save the workbook as "Income Statement" to your Data Files location.

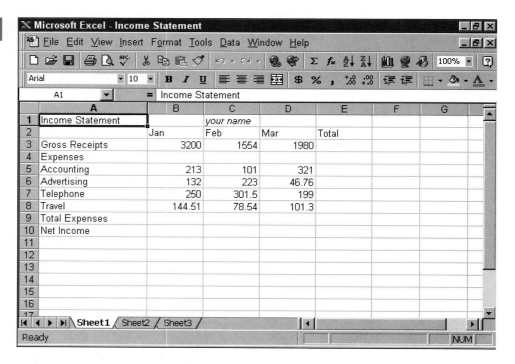

f. Insert one row between each of the following:

  - the "Income Statement" line and the month headings

  - the month headings and the "Gross Receipts" line

  - the "Total Expenses" line and the "Net Income" line

g. Select the cell range from B3 to E3.

h. Center the range and then make it bold and italic.

i. Select the cell range from A7 to A10.

j. Indent the entries by clicking the Increase Indent button (🔲) on the Formatting toolbar twice.

k. Make the primary headings—Gross Receipts, Expenses, Total Expenses, and Net Income—bold.

l. Make the title in cell A1 bold and assign a font of 14 points in size.

m. Use the AutoSum button to sum the expenses for each month and then display the sum of the Gross Receipts in cell E5.

n. Copy the function in cell E5 to cells E7 through E11 using the Copy (🔲) and Paste (🔲) toolbar buttons.

o. Enter a formula into cell B13 that subtracts the Total Expenses for January from the Gross Receipts.

p. Copy the formula from cell B13 through cell E13 using the fill handle.

q. Select the cell range from B5 to E13.

r. Apply a numeric format to insert commas and two decimal places.

s. Select the cell range from B3 to E3.

t. Place a border around these cells and then apply a background fill color and font color.

u. Select the cell range from B11 to E11.

v. Add a single line for the top border of this range.

w. Select the cell range from B13 to E13.

x. Add a single line for the top border and a double line for the bottom border.

y. Set the print area and then print the workbook centered horizontally on the page.

z. Save the workbook as "Income Statement" to your Data Files location.

2. This exercise uses the "Income Statement" workbook created in exercise 1. You modify the worksheet contents, apply names to cell ranges, and then create statistical functions.

a. If it's not already displayed, open the "Income Statement" workbook located in your Data Files location.

b. Select the cell range from B5 to D5.

c. Name this cell range "Receipts" using the Name box.

d. Name the following cell ranges:

Select the Range	Name the Range
B7 to D7	Accounting
B8 to D8	Advertising
B9 to D9	Telephone
B10 to D10	Travel
B11 to D11	Expenses

e. Move to cell F3 and create a heading called "Average."

f. Change the width of columns E and F to 12 characters.

g. Move to cell F5.

h. To average the Gross Receipts:
TYPE: =average(receipts)
PRESS: ENTER

i. Complete the column as follows:

Move to cell	*TYPE:*
F7	`=average(accounting)`
F8	`=average(advertising)`
F9	`=average(telephone)`
F10	`=average(travel)`
F11	`=average(expenses)`

j. Copy cell E13 to F13 using drag and drop.

k. Copy the formatting characteristics from column E to column F.

l. Set a new print area and then preview the worksheet. Your screen should now look similar to Figure 3.12.

m. Print the worksheet.

n. Save the workbook as "Income Statement" to your Data Files location and then close the workbook.

FIGURE 3.12

PREVIEWING THE "INCOME STATEMENT" WORKBOOK

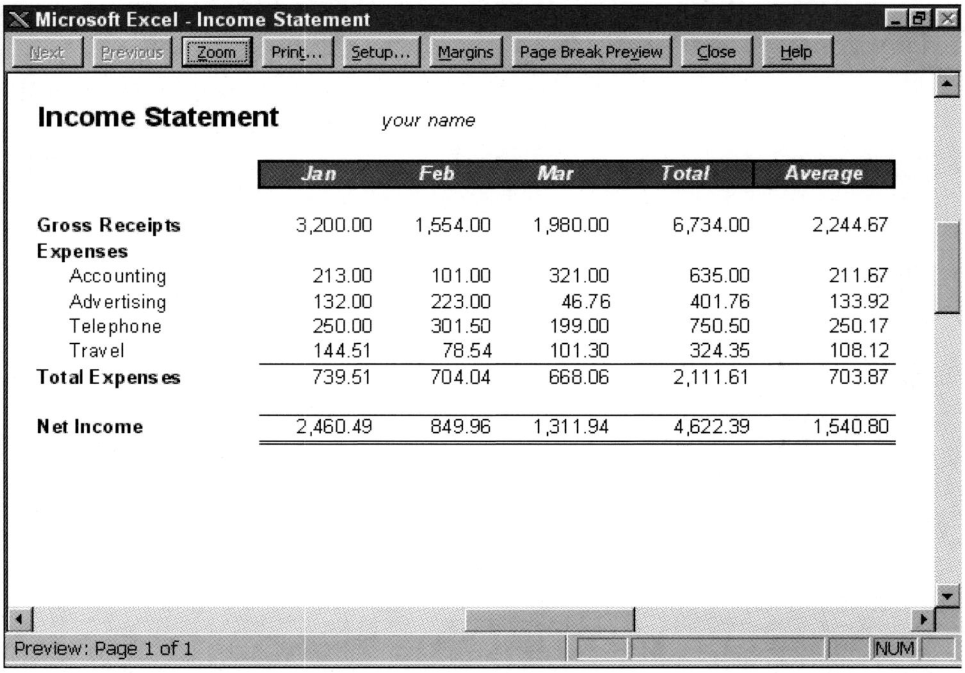
Microsoft Excel - Income Statement
Next
Previous
Zoom
Print...
Setup...
Margins
Page Break Preview
Close
Help
Income Statement
your name
Jan Feb Mar Total Average
Gross Receipts 3,200.00 1,554.00 1,980.00 6,734.00 2,244.67
Expenses
Accounting 213.00 101.00 321.00 635.00 211.67
Advertising 132.00 223.00 46.76 401.76 133.92
Telephone 250.00 301.50 199.00 750.50 250.17
Travel 144.51 78.54 101.30 324.35 108.12
Total Expenses 739.51 704.04 668.06 2,111.61 703.87
Net Income 2,460.49 849.96 1,311.94 4,622.39 1,540.80
Preview: Page 1 of 1
NUM

3. In this exercise, you create a workbook from scratch for computing a loan or mortgage table.

a. To begin, ensure that you have an empty worksheet.

b. Enter the textual information:

Move to cell	TYPE:
A1	MORTGAGE TABLE
D1	your name
A3	Principal Amount:
A4	Interest Rate:
A5	Years:
C4	Monthly Rate:
C5	Months:
C6	Payment:
A8	Payment #
B8	Principal
C8	Interest
D8	Balance

c. Change the column widths as follows:

Column	Width
A	18
B	15
C	15
D	15

d. Select the cell range from A3 to D8.

e. Right-align the entire range.

f. Select the cell range from A8 to D8.

g. Use bold and italic for the range and then apply an outline border with a background fill color and font color.

h. Enter the numeric information:

Move to cell	TYPE:
B3	150,000
B4	7.5%
B5	30
A9	0

i. Enter the formulas:

Move to cell	TYPE:
D4	=b4/12
D5	=b5*12
D6	=pmt(d4,d5,b3)
D9	=b3
A10	=a9+1

j. To calculate the amount of interest paid during each period (column C), move to cell C10 and enter the following formula:
    TYPE: =d9*d4
    PRESS: **ENTER**
    Notice that the monthly interest rate is an absolute cell reference. Since the formula will be copied down the worksheet, you must enter the formula with an absolute reference to ensure that the expression always refers to cell D4.

k. To calculate the amount of principal paid during each period (column B), move to cell B10 and enter the following formula:
    TYPE: =abs(d6)-c10
    PRESS: **ENTER**
    Again, the formula will always refer to the total payment amount when copied, so an absolute cell address is used in the expression.

l. To calculate the amount of principal left (the Balance for column D), move to cell D10 and enter the following:
    TYPE: =d9-b10
    PRESS: **ENTER**

m. Select the cell range from A10 to D10.

n. Format the numbers to appear with commas and no decimal places.

o. Select the cell range from A10 to D189.

p. CHOOSE: Edit, Fill, Down

q. Return to cell A1.

r. Change the loan principal amount from 150,000 to 175,000. Watch the worksheet recalculate the payments for each period.

s. Change the number of years to 25. Note the change in the ratio between the principal being paid back each period and the interest paid on the money borrowed.

t. Save the workbook as "Mortgage" to your Data Files location. Your worksheet should now look similar to Figure 3.13.

u. Print the worksheet.

v. Close the workbook and then exit Excel.

FIGURE 3.13

"MORTGAGE"
WORKBOOK

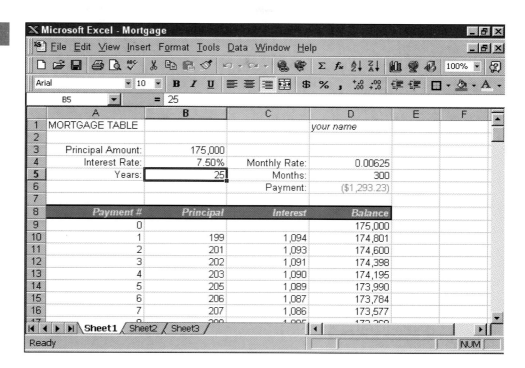

4. **On Your Own:** Your Personal Budget

Create a worksheet that contains your monthly budget information. Start by placing the months of the year across the top of the worksheet using the AutoFill feature. Create budget categories for each row, such as Food, Rent, Tuition, Loan, and Entertainment. At the far right of the worksheet, include a "Year-To-Date" column and an "Average" column. Enter the appropriate formulas for summing each month's total budget allowance and for calculating the summary columns. When finished, enter some sample figures to test your worksheet and then save it as "My Personal Budget" to your Data Files location.

5. **On Your Own:** Using Statistical Functions

Create a worksheet that contains a table of figures that spans four rows and three columns. Below this table, enter the name of each statistical function used in this session on a separate row. Beside the function name, enter the function equation using the entire table as the range value. Change numbers in the table to ensure that the figures flow through to the function equations correctly. Save the worksheet as "Using Functions" to your Data Files location.

CASE PROBLEM   **RIVERSIDE FORD, INC.**

(*Note:* In the following case problems, assume the role of the primary characters and perform the same steps that they identify. You may want to re-read the session opening.)

1. Zachary Rempel graduated from college in 1993 with a master's degree in economics. While his friends interviewed for entry-level jobs with larger companies, Zachary accepted the first position offered to him, as business manager for Riverside. Some of the reasons for Zachary's success at Riverside are that he willingly accepts new challenges and constantly looks for better ways of doing things. This was Zachary's attitude when Mr. Davies handed him the responsibility of generating all of the dealership's reports by computer.

    Upon reviewing the previous month's reports, Zachary identifies an opportunity for moving one particular report written in Microsoft Word to Microsoft Excel. The SOFIT report, which is Riverside's own abbreviation for a Summary of Finance and Insurance Totals, summarizes the number of new and used cars that are sold in a given month, including the number of financing, insurance, warranty, and rust protection packages. Currently, the report is manually typed into a Word document and then printed. All of the calculations are performed using a handheld calculator; so if one number changes, the entire report must be recalculated. Zachary decides that this report deserves his immediate attention.

    Assume the role of Zachary and convert the following SOFIT report for September into an Excel worksheet, complete with formulas for summing the columns. Save the document as "SOFIT - September" to your Data Files location.

Product Category	New Cars	New Dollars	Used Cars	Used Dollars
Retail Sales	20	492,000	15	138,000
Financing Packages	8	4,500	4	2,500
Life Ins. Policies	4	1,250	2	600
Option Packages	5	2,150	0	0
Ext. Warranties	3	1,800	0	0
Rust Protection	1	375	1	340
Totals				

2. Now that the original report has been converted into an Excel worksheet, Zachary decides to enhance the report and make better use of Excel's summary and reporting features. Perform the following modifications to the worksheet.

- Extend the report by two columns for "Total Cars" and "Total Dollars." Enter formulas on the Retail Sales row that add the New and Used values together for both the unit and dollar values. Copy these two formulas into the remaining rows of the table.

- Insert a row for "Accident & Health Ins." between "Life Ins. Policies" and "Option Packages." There are no sales figures for the month of September, so enter "0" in the appropriate cells.

- Insert two rows at the top of the worksheet for the name of the dealership and the name of the report. The first row of the worksheet should contain "Riverside Ford, Inc." and the second row should contain "SOFIT for September 1997."

- Format the worksheet by applying fonts, numeric styles, borders, fill colors, and font colors.

- Below the table, leave three blank lines and then enter the following information:

Packages:	Average	Total
New Cars		
Used Cars		
Total Cars		

- In the new table, calculate the average and total dollar value of all packages sold with vehicles. (*Hint:* Use the AVERAGE and SUM functions on the values extending from financing packages to rust protection.)

3. Zachary decides to enhance the report by adding the budget figures for Finance and Insurance to the worksheet. That way, Mr. Davies will be able to compare the actual results against the budget estimates on the same report. Having gone through this session, Zachary knows that the easiest method for copying a group of cells on a worksheet is using the drag and drop method. To prepare, he selects the entire cell range (including the titles at the top of the worksheet). He then presses the (**ALT**) key and holds it down as he drags the selection over top of the Sheet2 tab. Once the cell pointer is positioned at the top of Sheet 2, he releases the (**ALT**) key and the mouse button. He clicks the Sheet2 tab and then edits the title to read "Budget Estimates" instead of "Riverside Ford, Inc."

Complete the budget area on the worksheet for Zachary by editing the table to contain the figures shown in the table below. As a final step, print the report without gridlines, headers, or footers, and ensure that it appears centered horizontally on a single page. Save the workbook as "SOFIT - September" back to your Data Files location.

Product Category	New Cars	New Dollars	Used Cars	Used Dollars
Retail Sales	15	300,000	20	200,000
Financing Packages	10	5,000	8	2,500
Life Ins. Policies	5	1,500	4	1,200
Accident & Health Ins.	1	360	2	900
Option Packages	5	2,500	0	0
Ext. Warranties	5	1,800	0	0
Rust Protection	2	750	2	750

4. After explaining the finer points of Excel to Robyn Lombardi, a salesperson at Riverside, Zachary finishes the last bite of his sandwich. "Zak, what you've just finished describing sounds like something we can use on the floor," said Robyn excitedly. "Just imagine, we could calculate loan payments for customers while they are standing right in front of us! Can you design an attractive on-screen form if I provide you with a rough outline?" Zachary thought about what was involved in the project and ended up agreeing to create a simple form. At 4:30 PM, Robyn drops a handwritten form onto Zachary's desk with the following note. "Thanks, Zak. By the way, I mentioned our idea to Mr. Davies and he wants to see a sample of the form by tomorrow. Good luck!"

Create an on-screen form from the design sample that Robyn provided below. (*Hint:* Use the PMT function to perform the calculation.) Save your workbook as "Loan Form" to your Data Files location.

Riverside Ford, Inc.		**Loan Calculation**	
Salesperson:	*Robyn Lombardi*	**List Price:**	*$30,000*
Customer:	*Mr. Smith*	**Negotiated Price:**	*$25,000*
Year/Make/Model:	*97 Ford Explorer*	**Ann. Interest Rate:**	*10%*
Serial Number:	*XLT1001-880801*	**Term in Months:**	*48*

Your monthly payment is: $###.##

(Zak, this needs to be a formula!)

Microsoft Excel 97 for Windows

Managing a Workbook

SESSION

HTTP WWW

4

IRWIN
COMPUTER & INFORMATION TECHNOLOGY

SESSION OUTLINE

Freezing Titles
Splitting the Window into Panes
Filtering Worksheet Data
Working with Multiple Windows
Creating Multiple-Sheet Workbooks
Consolidating Your Work
What Is a Macro?
Creating Macros
Summary
Key Terms
Exercises

INTRODUCTION

What you've already learned to do with spread-sheets is quite sophisticated. Now we introduce some more commands to help you better manage your work. In this session, you will learn how to freeze titles on the screen, open windows to view different parts of a workbook, filter your data, create multiple-sheet workbook files, consolidate worksheets, and create simple macros. All of these features help you manage your workbooks more efficiently.

CASE STUDY	GINO'S KITCHEN

Gino Lerma is the owner of four pizza restaurants in the Boston metropolitan area. Starting with one restaurant 15 years ago, Gino was able to open a new restaurant every few years through hard work and careful planning. Gino now considers himself semiretired, even though he still works around the clock and requires a full-time assistant, Larry Ingla. Although he is no longer part of the daily activities, Gino fondly remembers his many years of working in the kitchens.

Each month, Gino's managers use Microsoft Excel and a custom-developed worksheet to report on their restaurants' activities. Each manager sends his or her workbook file to Larry Ingla for consolidation. To date, Larry has been printing each workbook separately and then manually consolidating a report for Gino's review. Hearing much about the consolidation capabilities of Excel, Larry wants to use the computer to combine each individual workbook into a summary workbook. From this one summary workbook, he could then print a monthly consolidated report. It would also be nice if the summary workbook contained a separate sheet for each month and a Year-to-Date sheet at the end. That way, Larry could analyze and compare sales and costs on a month-to-month basis. Unfortunately, Larry has only heard about Excel's capabilities and doesn't know how to create his dream workbook.

In this session, you and Larry will learn how to manage and extract information from worksheets. In addition, you learn how to consolidate data using formulas that link separate worksheets and workbooks. To improve the reliability and consistency of your daily procedures, this session also shows you how to compose macros that you can play back in the future.

FREEZING TITLES

Most worksheets display row and column titles to serve as a frame of reference for information contained in the worksheet. In a worksheet that stores address information, the column headings might be first name, last name, address, city, and phone number. Unfortunately, these titles can scroll off the screen as you move the cell pointer around the worksheet. Using the Window, Freeze Panes command, you can freeze specific rows and columns on the screen so that they appear at all times, regardless of where you move the cell pointer in the worksheet. Let's demonstrate.

 Perform the following steps . . .

1. Make sure that you've loaded Excel and know the storage location of your Advantage Files and your Data Files.

2. Open the "Planner" workbook, located in your Advantage Files location.

3. CLICK: cell B5

4. To quickly move to the end of the row:
PRESS: CTRL + ➡
The cell pointer moves to the end of the row, cell N5. Notice that you can no longer see the row titles in column A—they have scrolled off the screen. Assuming that you do not memorize your worksheets, you must return to column A to see what each row represents.

5. PRESS: CTRL + HOME
The cell pointer moves back to cell A1.

6. By freezing the window **panes,** you can lock the employee names in the first column no matter how far you move to the right. First, you position the cell pointer below the row and to the right of the column that you want to freeze. For this step, move the cell pointer to cell B7.

7. CHOOSE: Window, Freeze Panes

8. Position the tip of the mouse pointer below the scroll box on the vertical scroll bar and click once to move down the worksheet. Notice that the worksheet window scrolls down but leaves the top six rows visible.

9. Position the tip of the mouse pointer to the right of the scroll box on the horizontal scroll bar and click once to move across the worksheet. Again, notice that the worksheet scrolls but leaves the leftmost column of employee names visible. Your worksheet should now look similar to Figure 4.1.

10. To return to your starting screen position and unfreeze the panes:
PRESS: CTRL + HOME
CHOOSE: Window, Unfreeze Panes

FIGURE 4.1

THE "PLANNER"
WORKSHEET DIVIDED
INTO PANES

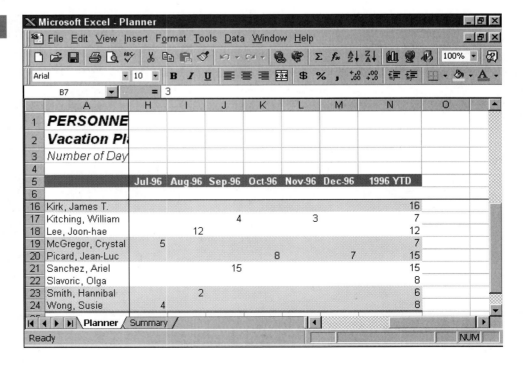

QUICK REFERENCE
Freezing Titles

1. **Position the cell pointer below and to the right of the row and column that you want to freeze.**
2. **To freeze the horizontal and vertical worksheet panes:**
   CHOOSE: Window, Freeze Panes
3. **To unfreeze the horizontal and vertical worksheet panes:**
   CHOOSE: Window, Unfreeze Panes

When a worksheet is relatively large and is organized under row and column headings, you freeze window panes to make it easier to work with your data. For a worksheet that is not grouped neatly into blocks or sections, you can use another tool. The next section explores the process of dividing a worksheet's document window into independent panes.

Splitting the Window into Panes

Similarly to freezing titles, you can manually split a worksheet's document window into two or four panes. This makes it easier to view and manage worksheets that cannot fit in a single window. You split the document window using the Split command or by dragging the **horizontal split box** or **vertical split box** at the end of each scroll bar (both are shown below).

Horizontal Split Box

Vertical Split Box

To use the Window, Split command, you first position the cell pointer below or to the right of the column and row where you want the split to occur—as you would setting titles. If you prefer using the mouse, drag the split boxes to the desired window location. Once in place, you can finalize the positioning of panes by dragging the actual split bars that appear in the document window. To move between two panes or among four panes, you simply click the mouse pointer in the desired pane.

In this exercise, you practice splitting the window into panes.

Perform the following steps . . .

1. Position the mouse pointer over the horizontal split box (above the vertical scroll bar) until the pointer changes to a black horizontal double line split by a two-headed arrow.

2. CLICK: left mouse button and hold it down
   DRAG: the split box downward to split the window in half

3. Release the mouse button. Notice that you now have two vertical scroll bars for controlling both panes independently.

4. Position the tip of the mouse pointer below the scroll box on the bottom vertical scroll bar and click once to move down the worksheet.

5. Position the tip of the mouse pointer below the scroll box on the top vertical scroll bar and click twice to move the viewing area in the top pane. As opposed to freezing titles, notice that you can change the viewing area in both panes.

6. Position the mouse pointer over the vertical split box (to the right of the horizontal scroll bar) until the pointer changes to a black vertical double line split by a two-headed arrow.

7. CLICK: left mouse button and hold it down
DRAG: the split box to the left to split the window in half

8. Release the mouse button. Notice that you have divided the current worksheet window into four panes with four separate scroll bars.

9. CLICK: anywhere in the bottom left-hand window pane
PRESS: (CTRL) + (HOME)

10. CLICK: anywhere in the bottom right-hand window pane
PRESS: (CTRL) + (HOME)

11. CLICK: anywhere in the top right-hand window pane
PRESS: (CTRL) + (HOME)

12. CLICK: anywhere in the top left-hand window pane
PRESS: (CTRL) + (HOME)
This example demonstrates that you must click in the pane before moving the cell pointer in the pane. Your worksheet should now appear similar to Figure 4.2.

13. To quickly remove panes from the window:
CHOOSE: Window, Remove Split
(*Note*: You can also double-click each split box to remove the panes.)

14. Save the workbook as "Vacation Planner" to your Data Files location.

FIGURE 4.2

DIVIDING THE
WORKSHEET'S
DOCUMENT WINDOW
INTO PANES

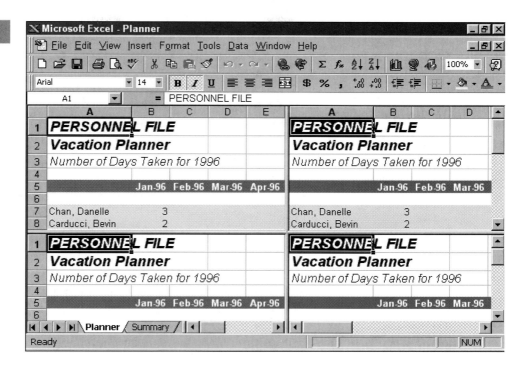

QUICK REFERENCE
Splitting the Window
into Panes

- **DRAG: horizontal and vertical scroll boxes to divide the current worksheet's document window into two or four panes**
- **To remove panes from the current window:**
  CHOOSE: Window, Remove Split

FILTERING WORKSHEET DATA

Excel's **AutoFilter** feature lets you find and retrieve data quickly from a worksheet list. Before you can use this feature, you must arrange your data in a particular way when constructing a worksheet. For example, you should leave several blank columns and rows between the data list and any other information in the worksheet. In the first row of a list, enter column headings or labels and then separate these headings from the data using a border. Finally, you need to design the list so that all columns contain the same type of information, such as text or numbers.

To start AutoFilter, select the desired cell range including the column heading labels and data and then choose the Data, Filter, AutoFilter command from the menu. When executed, AutoFilter analyzes the data and then displays a drop-down list arrow next to each column heading that contains its filtering options. To quickly filter and display data, you select a single criterion for a column from the drop-down list or choose to view a range of data, such as the top ten sales representatives based on units sold.

Let's practice filtering worksheet information.

Perform the following steps . . .

1. Ensure that the "Vacation Planner" workbook appears in the application window.

2. To start the AutoFilter command:
SELECT: cell range from A5 to N24
CHOOSE: Data, Filter, AutoFilter

3. To return to the top of the worksheet:
PRESS: (CTRL) + (HOME)
Notice that there are drop-down list arrows attached to each of the column headings in row 5.

4. To freeze the column headings in the worksheet window:
CLICK: cell B7
CHOOSE: Window, Freeze Panes

5. To move to the Year-to-Date column quickly:
CLICK: cell B5
PRESS: (CTRL) + (→)
Notice that the employee names in column A are still visible.

6. To select a filtering criterion:
CLICK: down arrow ([▼]) beside cell N5 to display its drop-down list
Your screen should now appear similar to Figure 4.3.

FIGURE 4.3

USING THE AUTOFILTER COMMAND

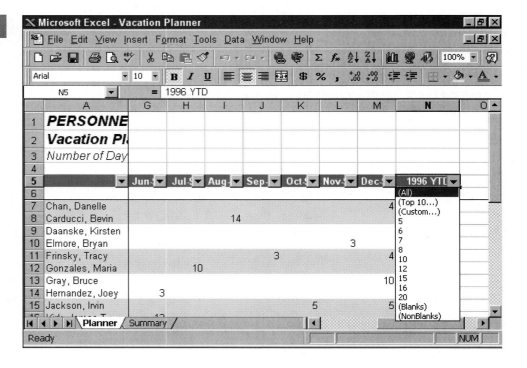

7. To display the three employees with the highest Year-to-Date figures for vacation days taken in 1996, do the following:
SELECT: (Top 10...) from the drop-down list
(*Note*: You can filter the list by two or more values, or apply more complex filtering options, by selecting the Custom option from a column's drop-down list box.)

8. In the dialog box that appears, specify that only the top three items (in this case, Year-to-Date vacation days) need to be displayed. Do the following:
SELECT: 3 in the *Show* spin box (Figure 4.4)

FIGURE 4.4

AUTOFILTER'S TOP 10
DIALOG BOX

9. To proceed with the filter operation:
PRESS: ENTER or CLICK: OK
The worksheet should now display only the following employees: Bevin Carducci, Maria Gonzales, and James T. Kirk. Also notice that the row numbers and drop-down arrow appear blue, as a reminder that you are currently viewing a subset of the total records.

10. To display all of the records once again:
CLICK: down arrow (▾) beside cell N5 to display its drop-down list
SELECT: (All) appearing at the top of the drop-down list
All of the records reappear in the worksheet window.

11. To remove the AutoFilter drop-down lists from the worksheet:
CHOOSE: Data, Filter, AutoFilter

12. To remove the window panes and return to the top of the worksheet:
CHOOSE: Window, Unfreeze Panes
PRESS: CTRL + HOME

QUICK REFERENCE
Filtering Data Using the
AutoFilter Command

1. Create a worksheet with column headings and ensure that each column contains the same type of information (i.e., sales units).
2. Select the cell range to be filtered, including the column headings.
3. CHOOSE: Data, Filter, AutoFilter
4. CLICK: down arrow (▾) beside the column or cell to display a drop-down list box of filtering options.
5. Select a value from the drop-down list box to filter the list.

Working with Multiple Windows

Using multiple document windows, you can load and display different workbook files at the same time or open different views of the same workbook. Multiple window views are useful when you have related information scattered in distant areas or across several worksheets in a large workbook, or perhaps stored in different workbooks. This section explains how to display and organize multiple windows in the Excel application window.

Before you can issue commands to affect a worksheet, its document window must be active. You activate a window by clicking on it in the document area or by choosing its name from the Window pull-down menu. If there is only one workbook open in the document area, it is active by default. To close a document window, you click its Close button (☒) in the upper right-hand corner of the window.

To automatically organize all the open windows in the document area, you can choose the Window, Arrange command to display the dialog box in Figure 4.5. The Arrange dialog box offers several options for arranging windows in the document area. The *Tiled* option lets you maximize the space for each window in a pattern similar to floor tiles. The *Horizontal* option places each worksheet in a horizontal strip in the document area while the *Vertical* option employs vertical strips. The *Cascade* option layers or fans the windows just as you would spread a deck of cards. Once you have selected an option, press (**ENTER**) or click on OK.

FIGURE 4.5

ARRANGE DIALOG BOX

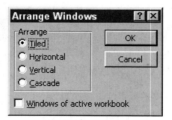

You will now practice working with multiple windows.

Perform the following steps . . .

1. Before proceeding, ensure that the "Vacation Planner" workbook is the only open document window. Do the following:
CHOOSE: Window
One entry should appear at the bottom of this pull-down menu called "1 Vacation Planner." If there are more entries, choose each additional workbook option on the menu and click its Close button ([✖]).

2. Let's practice working with document windows. A document window can be displayed as a window or it can be maximized to cover the entire document area. You can tell the difference by looking at the Title bar. If the name of the worksheet appears next to the words "Microsoft Excel" in the application's Title bar, then the document window has been maximized. If the name of the worksheet appears in its own Title bar within the document area, then the worksheet is displayed as a window. In this step, you practice manipulating the "Vacation Planner" worksheet window.
To tile the worksheet window, do the following:
CHOOSE: Arrange command from the Window pull-down menu
SELECT: *Tiled* option button
PRESS: [ENTER] or CLICK: OK

3. To maximize the worksheet window:
CLICK: document window's Maximize icon ([□])
(*Hint*: If you accidentally click the Minimize icon ([_]), you can restore the document window by clicking its Restore icon ([🗗]) or Maximize icon ([□]) in the Title bar that appears along the bottom of the document area.)

4. To minimize the worksheet window:
CLICK: document window's Minimize icon ([_])
(*Hint*: Make sure that you do not click Excel's Minimize icon. The worksheet window's icons will appear on the second row from the top of the screen.) When minimized, the Title bar for the window appears along the bottom of the document area, as follows:

5. To restore the worksheet window:
CLICK: document window's Restore icon ([🗗])

6. Practice changing the worksheet between a windowed view, a minimized view, and a maximized view.

7. CHOOSE: Window, Arrange
SELECT: *Tiled* option button
PRESS: [ENTER] or CLICK: OK

8. To open a second window on this worksheet:
CHOOSE: Window, New Window

9. The new document window appears over the top of the original window. To view both windows at the same time:
CHOOSE: Window, Arrange
SELECT: *Tiled* option button
PRESS: (ENTER) or CLICK: OK
Notice that the windows are identical, except for their Title bars. There are now two views of the "Vacation Planner" worksheet: "Vacation Planner:1" and "Vacation Planner:2" (Figure 4.6).

FIGURE 4.6

THE "VACATION PLANNER" WORKSHEET WITH TWO WINDOWS DISPLAYED

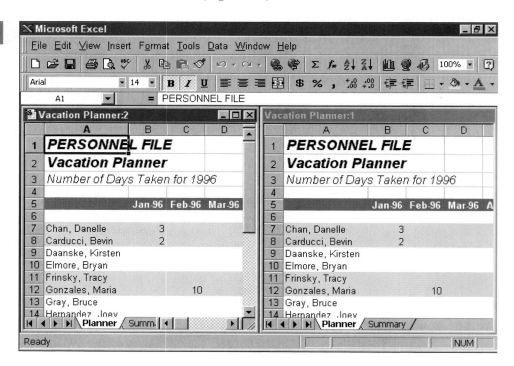

10. For a different window arrangement:
CHOOSE: Window, Arrange
SELECT: *Horizontal* option button
PRESS: (ENTER) or CLICK: OK

11. Practice switching between the two open windows using a mouse. Do the following:
CLICK: any part of a window in the document area to make it active
SELECT: each open window several times
With the possibility of having multiple windows open in the document area, it is important to be able to switch among them efficiently. You can execute commands or type information only in the active window, which is set apart from the rest by its solid or dark Title bar.

12. To switch to a worksheet window that is covered by another window, perform the following menu command:
CHOOSE: Window
CHOOSE: the window name that you want to make active

13. To make the first cell of the first window active:
CHOOSE: Window, 1
PRESS: CTRL + HOME

14. To make the second window active:
CHOOSE: Window, 2

15. The "Vacation Planner" workbook has a summary section located on the second worksheet tab. To move to this worksheet:
CLICK: Summary sheet tab (at the bottom of the document window)

16. Move back to the first window ("Vacation Planner:1") and then select cell B7.

17. In this step, you will change the number in cell B7 to see the effects of the change on the Summary section in the "Vacation Planner:2" window. Do the following:
TYPE: 5
PRESS: ENTER
The Average Vacation Days for Jan-96 changes from 3.00 to 3.67. Your screen should now appear similar to Figure 4.7.

18. To clean up the document area:
CHOOSE: File, Close
CLICK: No when asked to save changes

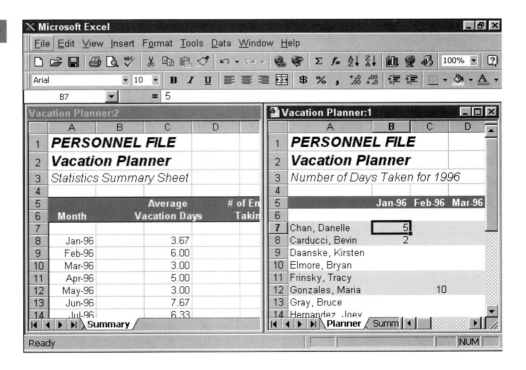

FIGURE 4.7

VIEWING TWO WORKSHEETS IN THE SAME WORKBOOK

- **To create a new window view for the active worksheet:**
  CHOOSE: Window, New Window
- **To arrange open windows in the document area:**
  SELECT: *Tiled, Horizontal, Vertical,* or *Cascade*
  PRESS: ENTER or **CLICK: OK**
- **To close a window:**
  CLICK: Close button (☒)

CREATING MULTIPLE-SHEET WORKBOOKS

In this section, you learn how to create and navigate a multiple-sheet workbook file. Multiple-sheet workbooks enable you to separate related information onto different pages in a single disk file. For example, imagine that you manage the advertising budgets for ten different brands of coffee. In addition to having individual reports for each brand, you need to produce a summary report that consolidates the budgets for the entire product line. Using a workbook, you can place the product summary report on the first worksheet and then each brand report on a subsequent worksheet. This three dimensional (3-D) capability enables you to easily manage and **consolidate** your information.

To access these additional sheets in a workbook, Excel provides tabs at the bottom of the document window. In a new workbook, Excel provides three worksheets by default. It may help you to think of a worksheet as a tear-off page on a notepad—the notepad representing the workbook. Although initially labeled Sheet1, Sheet2, and Sheet3, you can enter descriptive names for each worksheet. However, keep your sheet names under 30 characters, including spaces, for easy reference. You cannot use the asterisk (*), question mark (?), forward slash (/), backslash (\), or colon (:) in a worksheet's name. To move quickly to a particular worksheet, you scroll the tabs using the tab scroll buttons (shown below) and then click the desired sheet tab. You can also right-click any of the tab scroll buttons for a pop-up menu list of the available sheets in the current workbook.

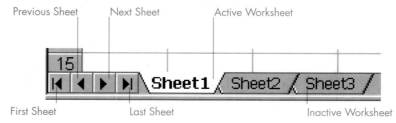

Excel's sheet tabs share the document window with the horizontal scroll bar. You can adjust how much room is devoted to each by dragging the tab split bar that is sandwiched between the two. Similar to creating window panes using the vertical split bar, the mouse pointer changes shape and color when positioned properly over the bar. You drag the tab split bar back and forth to increase and decrease the share of real estate given to each component. If you are working in a single-sheet workbook, you would normally drag the tab split bar to the far left. In this section, you will practice navigating worksheets and executing simple commands.

Let's create a multiple-sheet workbook.

Perform the following steps . . .

1. The document area in the Excel application window should be empty. To create a new workbook:
CLICK: New Workbook button (☐)

2. If the worksheet's document window is not maximized:
CLICK: Maximize button (☐)

3. To practice moving between the default worksheets:
CLICK: Sheet2 tab
CLICK: Sheet3 tab
If you had multiple sheets in the workbook, you could click the Next Sheet button (▶) to scroll through the worksheet tabs. The active worksheet would remain highlighted as you scrolled.

4. To move to Sheet1 and rename the tab:
DOUBLE-CLICK: Sheet1 tab
Notice that the "Sheet1" text is highlighted on the worksheet tab.

5. TYPE: Australia
PRESS: ENTER

6. To rename Sheet2:
DOUBLE-CLICK: Sheet2 tab
TYPE: New Zealand
PRESS: ENTER
(*Note*: You can also right-click a tab and then choose Rename from the shortcut menu that appears.)

7. Position the mouse pointer over the tab split bar until it changes to a black vertical double line split by a two-headed arrow.

8. DRAG: tab split bar to the left so that it rests to the right of the New Zealand tab (as shown below)

Tab Split Bar

9. Although not so important with only two worksheets in the file, let's practice selecting a worksheet using the shortcut menu:
RIGHT-CLICK: any one of the tab scroll buttons (◄◄, ◄, ▶, or ▶▶)
Notice that the first two menu choices are the new tabs, Australia and New Zealand.

10. To move to the Australia worksheet:
CHOOSE: Australia from the shortcut menu

11. To delete a worksheet in a workbook:
RIGHT-CLICK: any one of the tab scroll buttons
CHOOSE: Sheet3
RIGHT-CLICK: Sheet3 tab
CHOOSE: Delete from the shortcut menu
PRESS: (ENTER) or CLICK: OK to confirm the operation
The worksheet is permanently removed from the workbook.

12. To insert a new worksheet between Australia and New Zealand:
RIGHT-CLICK: New Zealand tab
CHOOSE: Insert
The Insert dialog box in Figure 4.8 appears. Notice that you can insert different types of sheets into the workbook, including worksheets and charts.

FIGURE 4.8

INSERT DIALOG BOX

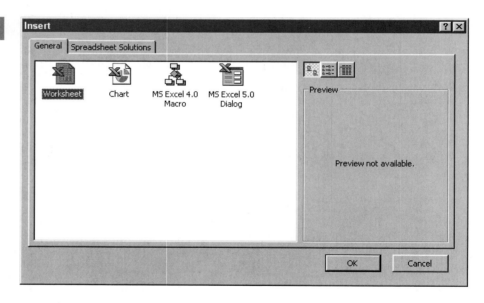

13. To insert a new worksheet:
DOUBLE-CLICK: Worksheet icon in the Insert dialog box
A new sheet, called Sheet4, appears next to the Australia tab.

14. To rename this worksheet:
DOUBLE-CLICK: Sheet4 tab
TYPE: Japan
PRESS: (ENTER)

15. Close the workbook and do not save the changes.

QUICK REFERENCE
Working With a
Multiple-Sheet Workbook

- Use the tab scroll buttons (⏮, ◀, ▶, or ⏭) to move through the available worksheets in a workbook file.
- Use the tab split bar to adjust the shared space for the sheet tabs and the horizontal scroll bar.
- RIGHT-CLICK: any one of the tab scroll buttons to display a pop-up menu showing all of the sheet names
- RIGHT-CLICK: a sheet tab to display a pop-up menu for inserting, deleting, and renaming sheets in a workbook
- DOUBLE-CLICK: a sheet tab to edit the tab name

CONSOLIDATING YOUR WORK

Whether you need to combine revenues from several regions or calculate produc-tivity statistics for several departments, Excel's consolidation tools allow you to better manage, organize, and present your information. In this section, you learn how to consolidate data using two methods. First, you use a single workbook file to summarize information. Second, you consolidate the results of individual work-books to produce a new summary workbook. To begin our discussion, you are intro-duced to the Group mode for working more efficiently with multiple-sheet files.

USING GROUP MODE

In a multiple-sheet workbook, the subsidiary sheets typically have a similar, if not identical, layout to the primary or summary worksheet. Therefore, you can copy the layout of the first worksheet to the remaining subsidiary worksheets and then enter the specific figures for each. Excel provides the **Group mode** to assist you in creating and formatting identical subsidiary worksheets. When you select more than one sheet tab, Group mode is automatically turned on and all the commands that you issue affect all the selected worksheets. For example, Group mode enables you to change a column's width in one worksheet and have that same modification made to all sheets in the workbook file. To understand the effects of Group mode, let's format a multiple-sheet file.

Perform the following steps to practice using Group mode.

Perform the following steps . . .

1. Close any workbooks that are currently open.

2. Open the "Shifts" workbook located on the Advantage Files diskette or in the Advantage Files folder. This workbook summarizes the production results for three shifts in a woodworking operation. The workbook file con-sists of four worksheets: one summary sheet and three detail sheets for each shift.

3. Let's start by renaming the sheet tabs:
DOUBLE-CLICK: Sheet1 tab
TYPE: Summary
PRESS: (ENTER)

4. To name the Sheet2 tab:
DOUBLE-CLICK: Sheet2 tab
TYPE: Shift 1
PRESS: (ENTER)

5. To name the Sheet3 tab:
DOUBLE-CLICK: Sheet3 tab
TYPE: Shift 2
PRESS: (ENTER)

6. To name the Sheet4 tab:
DOUBLE-CLICK: Sheet4 tab
TYPE: Shift 3
PRESS: (ENTER)

7. To select more than one worksheet at a time for Group mode:
CLICK: Summary tab
PRESS: (SHIFT) and hold it down
CLICK: Shift 3 tab
Notice that all four sheet tabs are highlighted and the word "[Group]" appears in the Title bar. (*Note*: To select multiple worksheet tabs that do not appear next to each other in a workbook, hold down the (CTRL) key and click the tabs individually.)

8. Release the (SHIFT) key.

9. With Group mode turned on, you can issue commands in the active worksheet which will carry through to the last selected worksheet in the workbook file. To begin, let's format the date headings to make them bold and italic:
SELECT: cell range from C4 to I4 on the Summary sheet

10. CLICK: Bold button (B)
CLICK: Italic button (I)
CLICK: Center button (≣)
These formatting commands are applied to all the sheets.
(*CAUTION*: Although the Group mode feature is very handy, it can also be quite dangerous. Remember that you can see the effects of the command only on the current worksheet. Without realizing, you can easily erase or reformat information on other sheets unintentionally. Make sure that selected sheets have a similar, if not identical, layout to the sheet in which you are making changes.)

11. To turn Group mode off:
RIGHT-CLICK: Summary tab
CHOOSE: Ungroup Sheets
Notice that there is no longer the word "[Group]" in the Title bar.

12. Browse through the worksheets to see the effects of the last few steps:
CLICK: Shift 1 tab
CLICK: Shift 2 tab
CLICK: Shift 3 tab
CLICK: Summary tab

CONSOLIDATING A MULTIPLE-SHEET WORKBOOK

One of the nicest features of working with a multiple-sheet workbook is that information in one sheet can automatically update information in another sheet. The "Shifts" workbook, for example, contains three subsidiary sheets for each shift. In the next section, you will create formulas that sum the values from each subsidiary worksheet into the first summary worksheet. Thereafter, any changes to values in the subsidiary sheets are immediately reflected in the summary.

Perform the following steps . . .

1. Move to cell C5 in the Summary sheet.

2. As discussed in past sessions, you can enter formulas by directly typing into a cell or by accessing the Formula Palette. The following steps show you how to use several different methods for summarizing data. In a real-world application, however, you would create the first formula and then copy it to the remaining cells. Do the following:
TYPE: =sum
CLICK: Edit Formula button (=)
The Formula Palette appears for the SUM function.

3. To select the cell range to sum:
CLICK: Dialog Collapse button (⊞) for the *Number1* text box
CLICK: Shift 1 tab
CLICK: cell C5 (20)
PRESS: SHIFT
CLICK: Shift 3 tab
Notice that we are grouping the worksheets from Sheet 1 to Sheet 3.

4. In Step 3, you selected a 3-D range for cell C5 on Sheet 1, Sheet 2, and Sheet 3. Let's see how Excel refers to this cell range in the Formula Palette. Do the following:
CLICK: Dialog Expand button (▣)
Your screen should now appear similar to Figure 4.9.

FIGURE 4.9

SELECTING A 3-D CELL
RANGE

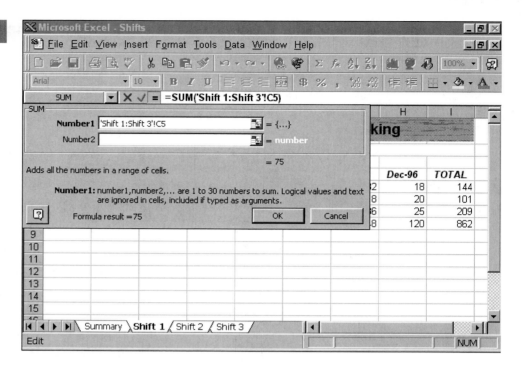

5. To complete the entry:
CLICK: OK command button
The answer of 75 appears in cell C5 on the Summary sheet.

6. Move to cell C6 in the Summary sheet.

7. To enter the SUM equation by typing, do the following:
TYPE: =sum('Shift 1:Shift 3'!c6)
PRESS: ENTER
An answer of 30 appears in the cell. Notice that you surround the tab range with single quotes and then separate the tabs from the cell address with an exclamation mark (!). If the tab names did not contain any spaces (for example, Shift1 instead of Shift 1), you could leave out the single quotes in the formula.

8. Move to cell C7 in the Summary sheet.

9. Let's create a formula by pointing to the cells without using the Formula Palette:
TYPE: =sum(
CLICK: Shift 1 tab
CLICK: cell C7
PRESS: SHIFT and hold it down
CLICK: Shift 3 tab
TYPE:)
PRESS: ENTER
An answer of 109 appears in the cell.

10. Let's copy the formula in cell C7 to cell C8 in the Summary worksheet. With cell C7 still selected, do the following:
CLICK: Copy button (📋)
CLICK: cell C8
PRESS: (ENTER)
An answer of 406 appears in the cell. Notice how the cell addressing changes *relative* to where it is copied.

11. Let's copy these formulas across the remainder of the worksheet:
SELECT: cell range from C5 through I8 on the Summary tab
CHOOSE: Edit, Fill, Right
PRESS: (CTRL) + (HOME)
Your worksheet should appear similar to Figure 4.10.

12. For practice, change some numbers in the subsidiary worksheets and then watch their effects on the Summary worksheet. Use your knowledge of arranging windows to best see the results of your changes. When finished, save the workbook as "Shift Summary" to your Data Files location and then close the workbook.

FIGURE 4.10

CONSOLIDATING A
MULTIPLE-SHEET
WORKBOOK

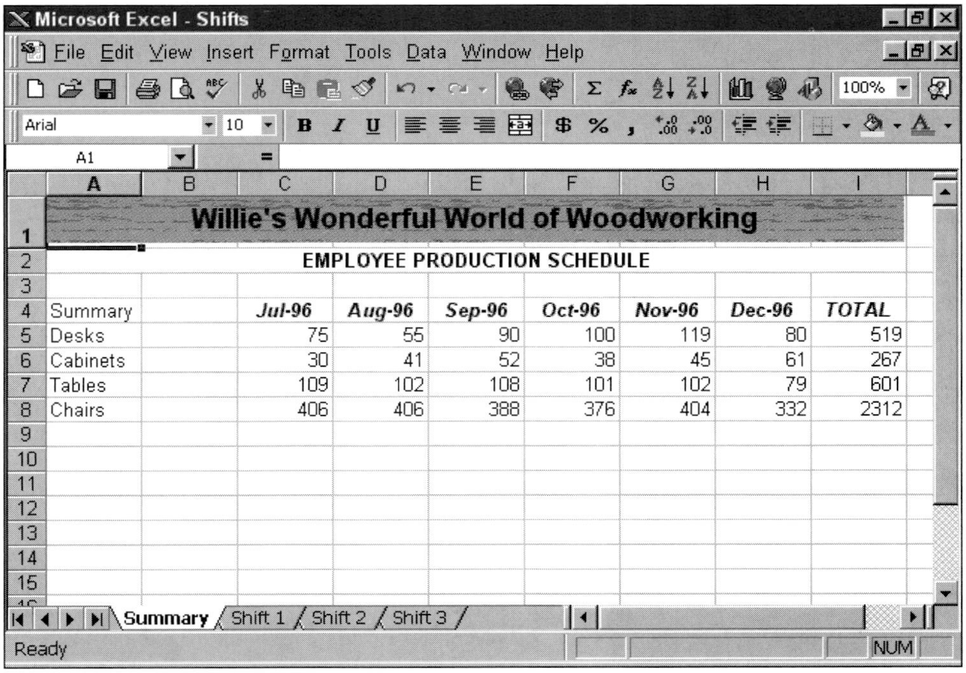

CONSOLIDATING MULTIPLE WORKBOOKS

In addition to consolidating a multiple-sheet workbook, you can link separate workbook files. Linking workbooks has two major advantages over using one large workbook. First, the subsidiary workbooks are smaller in size and therefore easier to manage on a daily basis. Second, subsidiary workbooks are not restricted to the same computer as the summary workbook. For example, each department may control its own workbook and submit the file once a month for consolidation, perhaps on a diskette, across the network, or via the Internet. To create a consolidated workbook, you open each subsidiary workbook in the document area, along with the summary workbook, and then create formulas as you did in the previous section.

In this example, you compile three departmental workbooks from XYZ Corporation into a single summary workbook.

Perform the following steps . . .

1. Close any workbook files that are currently open in the document area.

2. To open four workbook files in one command:
   CLICK: Open button (📂)

3. SELECT: your Advantage Files location
   The workbook files should appear sorted by name.

4. In the file display area of the dialog box:
   CLICK: XYZDept1
   PRESS: **SHIFT** and hold it down
   CLICK: XYZSumm
   The four files should all appear highlighted, as shown in Figure 4.11.

FIGURE 4.11

SELECTING MULTIPLE WORKBOOK FILES IN THE OPEN DIALOG BOX

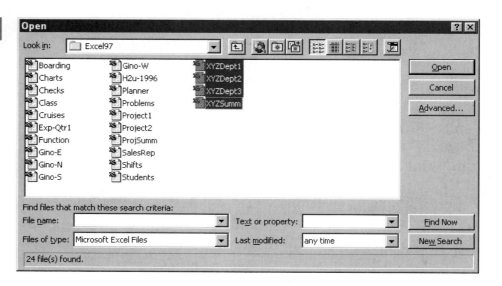

5. To open the selected files:
   CLICK: Open command button
   After a few seconds, the four files are loaded into Excel's document area.

6. To organize the windows within the document area:
CHOOSE: Window, Arrange
SELECT: *Tiled* option button
PRESS: **ENTER** or CLICK: OK
Your screen should now look like Figure 4.12.

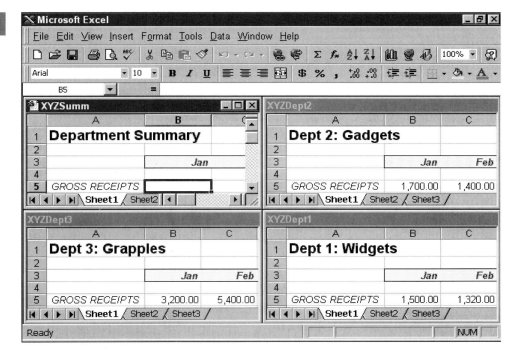

7. To move among the open windows in the document area, you position the mouse pointer on a visible part of the worksheet and click once. To practice, click the Title bars of the four worksheets. Notice that the solid or dark-colored Title bar represents the active worksheet window. When you are ready to proceed, ensure that the "XYZSumm" worksheet is active.

8. Before you consolidate the departmental workbooks into a consolidated workbook, notice that they share the same worksheet structure and layout. Although this is not necessary, it provides an instantaneous familiarity with each worksheet and makes entering the consolidation formulas much easier. To begin entering the first linking formula:
SELECT: cell B5 in the "XYZSumm" workbook

9. A formula that links subsidiary workbooks is entered the same as any other formula. To inform Excel that you are entering a formula:
TYPE: =
CLICK: the Title bar of the "XYZDept1" workbook
CLICK: cell B5 in the active workbook
(*Hint*: After selecting the "XYZDept1" workbook, you may have to use the scroll bars to move the worksheet window so that cell B5 is visible.) Notice the formula being constructed in the Formula bar.

10. To complete the formula:
TYPE: +
CLICK: the Title bar of "XYZDept2" workbook
CLICK: cell B5 in this workbook
TYPE: +
CLICK: the Title bar of the "XYZDept3" workbook
CLICK: cell B5 in this workbook
PRESS: (ENTER)
The summary worksheet calculates the answer to be 6,400.00. Notice the equation that appears in the Formula bar.

11. Maximize the "XYZSumm" document window. If the Maximize button (◻) is covered by the expression in the Formula bar, you can click a cell in the active worksheet and then click the Maximize button (◻).

12. Before you can copy this formula to the other cells, you need to remove the absolute references to cell B5:
DOUBLE-CLICK: cell B5

13. Use the arrow keys or the I-beam mouse pointer to highlight a dollar sign ($) and then press (DELETE). Perform this step for each dollar sign that appears in the formula and then press (ENTER). When finished, the formula should read as follows:
=[XYZDept1.xls]Sheet1!B5+[XYZDept2.xls]Sheet1!B5+[XYZDept3.xls]Sheet1!B5

14. Ensure that cell B5 is selected and then copy the formula to the Clipboard:
CLICK: Copy button (▣)

15. To paste the formula into all the remaining cells at the same time:
SELECT: cell range from B5 to D5
PRESS: (CTRL) and hold it down
SELECT: cell range from B8 to D11
RELEASE: (CTRL)
PRESS: (ENTER)
The formula is pasted to all the highlighted cells. Your worksheet should now appear similar to Figure 4.13.

16. To save and then close all of the open workbooks, do the following:
PRESS: (SHIFT)
CHOOSE: File, Close All from the menu
CLICK: Yes to All command button, if it appears

FIGURE 4.13

COPYING THE
CONSOLIDATION
FORMULA TO THE
REMAINING CELLS

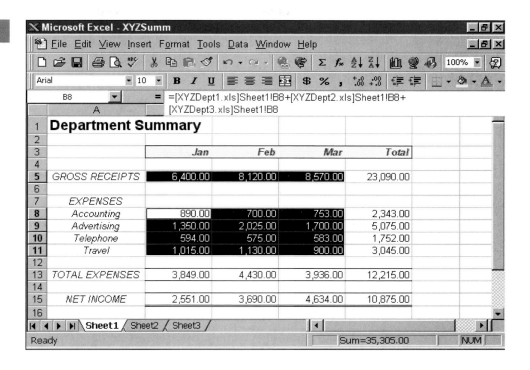

	A	Jan	Feb	Mar	Total
1	**Department Summary**				
2					
3		*Jan*	*Feb*	*Mar*	*Total*
4					
5	GROSS RECEIPTS	6,400.00	8,120.00	8,570.00	23,090.00
6					
7	*EXPENSES*				
8	*Accounting*	890.00	700.00	753.00	2,343.00
9	*Advertising*	1,350.00	2,025.00	1,700.00	5,075.00
10	*Telephone*	594.00	575.00	583.00	1,752.00
11	*Travel*	1,015.00	1,130.00	900.00	3,045.00
12					
13	*TOTAL EXPENSES*	3,849.00	4,430.00	3,936.00	12,215.00
14					
15	*NET INCOME*	2,551.00	3,690.00	4,634.00	10,875.00
16					

B8 = =[XYZDept1.xls]Sheet1!B8+[XYZDept2.xls]Sheet1!B8+[XYZDept3.xls]Sheet1!B8

QUICK REFERENCE
Consolidating Workbooks

1. **Open the summary workbook and the subsidiary workbooks.**
2. **Organize the workbooks in the document area using the Window, Arrange command.**
3. **Enter a formula in the summary workbook that references cells in the subsidiary workbooks.**

IN ADDITION USING EXCEL'S CONSOLIDATE COMMAND

Excel provides a Consolidate command for consolidating worksheets. This command was not covered in this section because it introduces new concepts. The formula method for consolidating your workbooks is simply an extension of the skills you already possess. For more information, ask the Office Assistant for help on "Data Consolidation."

WHAT IS A MACRO?

Many spreadsheet tasks are repetitive, such as enhancing titles with fonts and borders, formatting numbers, or printing cell ranges. For our benefit, Excel has assigned many of these monotonous tasks to toolbar buttons and "Auto" commands. However, there are still specific tasks that you may have to perform time and time again, such as entering and formatting your company name and address, that are not included as buttons on a toolbar. To save you time and improve the consistency of these operations, Excel enables you to store and play back keystrokes and commands in a **macro.** Using a special utility called the Macro Recorder, Excel writes the instructions for each task in the Visual Basic for Applications programming language. Using a macro, you can execute a series of instructions by pressing only two keys, clicking a toolbar button, or choosing a custom command from the Menu bar. You can even create custom command buttons and place them directly on a worksheet!

By incorporating macros into a worksheet, you make it easier to use for yourself and for others. Instead of having to remember all of the commands and keystrokes required to perform a procedure, you only have to remember a few simple keystrokes or which toolbar button to click. Furthermore, you can automate complicated tasks for co-workers or temporary personnel who are not familiar with using spreadsheets. If you are so inclined, you can even write your own Visual Basic code for creating menu commands, dialog boxes, and custom applications that don't even resemble Microsoft Excel.

CREATING MACROS

After planning the steps that you want performed in a macro, you simply record your keystrokes. The results are stored in a Visual Basic module. You can specify that macros be stored in the current workbook or in a special file called a **Personal Macro Workbook.** The Personal Macro Workbook is managed by Excel (you don't have to open or close this file) and provides a common area for storing macros that you will use with all your workbooks.

RECORDING A MACRO

The quickest method for creating a macro is to record the keystrokes that you press and the mouse clicks that you make while performing a procedure. Once recorded, the procedure may be executed again and again by selecting the macro. You turn on the Macro Recorder by choosing the Tools, Macro, Record New Macro command. When executed, the dialog box in Figure 4.14 appears.

FIGURE 4.14

RECORD NEW MACRO
DIALOG BOX

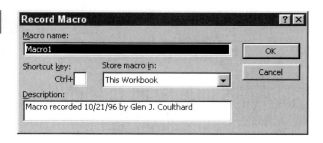

After entering a name for the macro, you select a shortcut key for implementing the macro and a location for storing the macro. After you click the OK command button, the recorder turns on and you perform the actions that you want included in the procedure. Once finished, you turn off the recorder by clicking the Stop button () or by choosing the Tools, Macro, Stop Recording command. Excel automatically writes the macro for you and stores it in a Visual Basic module.

You will now create a macro that automatically enters a company name and address into the worksheet and then formats the cells.

Perform the following steps . . .

1. Close any workbooks that may be open in the document area.

2. CLICK: New Workbook button ()

3. To create a macro, you must first turn on the Macro Recorder:
CHOOSE: Tools, Macro, Record New Macro
The Record Macro dialog box appears, as shown in Figure 4.14.

4. In the dialog box, type the name (without spaces) that you want to assign to the macro:
TYPE: CompanyName

5. From the *Store macro in* drop-down list box:
SELECT: This Workbook
PRESS: (ENTER) or CLICK: OK
Notice that the word "Recording" appears in the Status bar and that the Stop Recording button floats above the application window.

6. As the first recorded step in the macro:
PRESS: (CTRL) + (HOME)

7. Now enter the company name and address information:
TYPE: Sam's Superior Sailboats
PRESS: (↓)
TYPE: Suite 100, 2899 Seashore Drive
PRESS: (↓)
TYPE: Seattle, WA 98004
PRESS: (ENTER)

8. To format this information:
SELECT: cell range from A1 to A3
CLICK: Bold button ()
CLICK: Italic button ()
SELECT: Times New Roman from the Font drop-down list ([Arial ▼])
SELECT: 12 from the Font Size drop-down list ([10 ▼])

9. SELECT: cell A1
SELECT: 14 from the Font Size drop-down list ([10 ▼])

10. To stop the recording:
CLICK: Stop button ()
And that's all there is to recording a macro! In the next section, you will get an opportunity to play back a macro.

QUICK REFERENCE
Recording a Macro

1. **CHOOSE: Tools, Macro, Record New Macro**
2. **Enter a name for the macro.**
3. **PRESS: (ENTER) or CLICK: OK**
4. **Perform the procedure to be recorded.**
5. **CLICK: Stop button ( )**

PLAYING BACK A MACRO

There are several methods for playing back a macro. You can execute a macro by selecting it from a dialog box, by pressing a keystroke combination, by clicking a toolbar button, or by selecting a custom command from the menu. In this section, you learn how to run a macro from the Macro dialog box.

Perform the following steps . . .

1. CLICK: Sheet2 tab

2. To enter the company name and address at the top of this worksheet:
CHOOSE: Tools, Macro, Macros
The dialog box in Figure 4.15 appears.

FIGURE 4.15

MACRO DIALOG BOX

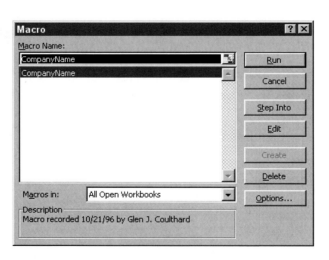

3. To run a macro from the *Macro Name* list box:
SELECT: CompanyName macro
CLICK: Run command button
The company information is automatically entered and formatted in the proper range of the worksheet. (*Note*: You can also double-click a macro name in the list box area to execute the macro.)

QUICK REFERENCE	1.	**CHOOSE: Tools, Macro, Macros**
Playing Back a Macro	2.	**SELECT: the desired macro from the list box**
	3.	**PRESS:** [ENTER] **or CLICK: Run**

REVIEWING YOUR MACROS

You can easily review and edit a macro using the Visual Basic Editor. In this section, you learn how to modify Excel's code and play back the new version of your macro.

 Perform the following steps . . .

1. To view the Visual Basic module:
CHOOSE: Tools, Macro, Macros
SELECT: CompanyName macro
CLICK: Edit command button
The Visual Basic Editor loads into memory and displays the macro module.

2. To see more of the macro:
CHOOSE: Window, Tile Horizontally
Your screen should now appear similar to Figure 4.16.

FIGURE 4.16

THE VISUAL BASIC
EDITING ENVIRONMENT

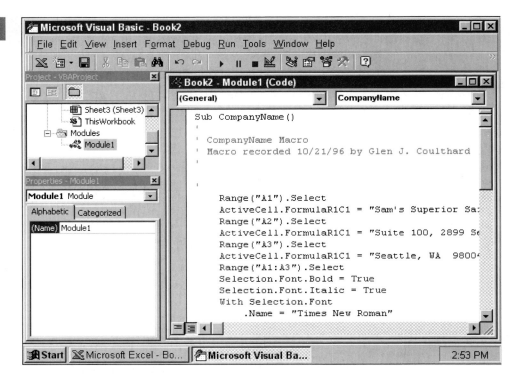

3. You edit the Visual Basic code as you would work with a word processing software program. For example, position the I-beam mouse pointer over the word "Suite" in the company's address. Do the following:
DOUBLE-CLICK: "Suite"
TYPE: **Room**
DOUBLE-CLICK: "Drive"
TYPE: **Road**

4. To see the results of our editing:
CHOOSE: File, Close and Return to Microsoft Excel

5. To run the macro:
CLICK: Sheet3 tab
CHOOSE: Tools, Macro, Macros
DOUBLE-CLICK: CompanyName macro in the list box
Notice that the new information is entered into the cells. This example demonstrates how quick and easy it is to edit the code created by Excel's Macro Recorder.

6. Save the workbook as "My Macros" to your Data Files location.

7. Close the workbook and then exit Microsoft Excel.

QUICK REFERENCE	
Editing a Macro	**1. CHOOSE: Tools, Macro, Macros** **2. SELECT: macro name from the list box** **3. CLICK: Edit command button** **4. Edit the Visual Basic code using basic wordprocessing keystrokes.** **5. CHOOSE: File, Close and Return to Microsoft Excel.**

SUMMARY

This session introduced you to several commands and procedures that increase your efficiency and productivity when working in Excel. The first part of the session concentrated on dividing the document window into panes for freezing titles on the screen. This technique is useful when your worksheet is organized under static column and row headings. When your application consists of separate but related areas, separating the workbook into multiple window views helps you keep track of the workbook's relationships. You also learned how to filter data and produce "top-ten" lists in your worksheet.

For consolidating worksheets or workbooks into a summary worksheet, the ability to organize and tile multiple windows in the document area is an incredible time-saver. The latter half of the session explored different methods for consolidating worksheet information. You also learned to use macros for automating common tasks and procedures. Excel's easy-to-use Macro Recorder gives everyone the ability to become a programmer using the Visual Basic for Applications language.

The Command Summary in Table 4.1 provides a list of the commands and procedures covered in this session.

TABLE 4.1 Command Summary	*Command*	*Description*
	Data, Filter, AutoFilter	Analyzes a column's data and produces a filter method that enables you to limit the display of information.
	File, Close All	Closes all open documents in the document area.
	Tools, Macro, Macros	Displays a dialog box for executing or editing macros.
	Tools, Macro, Record New Macro	Records keystrokes, commands, and procedures and saves them as a macro.
	Tools, Macro, Stop Recording	Turns off the recorder to finish creating the macro; you can also click the Stop button (◼).
	Window, Arrange	Arranges the open windows in the document area using square, horizontal, and vertical tiling options.
	Window, Freeze Panes	Lets you lock or freeze rows and columns on the screen so that they appear at all times.
	Window, New Window	Opens a new window in the document area for another view of the active workbook.
	Window, Remove Split	Removes panes created by choosing Window, Split or by dragging the horizontal and vertical split boxes.
	Window, Split	Splits the window into horizontal and vertical panes at the cell pointer.
	Window, Unfreeze Panes	Unfreezes the area that has been locked using the Window, Freeze Panes command.

EY TERMS

AutoFilter

In Excel, a software feature that makes it easy for you to select, filter, and display worksheet information quickly and easily.

consolidate

The process of combining smaller worksheet files into a single summary worksheet, making it easier to manage large amounts of data.

Group mode

A special mode for working with multiple-sheet workbooks; enables you to perform commands on a single sheet and have those commands reflected in all other sheets in the file.

horizontal split box

A small box located at the top of the vertical scroll bar; used to divide a window into panes.

macro

A collection of keystrokes, commands, or procedures that can be executed using two keystrokes, a mouse click, or a menu selection. Macros are recorded or written by the user, saved to the disk, and then repeatedly used to perform frequent tasks or commands.

panes

When a document window has been divided into separate areas using the Window, Freeze Panes command or the Window, Split command, these areas are called *window panes* or *panes*. A worksheet can have a maximum of four panes at any one time.

Personal Macro Workbook

A special workbook file, managed by Excel, for storing macros that you want made available to all your workbooks.

vertical split box

A small box located at the far right of the horizontal scroll bar in a document window; used to divide a window into panes.

EXERCISES

SHORT ANSWER

1. What is the main difference between freezing titles on a worksheet and dividing a window into panes?

2. What options are available using the Window, Arrange command?

3. Name some advantages of linking workbooks.

4. What is the significance of a solid Title bar in a window?

5. How do you change the name of a sheet tab?

6. What is a macro?

7. How do you create a macro?

8. How are macros commonly played back?

9. How can you view or edit the macros that you have recorded?

10. Name two examples of when you might want to use a macro.

HANDS-ON

(*Note*: Ensure that you know the storage location of your Advantage Files and your Data Files before proceeding.)

1. In this exercise, you retrieve a workbook and practice freezing titles and viewing the worksheet using panes.

    a. Load Excel and close all of the open windows in the document area.

    b. Open the "Checks" workbook located in your Advantage Files location. This worksheet is an incomplete cash disbursements journal.

    c. CLICK: cell A8

    d. To see how many checks have been posted in the first quarter:
        PRESS: CTRL + ⬇
        Notice how the column text headings have scrolled out of view.

    e. Return to the top of the worksheet.

    f. Your objective is to freeze the titles in Rows 1 through 6 at the top of the screen. Then, when you move to the bottom of the column to enter new checks, you will still be able to see the column headings. The first step is to move to cell A8.

    g. CHOOSE: Window, Freeze Panes

    h. To enter more checks into the journal:
        PRESS: CTRL + ⬇
        The titles remain at the top of the screen as the cell pointer is repositioned at the bottom of the column.

    i. Enter the following checks into the journal:

Check	Date	Amount
51	17-Mar-97	550.45
52	24-Mar-97	300.95
53	31-Mar-97	750.25

Your worksheet should now appear similar to Figure 4.17.

FIGURE 4.17

THE "CHECKS"
WORKBOOK

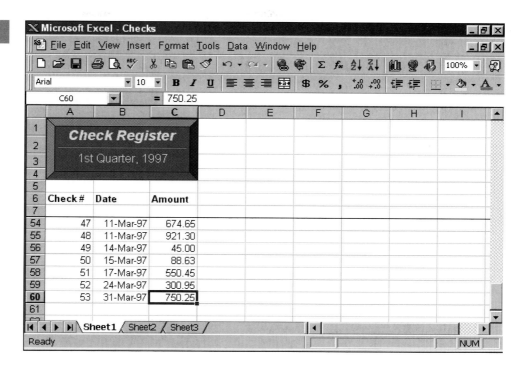

j. PRESS: [CTRL] + [HOME]

k. Unfreeze the row titles.

l. To create a new window onto the "Checks" workbook:
CHOOSE: Window, New Window

m. Arrange the open windows horizontally in the document area.

n. Arrange the open windows vertically in the document area.

o. Close the window titled "Checks:2" by clicking its Close button ([✗]).

p. Tile the single "Checks" window in the document area.

q. Save the workbook as "Check Register" to your Data Files location.

r. Close the workbook.

2. This exercise allows you to practice consolidating separate subsidiary workbook files into a summary workbook. The company, XYZ Developments, is currently working on two projects. Each project has a project manager responsible for hiring subcontractors and consultants. Fortunately, XYZ's project managers are experienced in using Excel and have set up tracking workbooks. Your objective is to complete a summary workbook that adds together the data from each project manager's file. (*Hint*: You will use linking formulas to consolidate these workbooks.)

a. Close all of the open windows in the document area.

b. Open the "Project1," "Project2," and "ProjSumm" workbooks that are stored in your Advantage Files location. Enter your name in cell E2 of the "ProjSumm" workbook.

c. Arrange the windows using the Tiled option.

d. Move to "Project1" and select cell B7.

e. Move to "Project2" and select cell B7.

f. Move to "ProjSumm" and select cell B7.
The last three steps ensure that cell B7 is visible in each worksheet.

g. Construct a formula to add together data from the two workbooks:
TYPE: =
CLICK: the Title bar of the "Project1" window
CLICK: cell B7
TYPE: +
CLICK: the Title bar of the "Project2" window
CLICK: cell B7
PRESS: ENTER

h. Modify the cell addresses to contain relative cell addresses rather than absolute cell addresses. (*Hint*: Remove the "$" symbols from the formula.)

i. Copy the formula in B7 to the cell range from B7 to M16.

j. PRESS: CTRL + HOME
CLICK: cell B7
Your screen should appear similar to Figure 4.18.

k. Save the workbook as "Project Summary" to your Data Files location.

l. Close all of the open windows.

FIGURE 4.18

"PROJECT SUMMARY"
WORKBOOK

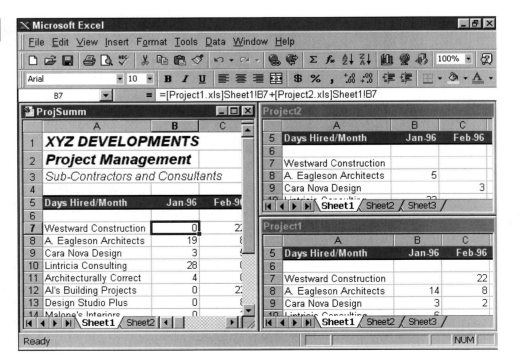

3. **On Your Own:** An Entertainment Review
Create a workbook that contains the following sheets: Music, Movies, and Books. For the Music sheet, add column titles for Title, Artist, Year, Producer, Label, and Rating. For the Movies sheet, add column titles for Title, Actors, Year, Director, Producer, and Rating. For the Books sheet, add column titles for Title, Author, Year, ISBN, Publisher, and Rating. Format all the worksheets using Group mode, and then add or edit the worksheet information as desired. When finished, enter some fictitious or real information with your personal rating system. Save the workbook as "Entertainment" to your Data Files location.

4. **On Your Own:** Macro Recordings
Open a new workbook and then create the following:

- a macro that enters your name into a worksheet cell and then assigns a Times New Roman font that is 12 points in size with a Bold and Italic style;

- a macro that enters the NOW function into two adjacent cells and then assigns one a date format and the other a time format;

- a macro that enters the following notice "© Copyright *Your Name, 1997*" and then assigns an Arial font that is 8 points in size with a Bold style.

Save the workbook as "More Macros" to your Data Files location and then close the workbook and exit Excel.

CASE PROBLEMS | **GINO'S KITCHEN**

(*Note*: In the following case problems, assume the role of the primary characters and perform the same steps that they identify. You may want to re-read the session opening.)

1. After a relaxing Christmas holiday, Larry arrives at the office to find the following note on his desk: "Larry, I trust you had a wonderful time on Nantucket Island. Sorry to be a pain, but I'd like the monthly restaurant report ASAP. Thanks. Gino." With his favorite mug in tow, Larry heads directly for the coffee machine, planning his strategy along the way. When he returns to his desk, Larry turns on the computer, launches Excel, and then locates the four managers' workbooks that are stored on the Advantage Diskette. These files are named "Gino-N", "Gino-S", "Gino-W", and "Gino-E". He loads all four workbooks into memory and then arranges the windows in a tiled pattern on the screen.

Leaning back in his chair, Larry ponders the task before him and then writes down the process on a piece of scrap paper. Before proceeding any further, Larry makes sure that the four restaurant workbooks appear tiled on the screen and then he performs the steps outlined in his list.

- Create a new workbook that contains a skeleton copy of the standard restaurant template. In other words, copy the contents of one restaurant's workbook to the new workbook and then delete the specific information. (*Hint*: Make sure that you leave the formulas in the new worksheet and delete only the financial information for the restaurant.)

- Edit the title in the new worksheet to read "Gino's Kitchen - All Restaurants."

- Consolidate the financial information from the four subsidiary workbooks.

- Format and print the new workbook for Gino's approval.

- Save the workbook as "Gino's Restaurants" to your Data Files location.

2. Having completed Gino's summary report, Larry decides to get a fresh start on 1996's year-end and create a summary workbook for his monthly reports. Using the same process as described in the previous case problem, Larry creates a new workbook with a skeleton copy of the standard restaurant template. Then, he renames and adds tabs in the workbook for Jan, Feb, Mar, and so on. He also inserts a new sheet at the very beginning of the workbook called "YTD" which he will use to sum the contents of the Jan through Dec sheets.

   Using Group mode, Larry copies the skeleton template to the other sheets in the workbook. Still in Group mode, he makes some formatting enhancements to the worksheet that flow through to all the worksheets in the stack. After previewing the formatting enhancements, Larry ungroups the worksheets. Moving to the YTD worksheet, Larry creates formulas for consolidating the values from Jan through Dec. Pleased with his new summary, Larry saves the workbook as "Gino's YTD 1996" to the Data Files location.

3. It's 5:30 PM and Larry is getting ready to leave the office after a productive day. Just as he closes his briefcase, Gino strolls into his office to share a few ideas. "Larry, you did a good job on that summary report. Marvelous, just marvelous. But Larry, I'm troubled by the numbers that some of our establishments are reporting. I'd like you to develop and print a first-quarter budget for me using these figures." Gino hands Larry a piece of paper with handwritten notes. "I think that I might have to visit our accountant tomorrow. Can you have this ready for me by 9:00 AM?" Larry assures Gino as he strolls back down the hallway that he'll finish the budget by tomorrow morning.

Larry returns to his desk and turns on his computer once again. He loads the "Gino's YTD 1996" workbook and then saves it as "Gino's Budget 1997" to the Data Files location. Using Gino's information (provided below), he enters the budget estimates, groups the first four sheets (YTD, Jan, Feb, and Mar), and then prints the sheets centered horizontally. Lastly, he saves the worksheet and exits Excel.

All Restaurants	Jan	Feb	Mar
Food Sales	75,000	90,000	110,000
Beverage Sales	95,000	120,000	145,000
Food Costs	40,000	54,000	65,000
Beverage Costs	32,000	40,000	52,000
Manager's Salary	16,000	16,000	16,000
Wages & Benefits	26,500	30,000	36,000
Administration	2,500	4,500	5,000
Laundry & Misc.	9,500	12,000	10,500
Occupancy Costs	15,000	15,000	15,000

Microsoft Excel 97 for Windows

Creating Charts

SESSION

5

IRWIN

COMPUTER & INFORMATION TECHNOLOGY

SESSION OUTLINE

INTRODUCTION

Most businesspeople recognize the benefit of using graphics to improve the effectiveness of their presentations. Clearly, a visual display is quicker in conveying information than rows and columns of tiny numbers. This session demonstrates how you can use Excel to produce visually stunning charts and data maps from basic worksheet information.

H2 UNDERSCAPING LTD.

In 1989 Chip Yee started H2 Underscaping Ltd. (H2U), a landscaping operation that specializes in the installation of underground sprinkler systems. Since that time, H2U has grown from annual sales of $30,000 to its current year's projection of over $700,000. This tremendous growth is due in large part to Chip's sound financial and marketing analysis of the landscaping industry. Just the previous year, Chip purchased a competing business, called Xeriscaping, Inc. (*xeriscaping* is a special form of landscaping for desert or low fresh-water areas), that was losing money and turned it around into a profitable business unit at H2U. One of the other keys to Chip's success is his ability to closely monitor the seasonal trends of his industry.

Having just completed entering a full year's information into an Excel worksheet, Chip wants to take advantage of his slow time this January to analyze the results and trends for 1996. In particular, he wants to compare the dollar sales from his sprinkler installations against his new xeriscaping business. He also wants to plot his combined sales revenues against his expenses for the year to get a feeling for the seasonal trends. Although most of these numbers appear next to each other in the worksheet, Chip feels that he could better understand the results if they appeared in a chart. Ever since he can remember, Chip has been a visual learner and understands charts and pictures better than text or numbers. Unfortunately, Chip's experience with Excel has been limited to entering information into worksheets, formatting cells, using functions, and linking workbooks.

In this session, you and Chip learn about the different charting formats available in Excel and how to create basic charts and data maps using worksheet information.

FORMS OF BUSINESS GRAPHICS

A graphic representation of worksheet data is far more effective than the numbers alone for the same reason that road maps are easier to follow than written directions. The majority of people are visual learners and seem to remember what they see better than what they hear or read. Everybody has seen some sort of business graphic used at one time or another, depicting everything from interest rate trends to unemployment statistics.

Graphics are produced in a variety of formats to suit the specific needs of the business professional. For example, microcomputer images can be displayed on a monitor, photographed, plotted on paper (black and white or color), or made into transparencies to be used with an overhead projector. There are several types of charts available for presenting information to different audiences such as engineers, statisticians, medical researchers, and business professionals. This section describes some of the most popular business graphics, namely line charts, column charts, pie charts, and XY or scatter plot diagrams.

LINE CHARTS

When you need to plot trends or show changes over a period of time, the **line chart** is the perfect tool. The angles of the line reflect variations in a trend, and the distance of the line from the horizontal axis represents the amount of the variation. An example of a line chart appears in Figure 5.1.

FIGURE 5.1

A LINE CHART SHOWING CHANGES IN TELEVISION VIEWERSHIP OVER A FIVE-YEAR PERIOD

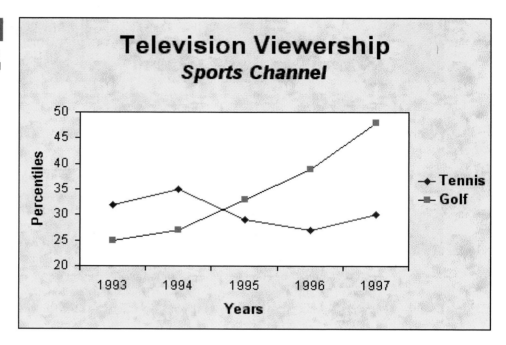

BAR OR COLUMN CHARTS

When the purpose of a chart is to compare one data element with another data element, a **column chart** is the appropriate form to use. A column chart also shows variations over a period of time, similarly to a line chart, and is one of the most commonly used graphs in business. An example appears in Figure 5.2. A *bar chart* also uses rectangular images, but they run horizontally rather than vertically.

FIGURE 5.2

A COLUMN CHART
COMPARING GOLF
VERSUS TENNIS
VIEWERSHIP OVER A
FIVE-YEAR PERIOD

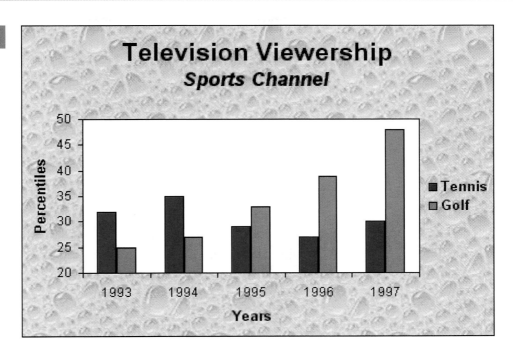

PIE CHARTS

A **pie chart** shows the proportions of individual components compared to the total. Similar to a real pie (the baked variety), a pie chart is divided into slices. An example of a pie chart appears in Figure 5.3.

FIGURE 5.3

A PIE CHART SHOWING
THE BREAKDOWN OF
EXPENSES FOR XYZ
COMPANY

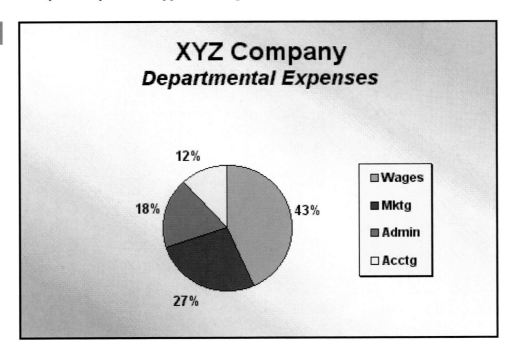

SCATTER PLOT CHARTS

XY charts, which are commonly referred to as *scatter plot diagrams*, show how one or more data elements relate to another data element. Although they look much like line charts, XY charts include a numeric scale along both the X and Y axes. Figure 5.4 shows an XY chart.

FIGURE 5.4

AN XY CHART
SHOWING THE
CORRELATION BETWEEN
WORKER STRESS AND
PRODUCTIVITY

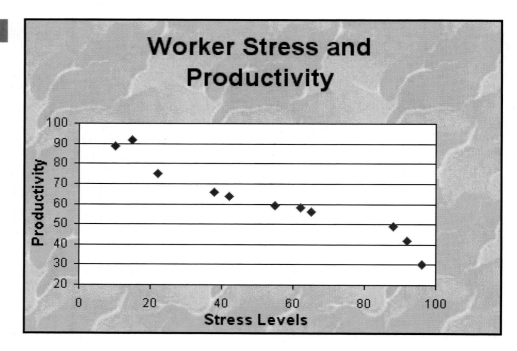

PRINCIPLES OF BUSINESS GRAPHICS

With graphics programs, there is often a tendency to overindulge in the various formatting and customizing options available. Although a picture may be worth a thousand words, it is probably wise not to test this adage with business graphics. Regardless of the sophistication of your graphics program, do not attempt to tell an entire history using a single chart. To assist your planning of when and how to apply business graphics, there are certain basic principles to follow:

- *Simplicity*   Do not put too much information and formatting onto a single chart. If you include too much detail, the visual aspects become muddled and the symbols become difficult to understand.

- *Unity*   A chart must clearly relate the data elements it contains—that is, it must appear as a unit. For instance, if you use too much space between the variables (such as between columns in a column chart), you will probably destroy the unity of your chart.

- *Emphasis* Use emphasis sparingly and correctly. Emphasis is used to draw one's attention to certain data elements or trends.

- *Balance* Your graph should look balanced—both as a unit and in the context of the rest of the page. Changing the position of text affects the balance of the graph, as does changing the shading, color, and thickness of the lines used in a graph.

These four principles will assist you in developing charts that are easily read and interpreted. The next section introduces the methods for creating charts using Microsoft Excel. The concepts presented in this past section should be applied in the following sections.

CHART METHODS AND TYPES

There are two methods for creating a chart in Excel, differing primarily in the way the chart is printed and stored.

- You can create a new chart as a separate sheet in a workbook. This method works well for creating computer-based presentations and electronic slide shows.

- You can also create an **embedded chart** that is layered on an existing worksheet. An embedded chart can be printed and saved alongside related or clarifying information in the worksheet.

Regardless of the above methods, you create a new chart by choosing the Insert, Chart command or by clicking the Chart Wizard button (⊞) on the Standard toolbar. The **Chart Wizard** guides you through the process of selecting a cell range to plot, choosing a chart type, adding elements to the chart, and, finally, selecting either a new sheet or an existing worksheet as the storage location for the new chart.

Excel's default chart type is a column chart. However, there are many additional chart types available in the gallery. Table 5.1 describes each type of chart. Many of these chart types have several formats, including three-dimensional (3-D) variations.

	Chart Type	*Description*
TABLE 5.1	Area	Compares the amount or magnitude of change in data elements over a period of time.
Chart Types	Bar	Compares data elements by value or time.
	Bubble	Plots the relationships between different sets of data like an XY chart, but includes a third variable whose value is shown by the size of the bubble.
	Column	Compares data elements over a period of time.
	Line	Shows trends in data over equal intervals of time.
	Pie	Shows the proportion of each individual element when compared to the total.
	Doughnut	Shows the proportion of each individual element when compared to the total; differs from pie chart in that you can display more than one data series.
	Radar	Shows each category as an axis or spoke from the center point, with lines connecting values in the same series.
	Stock	A high-low-close chart shows value ranges with a finite value, typically used for quoting stocks.
	Surface	Shows various combinations between two sets of data.
	XY (Scatter plot)	Plots the relationships between different sets of data, usually for scientific numerical analysis.

In the next section, you will create, print, and save a chart as a separate chart sheet in a workbook. Later, you will learn how to embed a chart on a worksheet and then print it with the worksheet data.

CREATING A CHART

You create a chart by selecting a range of cells to plot and issuing a menu command or by clicking the Chart Wizard button ( ). How does Excel know how to plot the information? What values does it place on the horizontal or **X-axis**? What values does it place on the vertical or **Y-axis**? Excel's decision process is examined in this section, along with the steps for creating a chart as a separate sheet in a workbook.

CHARTING A SINGLE RANGE

When you select a cell range to plot, Excel examines the shape of the highlighted area to determine which cells contain data and which cells contain headings or labels. If Excel finds text or dates in the left-hand column or in the top row, it then uses this information for the category and data labels. In other words, you should include the column headings and row labels when selecting a cell range so that Excel can automatically generate the labels for the X-axis and the legend.

In determining which information appears where, Excel counts the rows and columns in the selected range and plots the smaller dimension as the **data series** on the Y-axis. Excel always creates a chart based on the assumption that you want fewer data series than points along the X-axis. However, you can change this initial or default assumption in one of the dialog boxes displayed by the Chart Wizard.

Let's demonstrate using the Chart Wizard.

Perform the following steps . . .

1. Make sure that you've loaded Excel and know the storage location of your Advantage Files and your Data Files.

2. On the blank workbook that appears in the document window, create the worksheet appearing in Figure 5.5. Format cell A1 and then the table using the Table, AutoFormat command and Colorful 2 option. Then, change the column widths to 9.00 characters. When finished, save the workbook as "Employee" to your Data Files location.

FIGURE 5.5

"EMPLOYEE" WORKBOOK

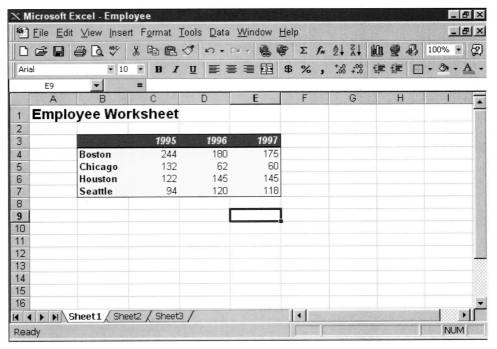

3. SELECT: cell range from B3 to E7
   Notice that there are more cities (4) than years (3) in this selection. There-fore, Excel will place the cities on the horizontal or X-axis and will plot the years on the vertical or Y-axis.

4. To plot the selected range as a new chart sheet in the workbook:
   CHOOSE: Insert, Chart
   The Chart Wizard displays the first dialog box in a series of four, as shown in Figure 5.6.

5. In the first dialog box, you select the type of chart that you want displayed from either the *Standard Types* tab or the *Custom Types* tab. Notice that the default type is a Column chart and that the first sub-type is selected. To see a sample of how the worksheet data will appear using this chart type:
   CLICK: "Press and hold to view sample" command button and hold it down

6. The *Chart sub-type* area is temporarily replaced by a *Sample* area for viewing a chart with your data. Release the mouse button to stop viewing the sample chart.

7. With the Column option selected in the *Chart type* list box:
   SELECT: "Clustered column with a 3-D visual effect" sub-type
   (*Note*: A description of the selected option appears below the list when you click on a chart sub-type.)

8. To continue to the next step:
   CLICK: Next >
   The Chart Wizard displays the second dialog box.

9. In Step 2 of 4, you select or modify the data range (Figure 5.7). You can also specify the desired data elements to display (on the *Series* tab) and the appropriate column and row orientation. The preview area helps you make the right decision. To accept the defaults and proceed:
   CLICK: Next >

FIGURE 5.7

CHART WIZARD:
STEP 2 OF 4 - CHART
SOURCE DATA

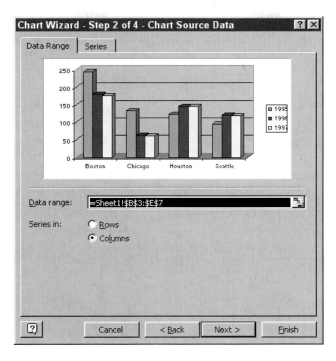

10. The Step 3 of 4 dialog box appears with a variety of formatting options, including tabs for adding and adjusting *Titles, Axes, Gridlines, Legend, Data Labels*, and *Data Table*. To add a title to this chart:
    CLICK: *Titles* tab

11. Position the I-beam mouse pointer in the *Chart title* text box and then click once to position the cursor.

12. TYPE: `Employee Levels`
    After waiting a few moments, you will notice that the title appears in the sample preview area. Your worksheet should now appear similar to Figure 5.8.

FIGURE 5.8

CHART WIZARD:
STEP 3 OF 4 - CHART
OPTIONS

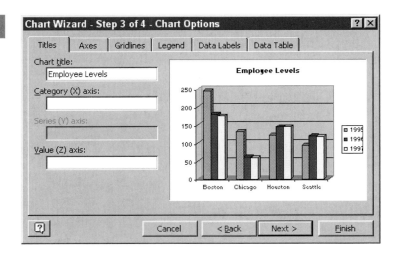

13. Since you will place this chart on a separate sheet in the workbook, let's include the table of worksheet numbers near the bottom of the chart. Do the following:
CLICK: *Data Table* tab
SELECT: *Show data table* check box so that a "✓" appears

14. You may notice that the sample preview looks crowded. Since we are displaying the table of numbers, let's delete the legend:
CLICK: *Legend* tab
SELECT: *Show legend* check box so that no "✓" appears

15. To proceed to the next step:
CLICK: Next >
The last dialog box appears (Figure 5.9).

FIGURE 5.9

CHART WIZARD:
STEP 4 OF 4 - CHART
LOCATION

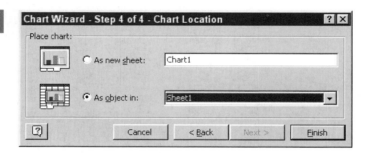

16. In the Chart Location dialog box, you specify where you want Excel to create and store the new chart. Do the following:
SELECT: *As new sheet* option button
TYPE: Levels Chart as the sheet tab's name
CLICK: Finish
The chart is displayed in a new sheet, called Levels Chart, in the same workbook file as the selected data.

17. To ensure that you are viewing all of the chart:
CLICK: down arrow beside the Zoom (100% ▾) drop-down list box
CLICK: Selection option
(*Note:* Your zoom factor may appear differently than the icon shown above.)

18. Ensure that the Chart toolbar appears docked below the Formatting toolbar. If not, drag it into place using the mouse.

19. Let's demonstrate the link between the worksheet data and the chart. First, take note of Seattle's 1995 bar in the chart. Then, do the following:
CLICK: Sheet1 sheet tab
CLICK: cell C7
TYPE: 300
PRESS: ENTER

20. To review the chart:
CLICK: Levels Chart sheet tab
Notice that the change in the worksheet data is immediately reflected in the chart. Your chart should now appear similar to Figure 5.10.

21. Save this workbook as "Employee" to your Data Files location and then close the workbook.

FIGURE 5.10

THE EMPLOYEE
LEVELS CHART SHEET

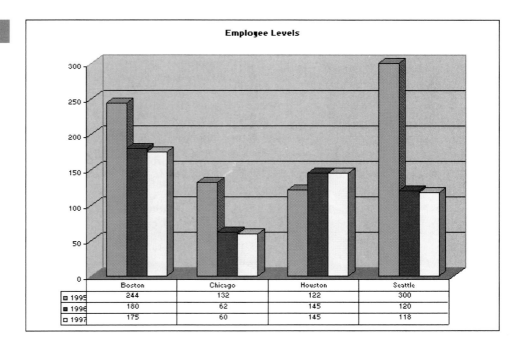

	Boston	Chicago	Houston	Seattle
☐ 1995	244	132	122	300
■ 1996	180	62	145	120
☐ 1997	175	60	145	118

QUICK REFERENCE
Creating a Chart

1. **SELECT: the cell or range of cells to plot in a chart**
2. **CHOOSE: Insert, Chart or**
   CLICK: Chart Wizard button (📊)
3. **Respond to the dialog boxes displayed by the Chart Wizard.**

CHARTING MULTIPLE RANGES

You can improve your productivity in Excel by reducing unnecessary keystrokes and commands. One method for reducing keystrokes is to select multiple cell ranges prior to formatting, deleting, or charting worksheet information. This allows you to place information anywhere in a workbook and still select it for charting. Because most worksheets are not as structurally perfect as the example in the last section, you must learn how to take advantage of this flexibility.

Perform the following steps . . .

1. Open the "XYZDept1" workbook located in your Advantage Files location.

2. To practice selecting multiple cell ranges, let's format the GROSS RECEIPTS line, TOTAL EXPENSES line, and NET INCOME line to display a currency format. Do the following:
   SELECT: cell range from B5 to E5

3. To select the range of cells from B13 to E13:
   PRESS: CTRL and hold it down
   CLICK: cell B13 and hold down the mouse button
   DRAG: mouse pointer from B13 to E13
   Notice that the original cell selection of B5 to E5 remains highlighted.

4. Release the mouse button and the CTRL key.

5. To select the range of cells from B15 to E15:
   PRESS: CTRL and hold down
   CLICK: cell B15 and hold down the mouse button
   DRAG: mouse pointer from B15 to E15

6. Release the mouse button and the CTRL key.

7. CLICK: Currency Style button ($)
   Each of the highlighted cells is formatted to the accounting format.

8. Now, we'll select some ranges for charting. To highlight the cell range for the horizontal or X-axis:
   SELECT: cell range from A3 to D3
   (*Note*: Column E is not included because it is a summed value and we want to compare the months only.)

9. When selecting the data ranges to plot, you must ensure that they are the same shape (for example, same number of rows and columns) so that they will contain the same number of items:
   PRESS: CTRL and hold it down
   SELECT: cell range from A5 to D5
   SELECT: cell range from A13 to D13

10. Release the CTRL key.
    At this point, there should be three cell ranges selected on the worksheet as shown in Figure 5.11.

FIGURE 5.11

SELECTING MULTIPLE
RANGES TO CHART

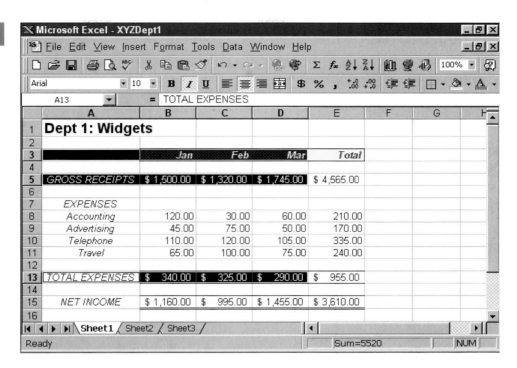

11. To produce a quick chart using the selected cell ranges:
CLICK: Chart Wizard button ( )

12. When the first Chart Wizard dialog box appears:
CLICK: Next > three times to move to Step 4 of 4

13. To complete the Chart Wizard:
SELECT: *As new sheet* option button
CLICK: Finish
A new chart sheet appears in the workbook. Notice that the Y-axis is formatted with dollar signs because of your earlier formatting of the GROSS RECEIPTS and TOTAL EXPENSES lines.

14. Let's rename the chart sheet's tab:
DOUBLE-CLICK: Chart1 tab
TYPE: Widgets
PRESS: ENTER

15. Save the workbook as "XYZ Chart" to your Data Files location.

The next section explains some general features of charts. Do not close the chart or workbook as they are referred to in the following sections.

WORKING WITH CHARTS

When the chart sheet is active, Excel modifies your work area slightly. In addition to the appearance of the Chart toolbar, you will find additional menu commands specific to formatting and manipulating charts. Because chart sheets are quite different from worksheets, you may find that it takes some time to adjust. For example, you no longer have the familiar rows and columns to guide your entry of information. Before learning how to format and enhance charts in the next sections, take a few moments to study the parts of a chart labeled in Figure 5.12 and described in Table 5.2.

FIGURE 5.12

PARTS OF A CHART

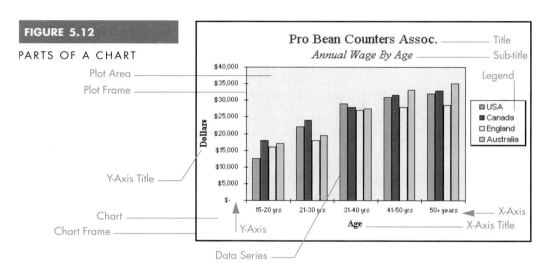

TABLE 5.2	*Component*	*Description*
Parts of a Chart Window	Chart and Chart Frame	The area inside a chart, including the **plot area,** titles, axes, legend, and other objects.
	Plot Area and Plot Frame	The area for plotting values from the worksheet. The plot area contains the axes and data series.
	Axes (X and Y) and Axes Titles	Most charts have a horizontal category axis (X) and a vertical value axis (Y) for plotting values.
	Data Marker	A single dot, bar, or symbol that represents one number from the worksheet.
	Data Series	A series of related values from the worksheet. A data series consists of related data markers.
	Legend	A key for deciphering the different data series appearing in the plot area.

SELECTING A CHART TYPE

By default, Excel selects a two-dimensional column chart for plotting your worksheet information. However, there are many different chart types and formats to choose from in the gallery, as summarized in Table 5.1. This section shows you how to access these different chart formats.

Perform the following steps ...

1. First, ensure that the chart sheet is the active sheet:
   CLICK: Widgets sheet tab

2. To select a different chart type:
   CHOOSE: Chart, Chart Type
   Notice that the first four menu items on the Chart menu correspond to the dialog boxes in the Chart Wizard.

3. In the Chart Type dialog box, you select a primary chart type and then a sub-type. You can also select from a list of custom types:
   SELECT: Cylinder in the *Chart type* list box
   SELECT: "Bar with a cylindrical shape" as the *Chart sub-type*
   CLICK: "Press and hold to view sample" command button
   The dialog box should appear similar to Figure 5.13.

FIGURE 5.13

CHART TYPE
DIALOG BOX

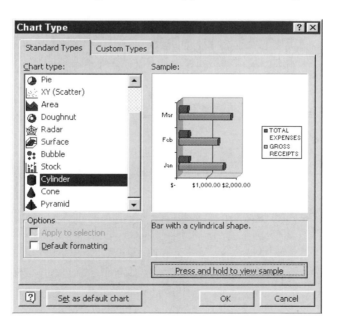

4.   Release the mouse button to stop viewing the sample.

5.   On your own, select the other chart types and then preview their sub-types using the "Press and hold to view sample" command button.

6.   To proceed:
SELECT: Column in the *Chart type* list box
SELECT: "Clustered column with a 3-D visual effect" sub-type
PRESS: **ENTER** or CLICK: OK

7.   Use the Chart Objects (Chart Area) drop-down list box on the Chart tool-bar to select individual chart objects. To demonstrate:
CLICK: down arrow adjacent to the Chart Objects (Chart Area) box
SELECT: Chart Area
Notice that small black selection boxes appear around the chart area.

8.   To ensure that you are viewing the maximum area of the chart:
CLICK: down arrow beside the Zoom (100%) drop-down list box
CLICK: Selection option
This command tells Excel to display all of the selected object, in this case the Chart Area, in the document area. Your screen should now appear similar to Figure 5.14.

9.   Save the workbook as "XYZ Chart" to your Data Files location.

FIGURE 5.14

WIDGETS CHART SHEET

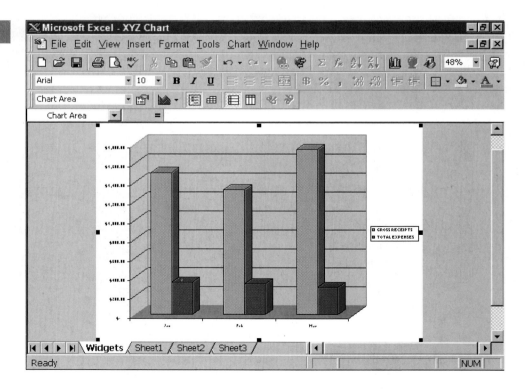

QUICK REFERENCE
Selecting a Chart
Type

1. **CHOOSE: Chart, Chart Type**
2. **In the dialog box, select the chart type and sub-type.**
3. **CLICK: "Press and hold to view sample" command button and hold it down to preview the format**
4. **Release the mouse button to proceed.**
5. **PRESS: ENTER or CLICK: OK**

CUSTOMIZING AND FORMATTING A CHART

Customizing a chart involves adding titles, legends, annotations, and arrows which emphasize certain aspects of the chart and improve its overall readability. Formatting a chart refers to setting the display options for each element of a chart. For example, if you are working on a color system, Excel differentiates each data series in a chart by assigning them different colors. When you print the chart to a non-color printer, however, the various colors appear as black or white. Therefore, you need to format the columns using patterns or shades of gray to differentiate the series. This section explores several methods for enhancing your chart.

To customize or format a chart, you must first select the chart object that you want to format. As demonstrated in the previous section, you can select objects using the Chart Objects (Chart Area ▼) drop-down list box on the Chart toolbar. You can also select an object by clicking on it using the mouse. The following sections demonstrate how to add titles, legends, free-form text, arrows, fonts, patterns, and backgrounds to your chart.

ATTACHING TITLES

Titles are used to state the purpose of the chart and to explain the scales used for the axes. After adding titles, you can format the text using a variety of fonts, styles, and shading. You will now add a title to the Widgets graph.

Perform the following steps . . .

1. Ensure that the chart sheet is active.

2. To add titles to the chart:
    CHOOSE: Chart, Chart Options
    CLICK: *Titles* tab

3. In the Chart Options dialog box:
    SELECT: *Chart title* text box
    TYPE: Receipts vs. Expenses
    SELECT: *Category (X) axis* text box
    TYPE: Months
    SELECT: *Value (Z) axis* text box
    TYPE: Dollars
    Your dialog box should now appear similar to Figure 5.15.

FIGURE 5.15

CHART OPTIONS
DIALOG BOX: *TITLES*
TAB

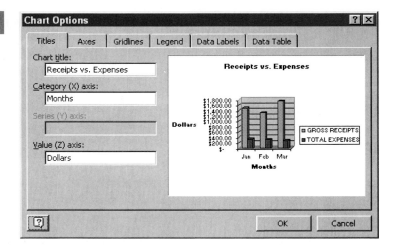

4. To accept the modifications:
PRESS: (ENTER) or CLICK: OK

5. Let's format the "Dollars" entry for the Value Axis title:
CLICK: Value Axis title once
Notice that it is surrounded by small black selection boxes.

6. To display the formatting options for this object:
CLICK: Format Object button (🗗) in the Chart toolbar
(*Note*: The name of the Format Object button changes according to the chart object that is selected. For example, the ToolTip will now read "Format Axis Title.")

7. To change the alignment or orientation of the title:
CLICK: *Alignment* tab
CLICK: the leftmost "Text" box in the *Orientation* group (displaying text running down a single column)
PRESS: (ENTER) or CLICK: OK

QUICK REFERENCE
Attaching Titles

1. CHOOSE: Chart, Chart Options

2. CLICK: *Titles* tab

3. Type the desired titles into the *Chart title, Value (X) axis,* and *Category (Z) axis* text boxes.

4. PRESS: (ENTER) or CLICK: OK

MODIFYING THE CHART LEGEND

A legend provides a key for the data series plotted in the chart. If you didn't specify a legend in the Chart Wizard dialog box, you can add one later using the Chart, Chart Options command. Although Excel places the legend at the right-hand side of the chart window by default, you can easily move the legend by dragging it using the mouse.

Perform the following steps . . .

1. To modify the legend:
CHOOSE: Chart, Chart Options
CLICK: *Legend* tab

2. To change the legend's location on the chart sheet:
SELECT: *Top* option button
Your screen should now appear similar to Figure 5.16.

FIGURE 5.16

CHANGING THE LEGEND PLACEMENT

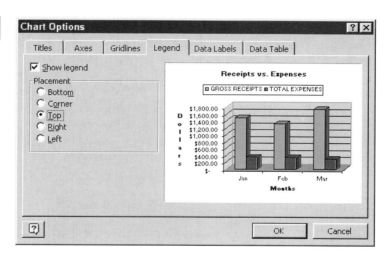

3. To accept the modifications:
PRESS: (ENTER) or CLICK: OK

4. To move the legend to the bottom right-hand corner of the sheet, position the mouse pointer on the legend:
CLICK: legend once and hold down the left mouse button
DRAG: legend to the bottom right-hand corner

5. Release the mouse button. Notice that this method for moving the legend does not result in the rest of the chart objects being resized.

6. Let's finalize the legend's position on the chart sheet using a shortcut pop-up menu:
RIGHT-CLICK: anywhere on the legend
CHOOSE: Format Legend
CLICK: *Placement* tab
SELECT: *Right* option button
PRESS: (ENTER) or CLICK: OK

ENTERING FREE-FORM TEXT

Using a text box, you can place free-form text anywhere in the chart area. You use free-form text to emphasize or draw attention to important areas of a chart or to add subsidiary information, such as copyright notices. Once text is entered, you can easily apply fonts and styles.

Perform the following steps . . .

1. For the next two sections, we access buttons on the Drawing toolbar. To display the Drawing toolbar:
   RIGHT-CLICK: on any toolbar
   CHOOSE: Drawing
   The Drawing toolbar should now appear on your screen. (*Note:* For a complete listing of the Excel toolbars and their buttons, refer to the Appendix at the end of this guide.)

2. If the Drawing toolbar appears in its own window, floating above the chart sheet:
   DRAG: Drawing toolbar downward to dock it near the Status bar

3. To provide a better view of your chart:
   CLICK: down arrow beside the Chart Objects (Chart Area ▼) box
   SELECT: Chart Area
   CLICK: down arrow beside the Zoom (100% ▼) box
   SELECT: 100%

4. Scroll the window to view the upper-right quadrant of the chart.

5. To enter free-form text, do the following:
   CLICK: Text Box button (▣) on the Drawing toolbar

6. Move the cross-hair mouse pointer into the chart area and drag a rectangle that is similar to the screen graphic in Figure 5.17.

FIGURE 5.17

CREATING A TEXT BOX

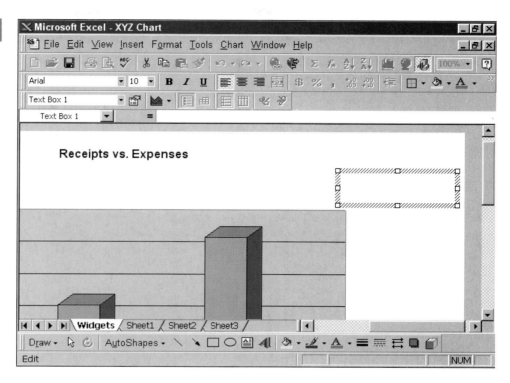

7. When you release the mouse button, you will notice a flashing insertion point. To enter the free-form text:
TYPE: After Training

8. To remove the insertion point and deselect the text box:
CLICK: on the white chart area surrounding the text box

USING ARROWS FOR EMPHASIS

Besides free-form text, you can use other types of objects to direct the reader's attention. Arrows are the most common means for focusing a viewer on certain locations in your chart. Let's add an arrow for emphasis.

Perform the following steps . . .

1. To add an arrow to the chart:
   CLICK: Arrow button ( ) on the Drawing toolbar

2. Position the cross-hair mouse pointer below and to the left of the letter A in the word "After."

3. DRAG: the cross-hair mouse pointer toward the March GROSS RECEIPTS column (see below)

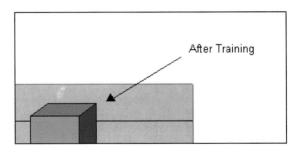

After Training

4. Release the mouse button. Your text box and arrow should appear similar to the above example.

5. To remove the selection boxes:
   CLICK: on the white chart area surrounding the arrow

6. Let's return to a full chart view:
   RIGHT-CLICK: Drawing toolbar
   CHOOSE: Drawing to remove the toolbar from view
   CLICK: down arrow beside the Zoom (100% ▼) box
   SELECT: Selection

QUICK REFERENCE
Adding an Arrow

1. **CLICK: Arrow button ( ) on the Drawing toolbar**
2. **DRAG: cross-hair mouse pointer in the chart sheet**

CHOOSING FONTS AND TEXTURES

Formatting a chart involves changing its background color and texture, choosing fonts for headings and other text, and selecting patterns for data series. Although most commands are available in the Menu bar, you will find that using the Format Object button (▣) and shortcut pop-up menus are much easier and more convenient.

Perform the following steps . . .

1. Position the mouse pointer over the chart title and click the right mouse button to display its pop-up menu.

2. To enhance the text:
   CHOOSE: Format Chart Title

3. Let's change the font and style for the title:
   CLICK: *Font* tab
   SELECT: Bold Italic from the *Font style* list box
   SELECT: 24 from the *Size* list box
   PRESS: **ENTER** or CLICK: OK

4. To format the free-form text in the text box, move the I-beam mouse pointer over the word "After" and then do the following:
   DOUBLE-CLICK: the word "After" continuing to hold down the mouse button as you drag the pointer to highlight "Training" as well

5. CLICK: Format Object button (▣)
   SELECT: Italic from the *Font style* list box
   SELECT: 14 from the *Size* list box
   PRESS: **ENTER** or CLICK: OK

6. To format the Category axis:
   CLICK: down arrow beside the Chart Objects (Chart Area ▾) box
   SELECT: Category Axis
   CLICK: Format Object button (▣)
   CLICK: *Font* tab
   SELECT: 14 from the *Size* list box

7. To format the Category axis title:
   CLICK: down arrow beside the Chart Objects (Chart Area ▾) box
   SELECT: Category Axis Title
   CLICK: Font Size (10 ▾) box on the Formatting toolbar
   SELECT: 14

8. On your own, format the Value Axis and its Title using the same options as chosen in Steps 6 and 7.

9. To apply a background color for the legend box:
RIGHT-CLICK: on the legend
CHOOSE: Format Legend
CLICK: *Patterns* tab
SELECT: *Shadow* check box
SELECT: a light yellow color in the *Area* group

10. To change the font and point size:
CLICK: *Font* tab
SELECT: Regular in the *Font style* list box
SELECT: 12 in the *Size* list box
PRESS: (ENTER) or CLICK: OK

11. To format the plot area background:
CLICK: down arrow beside the Chart Objects ([Chart Area ▼]) box
SELECT: Walls
CLICK: Format Object button (🖼)
CLICK: Fill Effects command button
CLICK: *Texture* tab
SELECT: a marble texture
CLICK: OK command button twice to save your choices

12. Save the workbook as "XYZ Chart" to your Data Files location. Your chart is now ready for printing and should look similar to Figure 5.18.

FIGURE 5.18

A FORMATTED AND
CUSTOMIZED CHART

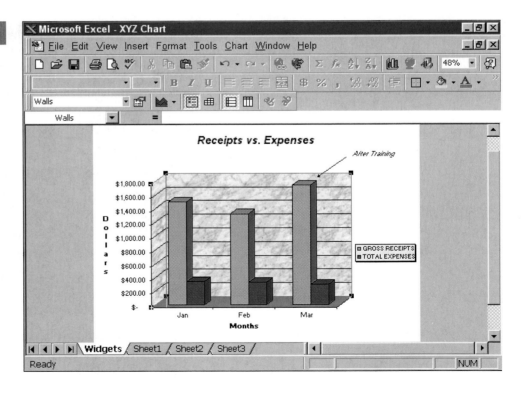

PRINTING A CHART

When a chart is created as a separate chart sheet, you print it directly from the sheet using the File, Print command. For the most part, the general print options are identical to printing a worksheet. However, there is one additional set of layout options for scaling the chart to fit on a page. Like a worksheet, remember to preview your charts prior to printing.

Perform the following steps to print the Widgets chart.

Perform the following steps . . .

1. Ensure that the chart sheet is active.

2. To adjust the page layout options:
   CHOOSE: File, Page Setup
   CLICK: *Chart* tab
   The Page Setup dialog box appears.

3. In this dialog box, you select the appropriate size option for printing the chart. The *Scale to fit page* option prints the chart using the current height to width ratio, and the *Use full page* option adjusts the ratio to maximize the print area. Try the following option on your printer:
   SELECT: *Scale to fit page* option button
   CLICK: Print Preview command button
   Your screen should now appear similar to Figure 5.19.

PRINT PREVIEWING THE
WIDGETS CHART SHEET

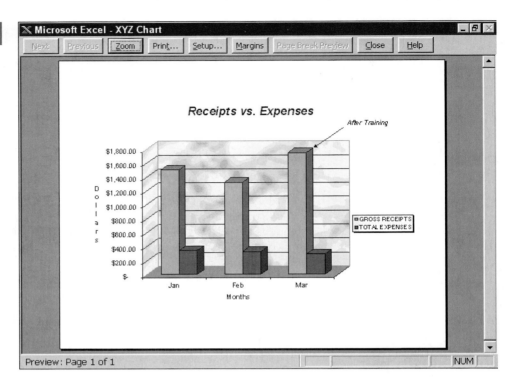

4. When finished viewing the chart, send it to the printer:
CLICK: Print command button (at the top of the window)
PRESS: (**ENTER**) or CLICK: OK

5. Save the workbook as "XYZ Chart" to your Data Files location, replacing
the existing version.

6. Close the workbook.

QUICK REFERENCE
Printing a Chart

1. **Ensure that the chart sheet is active.**
2. **CHOOSE: File, Page Setup**
3. **CLICK: *Chart* tab**
4. **SELECT: sizing options for printing the chart**
5. **CLICK: Print Preview command button to view the chart**
6. **CLICK: Print command button**
7. **PRESS: (ENTER) or CLICK: OK**

EMBEDDING A CHART

This section explains how to embed a chart into a worksheet. An embedded chart is placed over—not entered into—a cell range. All of the customizing and formatting for embedded charts is the same as for chart sheets. However, the method for printing the chart differs slightly from the previous section.

To create an embedded chart, you select the *As object in* option button during the fourth step of the Chart Wizard and then specify a particular destination worksheet. The worksheet is displayed with the embedded chart appearing in the middle of the worksheet window. You can then drag the chart to where you want it positioned. To remove an embedded chart, you select the chart by clicking on it and then press (DELETE). To print worksheet information along with the chart, you select a range that covers both areas of the worksheet and chart and then set the print area. To edit an embedded chart, you simply click the chart to make it active.

Let's practice embedding a chart in a worksheet.

Perform the following steps . . .

1. Open the "Cruises" workbook located in your Advantage Files location.

2. SELECT: cell range from A2 to D5

3. To use the Chart Wizard:
   CLICK: Chart Wizard button (📊)

4. In the first step of the Chart Wizard dialog box:
   SELECT: Column from the *Chart type* list box
   SELECT: "Stacked Column" (two dimensional) sub-type
   CLICK: Next >

5. Since the cell range was selected prior to launching the Chart Wizard, let's bypass Step 2 of 4:
   CLICK: Next >

6. In Step 3 of 4 of the Chart Wizard:
   CLICK: *Titles* tab
   SELECT: *Chart title* text box
   TYPE: Demographics
   SELECT: *Value (Y) axis* text box
   TYPE: Passengers
   CLICK: Next >

7. You'll now accept the default options for placing the chart as an object in Sheet1. Do the following:
   CLICK: Finish
   The embedded chart appears in the middle of the worksheet window. Notice that the Chart toolbar also appears.

8. To move the chart below the worksheet information, first select the chart by clicking in the middle of it and then drag it to a new location:
CLICK: embedded chart once and hold down the mouse button
DRAG: chart to line up the top left-hand corner with cell A7

9. To size the chart, position the mouse pointer over one of the boxes on the embedded chart's borders. The mouse pointer should change to a black double-headed arrow. Now drag the bottom right-hand corner's sizing box to stretch the chart down to cell F20. (*Note*: If you wanted to retain a constant height to width ratio, you would hold down the **SHIFT** key as you drag the mouse. If you wanted to align the chart with worksheet cells, you would hold down the **ALT** key.)

Your screen should appear similar to Figure 5.20 when completed.

FIGURE 5.20

MANIPULATING AN
EMBEDDED CHART

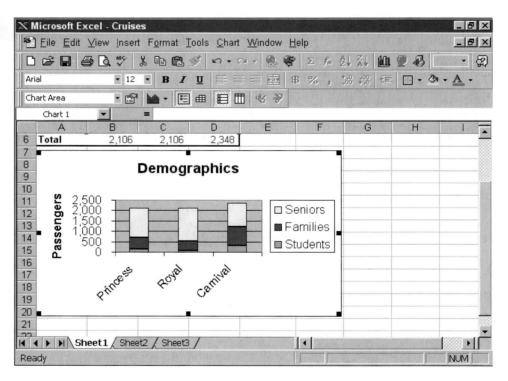

10. To return the focus to the worksheet:
CLICK: any visible worksheet cell
Notice that the selection boxes around the embedded chart and the Chart toolbar both disappear.

11. To edit or format the chart:
CLICK: on any part of the embedded chart once
Notice that it is now surrounded by the selection boxes and that the Chart toolbar reappears. All of the commands and procedures that you learned in previous sections (for example, adding titles, free-form text, and arrows) are available for use in formatting the embedded chart.

12. To print the worksheet along with the embedded chart:
SELECT: the entire cell range from A1 to the bottom right-hand corner of the embedded chart, F20
CHOOSE: File, Print Area, Set Print Area
CLICK: Print Preview command button

13. When you are satisfied with the preview:
CLICK: Print command button
PRESS: (ENTER) or CLICK: OK

14. Save the workbook as "Cruise Demographics" to your Data Files location.

15. Close the workbook.

<table>
<tr><td>QUICK REFERENCE
Creating an
Embedded Chart</td><td>

1. SELECT: the cell or range of cells to plot in a chart

2. CLICK: Chart Wizard button (📖)

3. Respond to the dialog boxes in the Chart Wizard. For Step 4 of 4, select the *As an object* option button and then specify a worksheet.
</td></tr>
</table>

USING MICROSOFT DATA MAP

Using a specialty charting tool called **Microsoft Data Map,** you can create a map to analyze your worksheet information geographically. For example, you could plot the number of UFO sightings by state or by country, assuming that you had a worksheet containing this information. Data Map also enables you to quickly analyze trends relative to a region's demographic breakdown. Existing demographic information is provided by Excel and is accessible from a special workbook called "Mapstats" located in the Datamap folder.

CREATING A DATA MAP

To use Data Map with Excel, you need to organize your worksheet data into columns. One column must contain geographic data such as the names of states or countries. This column determines the type of map that will be displayed (for example, a map of the United States, Canada, or the world.) To map your worksheet information, select the cell range that includes the geographic data and then click the Map button (🌐) on the Standard toolbar. You then drag the cross-hair mouse pointer on the worksheet to set the size and location of the map. When you release the mouse button, the selected cell range is analyzed and a map is displayed.

You will now practice creating a data map.

Perform the following steps . . .

1. Open the "Boarding" workbook, stored in your Advantage Files location. This worksheet provides a fictitious marketing report for a U.S. snowboarding manufacturer that wants to sell its products in the Canadian market.

2. To create a map showing the relative amount of money spent on snowboarding by each province, do the following:
   SELECT: cell range from A4 to B16
   Notice that you are including the column headings in the selection and that column A contains geographical information.

3. CLICK: Map button (🌐)
   (*Note*: If you do not see the Map button (🌐) on the Standard toolbar, you may not have this feature installed on your computer. If this is the case, you must re-install Microsoft Excel and select the Data Map utility before performing the steps in the remainder of this session.)

4. To place the map to the right of the worksheet information, first move the cross-hair mouse pointer to the middle of cell C4 and then click the left mouse button once. This method for embedding a map provides a "best-fit" size for the map.

5. If a dialog box appears with the title Multiple Maps Available, you must do the following:
   SELECT: Canada
   CLICK: OK command button
   The map will now appear embedded in the worksheet.

6. Scroll the document window so that you can view the entire map and move the Microsoft Map Control dialog box by dragging its Title bar. Notice that the map shows provinces with higher sales using a darker shade of gray. Your screen should now appear similar to Figure 5.21.

FIGURE 5.21

CREATING A MAP
FROM WORKSHEET
INFORMATION

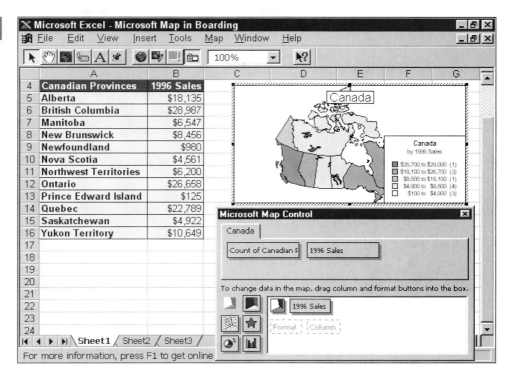

If the selected cell range contains ambiguous data or misspellings of geographic regions (states, provinces, or countries), a dialog box appears asking you for assistance. For the proper spellings and abbreviations of geographic regions, review the "Mapstats" workbook located in the "Program Files\Common Files\Microsoft Shared\Datamap\Data" folder. If you cannot locate the "Mapstats" workbook, choose the START, Find, Files or Folders command and perform a search of your hard disk.

QUICK REFERENCE	1. **Create a worksheet with at least one column containing geographic data such as names or abbreviations of states, provinces, and countries.**
Embedding a Data Map on a Worksheet	2. **Select the cell range to include in the data map.**
	3. **CLICK: Map button ( ) on the Standard toolbar**
	4. **CLICK: cell where you want to place the top-left corner of the map**

FORMATTING A DATA MAP

After embedding a data map on your worksheet, you can customize its appearance using the menu, toolbar, and Microsoft Map Control dialog box (shown in Figure 5.22). For example, you can color-code the geographic regions and change the way data is displayed on the map by simply dragging and double-clicking buttons in the Microsoft Map Control dialog box. However, be careful when dragging buttons in the work area. When you drag a new button onto an empty area, you are adding new formatting. When you drag a new button on top of an existing button, you are replacing the current formatting. In this section, you practice using some of the tools available for formatting a data map.

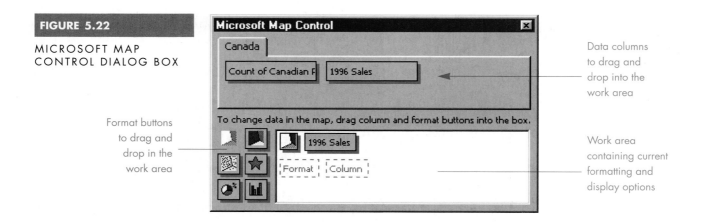

**Perform
the
following
steps . . .**

1. Ensure that the data map appears with a hatched border, indicating that it is active and ready for formatting. If no border appears, double-click the data map object. If the data map appears with a hatched border but the Microsoft Map Control dialog box shown in Figure 5.22 does not appear, do the following:
   CLICK: Show/Hide Microsoft Map Control button (▥) on the toolbar

2. To color-code the map of Canada:
   DRAG: Category Shading button (▨) over the existing format button in the work area
   (*Note*: You will know that you have positioned the mouse correctly when the row with the 1996 Sales button appears highlighted.)

3. Release the mouse button. Notice that the shades of gray are replaced by a color-coded map.

4. DRAG: Graduated Symbol button (★) over the existing format button in the work area

5. Release the mouse button. Now the map of Canada shows dots of varying sizes for each province, with each dot representing the relative dollar volume of 1996 Sales.

6. DRAG: Value Shading button (▨) over the existing format button in the work area

7. Release the mouse button to display the default map format.

8. To hide the Microsoft Map Control dialog box:
   CLICK: Show/Hide Microsoft Map Control button (▥) in the toolbar

9. To change the gray-scale shading in the map:
   CHOOSE: Map, Value Shading Options from the menu
   CLICK: *Value Shading Options* tab
   The dialog box in Figure 5.23 appears.

FIGURE 5.23

FORMAT PROPERTIES
DIALOG BOX

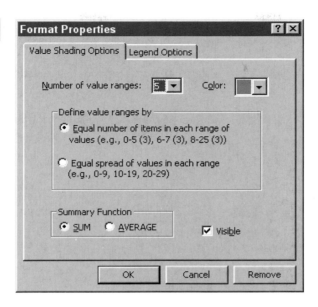

10. SELECT: 2 in the *Number of value ranges* drop-down list box
    PRESS: **ENTER** or CLICK: OK
    Notice that the map now displays the provinces using only two shading
    groups.

11. To display four shading categories:
    CHOOSE: Map, Value Shading Options
    SELECT: 4 in the *Number of value ranges* drop-down list box
    PRESS: **ENTER** or CLICK: OK

12. Let's display some additional features:
    RIGHT-CLICK: on any province in the map
    CHOOSE: Features from the shortcut menu

13. In the Map Features dialog box that appears:
    SELECT: *Canada Major Cities* check box in the *Visible* area
    PRESS: **ENTER** or CLICK: OK
    Now the map displays the locations of Canada's major cities (for example,
    Vancouver, Edmonton, Calgary, Toronto, and Montreal).

14. Position the mouse pointer over the black square appearing on the border in
    the bottom right-hand corner of the embedded map. To resize the map object,
    drag the border, with the mouse pointer on this black square, to cell G16.

15. To move the map to the left side, do the following:
CLICK: Grabber button () in the toolbar
CLICK: on any province in the map and hold down the mouse button
DRAG: the map to appear flush against the left and bottom borders

16. Release the mouse button.

17. DRAG: the legend to the top right-hand corner
DRAG: the title "CANADA" to the left slightly (if required)
Ensure that you can see the entire map of Canada and the title.

18. To finish editing the map and return to the worksheet:
CLICK: any cell in the worksheet
You are now ready to print the worksheet and data map.

QUICK REFERENCE
Customizing a Data Map

- **Use the Microsoft Map Control dialog box to change the way data is displayed in the map.**
- **CHOOSE: Map, Value Shading Options to change the number of categories displayed in the map**
- **CHOOSE: Features from the map shortcut menu to add landmarks to the data map such as cities, highways, and lakes**

PRINTING A DATA MAP

You print a data map as you would print any other embedded chart on your worksheet.

Perform the following steps . . .

1. To print the worksheet with the data map:
SELECT: the entire cell range from A1 to the bottom right-hand corner of the embedded map, approximately cell H17
CHOOSE: File, Print Area, Set Print Area

2. Let's print this worksheet with a landscape orientation:
CHOOSE: File, Page Setup
CLICK: *Page* tab
SELECT: *Landscape* option button in the *Orientation* group
CLICK: Print Preview command button
Your screen should now appear similar to Figure 5.24.

FIGURE 5.24

PREVIEWING THE
COMPLETED DATA
MAP

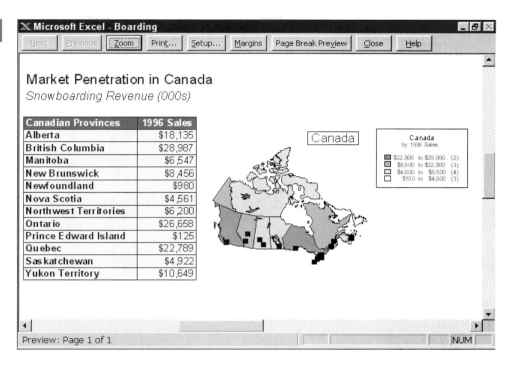

3. To send the worksheet to the printer:
   CLICK: Print command button (at the top of the window)

4. When the Print dialog box appears:
   PRESS: (ENTER) or CLICK: OK
   The worksheet and data map are sent to the printer.

5. Move to cell A1 to remove the highlighting.

6. Save the workbook as "Snowboarding" to your Data Files location.

7. Close the workbook and then exit Excel.

QUICK REFERENCE
Printing a Data Map
with Worksheet Information

1. Select the cell range containing the worksheet information and the embedded data map.

2. CHOOSE: File, Print Area, Set Print Area

3. CHOOSE: File, Print

4. PRESS: (ENTER) or CLICK: OK

SUMMARY

This session discussed the benefits of using graphics to present worksheet information. Besides introducing several types of business graphics, the basic principles of graphing, including simplicity, unity, emphasis, and balance, were explained. In Excel, there are two methods for creating charts from worksheet information. A chart can be created, printed, and saved as a separate sheet in a workbook or embedded into an existing worksheet. In this session, you practiced both methods for creating a chart.

Excel provides several customizing and formatting options for enhancing a chart, including fonts, patterns, textures, titles, legends, and annotations. With over 90 different charting formats, it is guaranteed you will find the perfect tool to help you make that winning presentation! Table 5.3 summarizes the commands introduced in this session.

TABLE 5.3 Command Summary	*Command*	*Description*
	Chart, Chart Options	Displays a dialog box for modifying the selected chart's titles, legend, gridlines, and data labels. Same as the third step in the Chart Wizard.
	Chart, Chart Type	Selects the type and format of chart to display. Same as the first step in the Chart Wizard.
	Insert, Chart	Launches the Chart Wizard for creating a chart as a separate chart sheet or as an embedded object. Same as clicking the Chart Wizard button ([📊]).
	Map, Value Shading Options	Displays a dialog box for changing the number of categories displayed on a data map.

KEY TERMS

Chart Wizard
A collection of dialog boxes that leads you through creating a chart in a workbook.

column chart
A chart that compares one data element with another data element and can show variations over a period of time.

data series
A series of values from the worksheet that are related.

embedded chart
A chart that is placed over worksheet cells and printed and saved along with the worksheet.

graphics

The pictorial representation of words and data.

legend

A key for deciphering the data series appearing in the plot area of a chart.

line chart

A chart that plots trends or shows changes over a period of time.

Microsoft Data Map

A special charting utility that enables you to create an embedded map from geographic data stored in a worksheet.

pie chart

A chart that shows the proportions of individual components compared to the whole.

plot area

The area for plotting values from the worksheet. The plot area contains the axes and data series.

X-axis

The horizontal or Category axis that shows the categories for which the chart is making comparisons.

XY charts

Charts that show how one or more data elements relate to another data element. Also called *scatter plot diagrams*.

Y-axis

The vertical or Value axis in a two-dimensional chart that shows the value or measurement unit for making comparisons among the various categories. The value axis in a three-dimensional chart is called the Z-axis.

EXERCISES

SHORT ANSWER

1. Describe the basic principles of using graphics.

2. Describe the four steps in creating a chart using the Chart Wizard.

3. List the different types of charts found in the Chart Type dialog box.

4. How do you select multiple ranges in a worksheet?

5. What are some placement options for a chart's legend?

6. Describe the process of adding free-form text to a chart.

7. Describe the process of adding an arrow to a chart.

8. How do you move an arrow once it has been placed on a chart?

9. How do you print an embedded chart without the worksheet data?

10. How must you organize a worksheet if you want to create a data map?

HANDS-ON

(*Note*: Ensure that you know the storage location of your Advantage Files and your Data Files before proceeding.)

1. The objective of this exercise is to create a worksheet and an embedded pie chart that show the breakdown of your total monthly expenses.

   a. Ensure that you have an empty workbook.

   b. Enter your name in cell A1.

   c. Create a worksheet that lists the following expense headings on separate rows within a column: RENT, FOOD, GAS, and FUN.

   d. Enter your monthly expense amounts in the column to the right of the row headings. (You may enter any values, not necessarily your own.)

   e. Select the row headings and values to produce an embedded chart.

   f. CLICK: Chart Wizard button (▣)

   g. Following the steps for each dialog box, select a 3-D pie chart that displays the names beside each pie wedge. Add a title to the chart that has the words "Monthly Expenses" on the first line. Delete the legend, if one appears.

   h. Once the chart appears on the worksheet, move it to the right of the present worksheet information and size it to cover fifteen rows by five columns.

   i. Select different textures, not just colors, for the various pie wedges.

   j. Print the worksheet and chart on the same page.

   k. Save the workbook as "My Pie Chart" to your Data Files location.

2. In this exercise, you retrieve a workbook and then create a line chart, stacked column chart, and a 3-D column chart.

   a. Close all of the open windows in the document area.

   b. Open the "Charts" workbook located on the Advantage Files diskette or in the Advantage Files folder. This worksheet is a planning tool used by XYZ Company to project sales and production. (Make sure to type your name into cell A3.)

   c. Create one line chart, in a separate chart sheet, showing the number of units sold for each product over the five-year period.

   d. Add an appropriate title to the chart.

   e. Name the sheet's tab LINE.

   f. Print the chart using the *Scale to Fit Page* option.

   g. Create one stacked column chart, in a separate chart sheet, that displays the revenue for each product over the five-year period. A stacked chart displays each product's portion of the total revenue in a single column for each year.

    h.   Add an appropriate title to the chart.

    i.   Name the sheet's tab STACK.

    j.   Print the chart using the *Use Full Page* option.

    k.   Create one 3-D column chart, in a separate chart sheet, to compare the Total Revenue versus the Total Costs over the five-year period.

    l.   Add an appropriate title to the chart.

    m. Name the sheet's tab COLUMN.

    n.   Print the chart using the *Scale to Fit Page* option.

    o.   Save the workbook as "Charting" to your Data Files location.

    p.   Close all of the open windows in the document area.

    q.   Exit Excel.

3. **On Your Own**: Charting Your Personal Budget
Open the workbook called "Your Personal Budget" that you created in Hands-On Exercise 4 in Session 3. If you did not create this workbook, do so before proceeding. On a separate sheet, create a pie chart that shows the distribution of your expense categories using the Year-to-Date column as the data series. Create a stacked column chart, also on a separate sheet, that compares your total monthly expenses. Save this workbook as "Personal Budget Charts" to your Data Files location.

4. **On Your Own**: Creating a Population Data Map
Using the "Mapstats" workbook mentioned in this session, create and then format a data map of the United States showing the population per state. Use the Graduated Symbol format. Save the new workbook as "US Data Map" to your Data Files location.

CASE PROBLEMS   **H2 UNDERSCAPING LTD.**

(*Note*: In the following case problems, assume the role of the primary characters and perform the same steps that they identify. You may want to re-read the session opening.)

1. Chip finishes his conversation with Kayla Parker at the local bank and then places the phone gently into its cradle. He glances down at the notes that he scrawled on the borders of the Canadian *Globe and Mail* newspaper. Although thinking to himself, Chip shakes his head and speaks aloud, "So, Kayla wants a financial plan after seven years of doing business." Chip isn't really *that* surprised with Kayla's request; but, perhaps, he's just a little annoyed with his longtime friend and business advisor. Kayla has been there for him since his company's inception and has helped guide him through complicated financing issues, debtor problems, and investment opportunities. But with his latest acquisition of Xeriscaping, Inc., even Kayla must watch Chip and his company's performance with a lot closer scrutiny than before.

Fortunately, Chip just completed entering his past year's results into an Excel workbook called "H2U-1996," stored with the Advantage Files. He loads the worksheet and then decides to perform some additional formatting, wanting to ensure that it looks its best for Kayla. After customizing the page setup to a landscape orientation and inserting the current date in the footer, he prints the worksheet on a single page.

Upon reviewing the printout, Chip decides to impress Kayla even further by embedding a column chart, on the same page, showing comparative sales for the sprinkler installations versus the xeriscaping projects. He adds a title and legend to the chart and then prints the entire worksheet and chart onto a single page. Finally, Chip saves the workbook as "H2 Underscaping 1996" to his Data Files location.

2. Impressed with his first printout for Kayla, Chip decides to create a new chart (on a separate sheet in the workbook) and attach it to the first page. Wanting to inform Kayla of the seasonal trend lines for his business, Chip creates a line chart showing the Total Sales, Cost of Sales, and Total Expenses for the entire year. Chip annotates the chart with an arrow and text box pointing out the high and low seasons, in addition to adding titles and a legend to the chart. When finished, Chip prints the chart to fit on a single landscape page and then saves the workbook back to his Data Files location.

3. Arriving quite early the next morning, Chip notices that the answering machine's message indicator light is flashing at the receptionist's desk. Hitting the appropriate button, Chip plays back the following message: "Hi Chip, this is Kayla, down at the bank. I received your financial analysis yesterday and just wanted to commend you on your work. This report is far better than I've seen from most accountants, let alone business owners. I don't see a problem with your seasonal business trends, but I would like you to break down your Total Expenses into a pie diagram for me. That way, I can suggest ways for you to cut your fixed costs during the low period. Thanks again for the report. Bye for now."

Chip is glad to hear that Kayla approved of his analysis and decides to tackle the expense breakdown right away. After loading the "H2 Underscaping 1996" workbook, Chip enters the following year-to-date expense information into the worksheet:

Administration	25,000
Marketing	60,000
Rent	36,000
Wages	24,000
Total Expenses	**145,000**

After looking through the available chart formats, Chip decides to create a 3-D pie chart with percentages appearing beside each wedge. He adds a title to the chart and a legend, and then prints the chart to a single landscape page. When finished, he saves the workbook back to his Data Files location.

Appendix

Microsoft Excel 97
Toolbar Summary

STANDARD

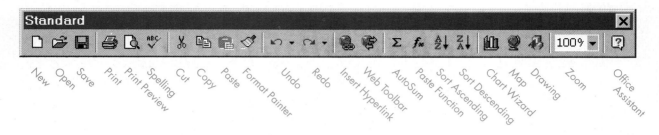

FORMATTING

CHART

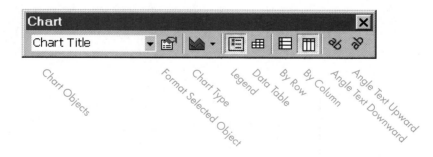

DRAWING

WEB

Index

The page numbers in boldface indicate Quick Reference procedures.

Addendum

Microsoft Excel 97 for Windows: Additional Microsoft Office User Specialist Certification Topics

SESSION OUTLINE

ABOUT THE ADVANTAGE FILES

A few sections in this appendix require that you open an Advantage File. Before proceeding, we recommend that you download these files from the Advantage Online site at *http://www.mhhe.com/cit/apps/adv*, in the Download area.

SORTING DATA

Sorting your worksheet data into a particular order is often the first step in making information out of the raw data. Not only does sorting allow you to better organize data, it makes it much easier to find information by scanning the worksheet. The general process for sorting data is to first select any cell in the column whose contents you want placed into a particular order. To sort the records into ascending order (0 to 9, A to Z), click the Sort Ascending button (⬆⬇) on the Standard toolbar. To sort the records into descending order (9 to 0, Z to A), click the Sort Descending button (⬇⬆). Regardless of the sort order chosen, blank entries in the worksheet are always placed at the bottom. You can also sort data by the contents of more than one column using the Data, Sort command.

In the following exercise, you practice sorting the worksheet data appearing in the "Checks" workbook.

Perform the following steps . . .

1. Launch Microsoft Excel 97 and ensure that there are no worksheets open in the application window. Then, open the "Checks" workbook that is stored in the Advantage Files location. This workbook contains a single worksheet for entering check numbers, dates, and amounts.

2. To sort the register from the lowest amount to the highest amount:
   SELECT: cell C8
   CLICK: Sort Ascending button (⬆⬇) on the Standard toolbar
   Notice that each column is correctly sorted, even though you selected a single cell.

3. To sort the register from the most recent date to the earliest date:
   SELECT: cell B8
   CLICK: Sort Descending button (⬇⬆)
   The list is now sorted into descending order by date.

4. To return the register to the original sort order:
   SELECT: cell A8
   CLICK: Sort Ascending button (⬆⬇)

5. Close the worksheet without saving the changes.

QUICK REFERENCE
Sorting Worksheet Data

1. **SELECT: a cell in the column whose contents you want sorted**
2. **CLICK: Sort Ascending (⬆⬇) or**
   CLICK: Sort Descending (⬇⬆)

OUTLINING A WORKSHEET

Outlining lets you view your data differently by displaying or hiding worksheet details. For example, a company president might prefer to review only the total sales figures from each of its regions, while each regional manager requires a more detailed analysis by salesperson. Using outlines, the worksheets used to generate these reports can be one and the same. Outlining lets you summarize and report the same information using different views for different needs.

Excel can automatically outline a worksheet based on your use of summary formulas, such as the SUM function. When you select a range and issue the Auto Outline command, Excel inserts outline levels at each subtotal formula and for the grand total. If your worksheet does not contain such formulas, you will need to manually group the detail sections that you want outlined. Once outlined, you can print a worksheet or plot a chart using only the visible data at a specific level in the outline.

In this section, you practice outlining a worksheet.

Perform the following steps . . .

1. Ensure that there are no open worksheets in the application window. Then, open the "XYZDept1" workbook that is stored in the Advantage Files location. This workbook contains a simple income statement layout for a three-month period.

2. Let's review the design of this worksheet:
   CLICK: cell E5
   Notice in the Formula bar that this cell contains a SUM function.

3. CLICK: cell B13
   Each cell in Row 13 contains a SUM function that totals the expenses for each month and for the quarter.

4. CLICK: cell B15
   Notice that this cell contains a subtraction formula.

5. Excel can use these formulas in determining an outlining format for the worksheet. To demonstrate:
   CHOOSE: Date, Group and Outline, Auto Outline
   Your screen should now appear similar to Figure A.1.

6. To collapse some of the detail in the worksheet:
   CLICK: Row-Level 2 button (2)
   The expense detail should disappear.

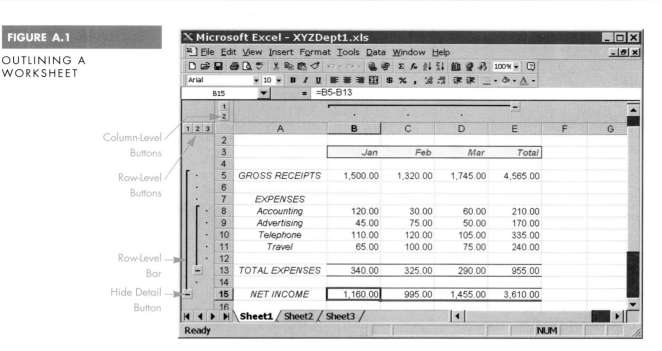

7. To return to viewing the individual expense rows:
CLICK: Row-Level 3 button (⬛3)
You can also click the Show Detail button (⬛+) to display these rows.

8. To display only the "Total" values for the worksheet:
CLICK: Column-Level 1 button (⬛1)
CLICK: Row-Level 1 button (⬛1)
The entire worksheet is now collapsed to display the grand totals. You can
also click the Hide Detail buttons (⬛−) in the Column and Row areas to
temporarily hide this information.

9. To remove the outline:
CHOOSE: Data, Group and Outline, Clear Outline
The original worksheet display appears.

10. Keep the workbook open and proceed to the next section.

QUICK REFERENCE
Outlining a Worksheet
Automatically

1. **SELECT: any cell within the worksheet table area**
2. **CHOOSE: Data, Group and Outline, Auto Outline, or**
   CHOOSE: Data, Group and Outline, Clear Outline

FORMATTING TEXT

In addition to the basic cell formatting options for labels, you can indent and rotate text in your worksheet. To indent a text label within a cell, you select the cell and then click the Increase Indent button (⊞) on the Formatting toolbar. If you get carried away when indenting an entry, you can always click the Decrease Indent button (⊞). To rotate text, you use the alignment tab of the Format Cells dialog box to change a cell's orientation. In this section, you practice indenting and rotating text.

Perform the following steps . . .

1. Ensure that the "XYZDept1" workbook appears open in the application window and that the *Sheet1* tab is displayed.

2. To begin, let's change some of the existing formatting:
   SELECT: cell range from A5 through A15
   CLICK: Align Left button (▤) on the Formatting toolbar

3. Now you will indent the expense categories under the "EXPENSES" heading label. Do the following:
   SELECT: cell range from A8 through to A11
   CLICK: Increase Indent button (⊞) twice
   The text now appears indented in the cell range.

4. To remove the indent level by one:
   CLICK: Decrease Indent button (⊞) once

5. To practice rotating text labels in a cell range:
   SELECT: cell range from B3 through to E3
   Notice that this cell range has a border and fill color applied.

6. To rotate the selection's contents:
   CHOOSE: Format, Cells
   CLICK: *Alignment* tab

7. In the *Orientation* area of the dialog box:
   SELECT: 33 in the *Degrees* spin box
   CLICK: OK command button
   Notice that the sample area also shows the text angled to 33 degrees, as shown in Figure A.2.

FIGURE A.2

ROTATING TEXT IN THE
FORMAT CELLS DIALOG
BOX

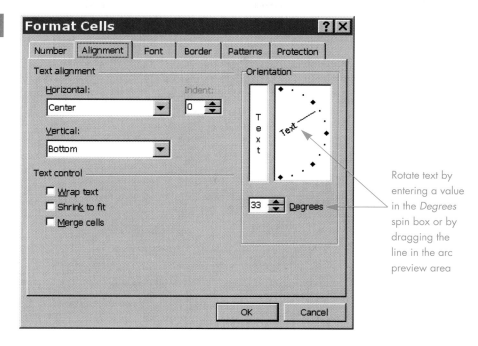

Rotate text by
entering a value
in the *Degrees*
spin box or by
dragging the
line in the arc
preview area

8. Save the workbook as "XYZ Labels" to your Data Files location.

9. Close the workbook before proceeding.

QUICK REFERENCE	• **CLICK: Increase Indent button ( ) to increase an indent**
Indenting Text	• **CLICK: Decrease Indent button ( ) to decrease an indent**

QUICK REFERENCE	1. **SELECT: the cell whose label you want to rotate**
Rotating Text	2. **CHOOSE: Format, Cells**
	3. **CLICK: *Alignment* tab**
	4. **SELECT: the desired options from the *Orientation* area**
	5. **CLICK: OK command button**

WORKING WITH OBJECTS

Think of each worksheet as a single piece of paper that you can add and remove from a workbook as you would using a three-ring binder. For each worksheet page, you can specify whether the paper is lined (gridlines) or textured (background graphic.) In addition to entering labels, values, and formulas, you can paste or stick elements called **objects** onto the paper. A chart object, for example, that is pasted on top of a worksheet is called an embedded chart. Other objects that you can place onto a worksheet include graphic images, photographs, slides, lines, arrows, and other shapes. These objects sit on top of the worksheet paper in layers.

THE CELL LAYER

The **cell layer** in a worksheet holds the data and formatting attributes for a particular cell address. Both of these elements can be changed without affecting the other. For example, you can apply formatting to a cell without changing its contents. Unfortunately, many users find it confusing that a cell without data is not the same as an empty cell. Understand that a cell without data can still store formatting information.

THE DRAW LAYER

The second layer in a worksheet, which we will call the **draw layer**, exists as an invisible surface above (and mostly independent of) the worksheet cells. This layer holds embedded objects, such as lines and 3D shapes, that you place onto a worksheet. You can size, move, and delete objects on this layer without affecting the data stored in the underlying cells. In this section, you add and format objects using the Drawing toolbar.

Perform the following steps . . .

1. Ensure that there are no open worksheets in the application window. Then, open the "Cruises" workbook that is stored in the Advantage Files location. This workbook contains a simple table summarizing the number of travellers and their cruise line preferences.

2. To emphasize a particular portion of the worksheet, you can add objects to the draw layer. (*Note*: Refer to Figure A.3 to view the completed worksheet.) Begin by displaying the Drawing toolbar:
RIGHT-CLICK: *any button on the Standard toolbar*
CHOOSE: Drawing
The Drawing toolbar should appear on the screen.

3. If it does not already appear docked at the bottom of the application window, drag the toolbar to that location and dock it.

4. To add an oval around the value "71" in cell C3:
CLICK: Oval button (⬭) on the Drawing toolbar

5. Move the cross-hair mouse pointer to the top left-hand corner of cell C3 in the worksheet. When ready, drag the mouse pointer to the bottom right-hand corner of the same cell. Release the mouse button to complete the oval. You will notice that the oval is colored white and appears to overwrite the contents of the cell. In actuality, the oval is layered over the cell contents.

6. To make the oval transparent:
CLICK: down arrow attached to the Fill Color button (🎨▾)
CHOOSE: No Fill
You should now be able to see the cell contents behind the oval.

7. On your own, drag the white selection boxes to size the oval around the value in cell C3.

8. To make the line style more pronounced:
CLICK: Line Style button (▤)
SELECT: 1 pt
CLICK: down arrow attached to the Line Color button (🖌▾)
SELECT: a dark red color
The oval should now appear vivid on the worksheet.

9. Let's add a callout to the oval object:
CLICK: Line button (◥)

10. Position the cross-hair mouse pointer on the bottom of the oval and drag downwards to the middle of cell D8. Release the mouse button to complete the line.

11. On your own, format the line object to appear similarly to the oval object—with a 1 pt line style and a dark red color.

12. Add a rectangle object that will contain a text box describing the value emphasized in cell C3. Do the following:
CLICK: Rectangle button (▭)

13. Position the cross-hair mouse pointer to the left of cell D8 and immediately below the bottom of the line object. Then, drag the mouse pointer to the right in order to size the rectangle across two columns and three rows.

14. With the object still selected, let's add some special effects:
CLICK: 3-D button (▣)
CHOOSE: 3-D Style 1 in the top left-hand corner
You will see the rectangle transformed into a three-dimensional box.

15. Notice that the selection handles for the 3-D object remain as the rectangular object. On your own, attempt to size the object by dragging these selection boxes. Then, do the following:
CLICK: 3-D button (▣)
CHOOSE: 3-D Style 7

16. Let's place text in the 3-D object:
RIGHT-CLICK: inside the selection handles for the 3-D object
CHOOSE: Add Text
TYPE: Students prefer the Carnival cruise line to the Royal package.

17. To stop editing text in the object:
CLICK: cell A8
Your worksheet should now appear similar to Figure A.3.

FIGURE A.3

ADDING AND
FORMATTING OBJECTS

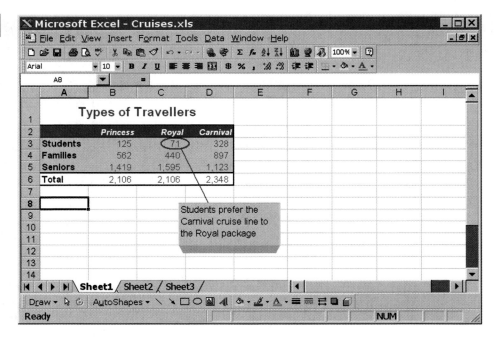

18. On your own, practice sizing and moving the 3-D shape.

19. Save the worksheet as "Formatted Cruises" to your Data Files location.

20. Close the workbook and exit Excel.

QUICK REFERENCE
Manipulating
Drawing Objects

1.   **CLICK: the desired object button on the Drawing toolbar**
2.   **CLICK: in the worksheet to create a default-sized object**
3.   **DRAG: the selection handles to size the object**
4.   **DRAG: the center of the object to move the object**

Summary

This Appendix provides some additional practice working with Microsoft Excel 97. In addition to performing a sort operation using toolbar buttons on the Standard toolbar, you learned how to create and use an outline to collapse and expand a worksheet's details. You also practiced rotating and formatting the appearance of text. And, lastly, you inserted and manipulated graphic objects and 3-D shapes using the Drawing toolbar.

Many of the procedures appearing in this session are summarized in Table A.1, the Command Summary.

TABLE 5.3	To do this . . .	Do the following . . .
Command Summary	Sort worksheet data into ascending or descending order	SELECT: a cell within the column to sort by CLICK: Sort Ascending button (⧉) or CLICK: Sort Descending button (⧉)
	Outline a worksheet automatically	CHOOSE: Data, Group and Outline, Auto Outline
	Clear an outline	CHOOSE: Data, Group and Outline, Clear Outline
	Rotate a text label within a cell	CHOOSE: Format, Cells CLICK: *Alignment* tab SELECT: the desired orientation
	Display the Drawing toolbar	RIGHT-CLICK: any button on any toolbar CHOOSE: Drawing
	Insert graphic objects onto a worksheet	CLICK: the desired object button on the Drawing toolbar DRAG: the cross-hair mouse pointer in the worksheet area
	Size and move graphic objects on the draw layer of a worksheet	CLICK: the object to select it DRAG: its center to move the object DRAG: its selection handles to size the object

KEY TERMS

cell layer
In Excel, the layer for worksheet cells; this layer holds data, calculated expressions, formatting attributes, and cell notes for cells.

draw layer
In an Excel worksheet, the invisible surface that exists above the cell layer and which holds embedded charts and other objects.

object
Any type of data, such as a document, slide, picture, or shape, that has been pasted or embedded into a worksheet.

EXERCISES

SHORT ANSWER

1. What is meant by sorting data into *ascending* order?

2. What must you do before clicking a sort button on the toolbar?

3. When might you want to use Excel's outlining feature?

4. How can you quickly remove an outline that you've applied?

5. How would you rotate a text label onto a 45-degree angle?

6. What happens to the borders and shading that are applied when you rotate a cell's text label?

7. How do you make a line thicker once you've added it to the worksheet?

8. How do you make a rectangle appear three-dimensional once you've added it to the worksheet?

9. How do you change the fill color of a graphic object?

10. How do you add text to a rectangular graphic object?

HANDS-ON

1. In this exercise, you practice sorting data in a worksheet.

   a. Load Microsoft Excel and ensure that there are no workbooks open in the application window.

   b. Open the "Project1" workbook that is stored in your Advantage Files location.

   c. To sort the list of sub-contractors and consultants:
   SELECT: cell A7
   CLICK: Sort Ascending button (⬚)
   The worksheet appears sorted alphabetically.

   d. To sort the list of sub-contractors by descending name:
   CLICK: Sort Descending button (⬚)

   e. Return the list to ascending alphabetical order.

   f. Keep the workbook open to use in the next exercise.

2. In this exercise, you practice outlining a workbook.

   a. Ensure that the "Project1" workbook appears open in the application window.

   b. To enter a summary row:
   CLICK: Bold button (**B**)
   SELECT: cell A17
   TYPE: Work Days in Month
   PRESS: ➡

    c.   You will now enter a formula:
SELECT: cell range from B17 through to N17
TYPE: `=sum(b7:b16)`
PRESS: **CTRL** + **ENTER**
The formula is entered into each cell in the selected range.

    d.   To return to Column A:
PRESS: **HOME**

    e.   To automatically outline the worksheet:
CHOOSE: Data, Group and Outline, Auto Outline
The outline is added to the worksheet.

    f.   In the Column-Level area:
CLICK: Column-Level 1 button (**1**) to collapse the columns
You should see a gap between Column A and the Year-to-Date column (N).

    g.   Keep the worksheet open and proceed to the next exercise.

3. In this exercise, you practice formatting a worksheet.

    a.   Ensure that the "Project1" workbook appears open in the application window.

    b.   Center the text labels in Row 5.

    c.   For these same column headings in Row 5, rotate the text to a 45-degree angle.

    d.   SELECT: cell A1

    e.   To remove the outline:
CHOOSE: Data, Group and Outline, Clear Outline
Notice that the months also appear on an angle.

    f.   Close the workbook without saving the changes.

4. **On Your Own:** Inserting and Formatting Graphic Objects
Since the insertion and manipulation of graphic objects enables you to express your personal creativity, this exercise lets you open any file from the Advantage Files location and enhance it for presentation. In your efforts, make sure to include a line, oval, and rectangle object at the bare minimum. You should also attempt to format the objects using the fill color, line style, and 3-D options that are available. Save the revised workbook to your Data Files location as "My Objects" and then exit Microsoft Excel.